Gambling and Survival in Native North America

Paul Pasquaretta.

Gambling and Survival in Native North America

The University of Arizona Press
Tucson

The University of Arizona Press

© 2003 The Arizona Board of Regents

First printing

♾ This book is printed on acid-free, archival-quality paper.

Manufactured in the United States of America

08   07   06   05   04   03   6   5   4   3   2   1

LIBRARY OF CONGRESS CATALOGING-IN-PUBLICATION DATA

Pasquaretta, Paul, 1962–

Gambling and survival in Native North America / Paul Pasquaretta.

p. cm.

Includes bibliographical references and index.

ISBN 0-8165-2289-8 (alk. paper)

1. Gambling on Indian reservations—United States.

2. Pequot Indians—Gambling.   3. Mohegan Indians—Gambling.

4. Mohawk Indians—Gambling. I. Title.

E98.G18 P37   2003

306.4'82'089973–dc21   2003002457

BRITISH LIBRARY CATALOGUING-IN-PUBLICATION DATA

A catalogue record for this book is available from the British Library.

Publication of this book is made possible in part by the proceeds of a permanent endowment created with the assistance of a Challenge Grant from the National Endowment for the Humanities, a federal agency.

This book is dedicated to my parents,
Emanuel Robert Pasquaretta and Rita Sottile Pasquaretta.

Contents.

Acknowledgments.

As this ten-year odyssey comes to an end, there are many I wish to acknowledge for their time and assistance: Charlene Jones (nee Prince), of the Mashantucket Pequot Tribal Council; Mike McDonald, Tom Porter, Barbara Barnes, Jim Ransom, and Barbara Gray, of the Mohawk Nation Council; Rowena General and Loran Thompson, of the St. Regis Tribal Council; Kevin McBride, Paul Costas, Helene Tigar, and Kate April, of the Mashantucket Pequot Library and Research Project; Arnold Krupat, of Sarah Lawrence College, for his extraordinary assistance in navigating the difficult waters of academic publishing; Katherine A. Spilde, former Director of Research for the National Indian Gaming Association and current Senior Research Associate with the Harvard Project on American Indian Economic Development, for her timely assistance and encouragement; Duane Champagne, Director of the American Indian Studies Center at UCLA, for first recognizing my work; Barry O'Connell, of Amherst College, for his careful reading of earlier versions of chapter 3; Patti Hartmann, of the University of Arizona Press, for going to bat for the manuscript; Dennis and Maria Gillan, for the quiet place to think, write, and grow; my dissertation committee at SUNY Stony Brook: Gerald B. Nelson, David Sheehan, and Timothy Brennan; and Jennifer Gillan, my friend, companion, and inspiration through the most difficult years of this writing.

Introduction.

In the opening pages of Okanogan writer Mourning Dove's 1926 novel *Cogewea, the Half-Blood,* the title character is found considering her options in life. "Life is a gamble," reflects the young woman of mixed tribal and European American descent, "a chance, a mere guess. Cast a line and reel in a splendid rainbow trout or a slippery eel."[1] As evidenced by the novel's Indian and non-Indian characters' nearly continuous engagement with games of skill and chance, Cogewea's metaphors are no random association. Rather, as a ubiquitous element of the text, gambling is identified as a fundamental and universal human activity engaged in by individuals and groups competing for a variety of social, economic, and political prizes. Concerned primarily with the choices before its Indian characters, the novel demonstrates how gambles involving work, marriage, lifestyle, and belief systems provide a critical context for understanding the Indian community's ongoing struggle against its aggressive and predatory adversaries.

In *Cogewea,* these competitions often involve issues relating to the control and ownership of land. Written during the allotment period in American Indian history, the text represents land claims issues in terms of gambling scenarios. Allotment, also known as the Dawes Severalty or General Allotment Act of 1887, was a government-initiated policy that divided reservation lands among tribal members, the standard measure being 160 acres per person.[2] According to its sponsors, transferring title to individual Indian patentees promoted the advancement of civilization among Native peoples by making them property owners. As such, the government reasoned, Indians would no longer be constrained by the believed-to-be limiting effects of the traditional practice of holding lands in common. As patentees of individual allotments, they would be free to profit from the farming, grazing, renting, or selling of their lands, and would therefore develop the entrepreneurial spirit they needed to thrive in a modern American democracy.

From an assimilationist's perspective, allotment was a good bet for Indian peoples, and there is some evidence to suggest that some individuals and tribal groups benefited from it. For the most part, however, allotment contributed to the demise of Indians and Indian culture by creating effective legal mechanisms by which the tribes were separated from the land. The Dawes Act stipulated that excess reservation lands not allotted to individual Indian patentees could be secured by the United States for use by whites.[3] As Flathead writer D'Arcy McNickle explains, allotment thus became "an efficient mechanism for separating the Indians from their lands and pauperizing them."[4] In 1887, when the Dawes Act was passed, 140 million acres were held in common by the Indians of the United States. Over the next forty-five years, some ninety million acres were transferred from Indian to white hands.[5] For Native peoples, betting on allotment was like gambling against the house; while a few individuals were lucky enough to turn a profit, the very nature of the game assured that most would lose. To pursue Mourning Dove's metaphor, allotment was presented to Indians as a rainbow trout; what they got was a slippery eel.

In associating gambling metaphors and practices with the social, political, and economic concerns of Native peoples, Mourning Dove introduces the twin themes that are the focus of this study: the survival of indigenous peoples in the face of the European invasion of North America and the ongoing and open-ended contest of Natives and newcomers that has transpired in the marketplace, on the battlefield, and in the courts. In exploring these themes, I consider the impact of reservation gambling on the development of contemporary tribal communities and the important role of traditional Indian gambling practices and stories in the survival of indigenous cultural traditions. Two key signs will receive particular attention: the Pequot and the Gambler. As we shall see, the Pequots have an iconic status in American culture related to the ongoing controversy surrounding the circumstances and execution of the Anglo-Pequot War of 1636–37. *Pequot,* a term of uncertain origin, identifies both an actual people and their history *and* abstract ideas about the assumed qualities of Indians. The

Gambler is likewise an iconic figure in Indian and non-Indian societies that can embody a variety of meanings. Both hero and villain, the Gambler calls attention to a variety of social and economic concerns and tensions that remain unresolved in American culture.

This project grew out of questions I had about the dramatic rise of Pequot gambling that occurred in the 1980s and 1990s. Owned and operated by the Mashantucket Pequot Tribal Nation, Foxwoods Resort Casino opened its doors in 1992, the same year that marked the quincentennial of Columbus's voyage of discovery. The irony of this development was obvious to anyone with a basic knowledge of colonial American history. One of the continent's most storied Indian nations, the Pequots were best known for having disappeared. As Ishmael tells us in *Moby-Dick,* by the mid-nineteenth century, the Pequots were remembered as "the name of a celebrated tribe of Massachusetts Indians, now extinct as the ancient Medes."[6] The existence of a contemporary Pequot community revealed that important information had been omitted from the history books.

It was with these thoughts in mind that I visited the Mashantucket Pequot tribal offices in January of 1992. On that occasion, I had the good fortune to meet Kate April, a non-Indian librarian, and her assistant, Charlene Jones, a tribal member who has since been elected to the Tribal Council. Our discussions over the next two years provided the basis for the partial study of Pequot history that follows. Focusing on the reemergence of the tribal community in the 1970s and 1980s, they conveyed a story of progress, optimism, and good fortune that, given the history of violence and oppression that had marked Pequot experience since the early seventeenth century, made the extraordinary turn of events all the more poignant and dramatic. I am especially indebted to Ms. Jones for the generous attention she paid to my visits and for allowing me access to the library's special resources. It was through our conversations that my understanding of the Pequot resurgence developed, forming the core field of this book. My meetings with her led to discussions with Kevin McBride, Paul Costas, and other researchers then working with the Mashantucket Pequot Ethnohistorical Project.

In some ways, the Mashantucket Pequots provided a case study of certain concepts that had been developed by Gerald Vizenor, the renowned writer of Ojibwa tribal descent. As I understand it, Vizenor's central project is to provide a new vocabulary and conceptual framework for articulating the processes of survival and change that affect tribal communities. For Vizenor, the principle of survival is signified in the trope of the trickster. Distinguishing the archetypal character of tribal stories from the storytelling process itself, he describes the trickster as a "liberator and healer in narrative."[7] Thus, rather than being a character in a story, Vizenor's trickster, or tricksterism, is associated with a mode of discourse that functions to liberate and heal both listeners and speakers. Agonistic, aggressive, and open–ended, trickster discourse provides a means to contest tragic narratives on Indian history, social science monologues on Indianness, and a belief in the ultimate extinction of the tribes.[8] It is thus a comic mode of discourse that emphasizes survival, adaptability, and humor. As a product of trickster modes of thinking, speaking, and behaving, crossbloods are described as the "agonistic survivors" of "racialism, colonial duplicities, sentimental monogenism, and generic cultures."[9] Crossblood stories are comic and communal; crossblood cultures are a creative response to colonial domination. In this context, Vizenor has coined the term "survivance" to emphasize deliberate strategies of survival, as opposed to mere accidents of history.

Vizenor's theories didn't tell the whole story of tribal gambling. Looking beyond the borders of Mashantucket revealed that, in other tribal contexts, the dynamic potential of tribal gambling had had more destructive and troubling effects. Such was the case at Akwesasne, the Mohawk Reserve in upstate New York and Canada. Beginning in the late 1980s, the development of high–stakes gambling operations led to a troubling rift within this close–knit community. The violent effects of these divisions had been widely reported in the press. It was with the view of getting a firsthand, insider perspective on the gambling war that I traveled to Akwesasne in June of 1992. On that visit, I met with Tom Porter and Mike McDonald, antigambling activists with the North American Indian Travelling College on Cornwall Island, Ontario. According to its own informational brochure, the Travelling College is "a non–profit cultural center that is dedicated to the preservation of native culture in the modern world." The college describes its members as Akwesasne Mohawks of the Haudenosaunee Iroquois Confederacy. Porter is a retired chief of the Mohawk Nation Council and the founder of Kanatsiohareke, the "Clean Pot," near Amsterdam, New York. McDonald is also affiliated with the Mohawk Nation Council. I am especially indebted to Mr. McDonald for the time he spent with me. During my brief visit, he led me through a tour of the Mohawk Nation Longhouse, introduced me to the teachings of Handsome Lake, and offered me a crash course in the role of gambling in traditional Haudenosaunee culture. Ten years later, in May of 2002, I returned to Akwesasne. In an effort to update this study and gain a broader perspective on the reserve's politics, I met with Jim Ransom, an antigambling activist with the Mohawk Nation Council, and Rowena General and Loran Thompson, pro-gambling Mohawks with the St. Regis Tribal Council.

The situation described by these Mohawks was in sharp contrast to the good news at Mashantucket. Rather than providing a boon for a struggling tribal economy and a new focal point of community solidarity, high-stakes gambling at Akwesasne aggravated social and political tensions to the point where outbreaks of violence occurred. At least two people were killed as a result of these internal conflicts. Thus, while crossblood theory provided a framework for understanding the surprising ways in which Native peoples like the Pequots had transformed and had been transformed by new languages, technologies, and social traditions, it did not account for the stance of Handsome Lake traditionals and others who were wary of the changes wrought by for-profit gambling. For antigambling Mohawks, high-stakes reservation gambling aggravated the ongoing debate on assimilation, self-determination, and the role of traditional culture in the modern world. As McDonald pointed out to me, indigenous gambling practices have an entirely different social role than the type of gambling that occurs in modern American casinos. These differences indicate larger differences in lifestyle and philosophy. As I found in my readings of American Indian novels, tribal gambling practices are key indicators of indigenous cultural traditions.

Divided into three parts, this book traces its themes through close readings of texts produced in the seventeenth, eighteenth, nineteenth, and twentieth centuries. Part 1, "Pequots," examines the famous Pequot War of 1636–37 through readings of Puritan war chronicles and nineteenth-century frontier romances. Chapter 1 reads the contemporary, firsthand accounts of the conflict written by John Underhill, John Mason, and Lion Gardener, colonial soldiers and participants in the fighting. Despite a general tendency to silence Pequot voices, the Pequot War narratives actually record the dialogue with indigenous peoples that occurred over the course of the war. By emphasizing this aspect of these texts, my reading provides the basis for dialogic readings of Pequot and non-Pequot responses to the war and its legacy, and how those responses informed the development of American literature. Emphasizing the legal aspects of Mason's and Gardener's narratives, this chapter also sheds light on the beginnings of Anglo-Indian relations in southern New England and how they were influenced by intracolonial conflicts and dialogues.

Chapter 2, offering a reading of Catharine Maria Sedgwick's 1827 novel *Hope Leslie; or, Early Times in the Massachusetts,* bridges the gap between seventeenth-century texts and fictional narratives that revitalized colonial history for American readers in the early nineteenth century. *Hope Leslie* was written at a time when America sought to establish its literary voice. In that same period, the country was deciding the question of removal to lands beyond the Mississippi River for Cherokee and other Indian nations. Partly through an imagined Pequot voice, the Princess Magawisca, *Hope Leslie* engaged this debate at the same time that it contributed to the cause of a national literature. Focusing on the history of Sedgwick's hometown of Stockbridge, Massachusetts, and its roots as an Indian town, my reading applies modern ethnohistorical accounts of Stockbridge history to an analysis of the model of Anglo-Indian relations put forth in the novel. In examining Sedgwick's manipulation of the captivity narrative and her treatment of Indian-white marriages, I explore the real-life experiences of Eunice Williams, an ancestor of Sedgwick, and Mary Jemison, whose life story was published in 1824, three years before *Hope Leslie* appeared.

In part 2, "Crossbloods," Pequot adaptations to Anglo-American culture are examined through close readings of Pequot advocacy texts. In Chapter 3, Pequot history from the conclusion of the war through the removal period is examined primarily through eighteenth- and nineteenth-century Pequot texts that detail the group's efforts to resist the further appropriation of its few remaining territories and to acquire civil rights. The texts examined include Pequot memorials and petitions from the seventeenth and eighteenth centuries and the later writings of nineteenth-century Pequot advocate William Apess. In recent years, a great deal has been written and said about Apess's life and work. My analysis focuses on the development of literacy among eighteenth-century Pequots, and how the development of a distinctly Pequot tribal discourse sheds light on Apess's efforts to advance tribal rights in the removal period.

In chapter 4, the discussion returns to Mashantucket and the contemporary Pequot renaissance. The analysis begins with a consideration of Indian activism nationwide and how it affected tribal peoples living in Connecticut. It was within these national and statewide movements that Mashantucket first began to emerge as a regional power. Exploring these developments, the chapter examines how a new generation of Pequot leadership has appropriated the political, corporate, and academic discourses of the mainstream to fashion a new tribal nation and a modern Pequot identity.

Pursuing this line of inquiry quite naturally leads to a discussion of identity politics. Because the Pequots do not appear or act in stereotyped Indian mannerisms, their legitimacy as a tribal nation has sometimes been questioned. This suspicion is partly fed by a general misunderstanding of tribalism and Native history. To address this issue, I examine Gerald Vizenor's essays on "crossbloods" and offer a reading of his 1991 novel, *Heirs of Columbus,* works that demand new ways of understanding Native peoples and what constitutes a modern, tribal community.

Thus, in part 3, "Gamblers," the discussion turns to an examination of Indian gambling in history, politics, and literature. Toward that end, chapter 5 focuses on Akwesasne, this project's other Native context. By exploring the role of traditional and appropriated forms of gambling in Mohawk society, the discussion reveals sources of tension within the Native American community. Since the early 1980s, high-stakes reservation gambling has sponsored debates among tribal people everywhere. Some of the key issues involve the meaning and use of tribal sovereignty and the difference between the community-centered economies of traditional tribal cultures and the individualism of modern capitalism. Divided between pro- and antigambling factions, the Mohawk community at Akwesasne dramatizes the struggles of indigenous communities threatened by, but enticed to emulate, the dominant socioeconomic order. To focus this broad issue, the discussion considers an interlocking matrix of gambling practices that includes traditional Iroquois gambling practices sanctioned by the Code of Handsome Lake, Euro-American games of chance, and the American gambling industry. This provides the basis for a discussion on the issues that separate Handsome Lake traditionals from the entrepreneurial Mohawks involved in the gambling and smuggling trades.

A related field of inquiry is pursued in chapter 6 through an analysis of the gambling motif in several Native American Indian novels, including Yellow Bird's *The Life and Adventures of Joaquin Murieta,* Mourning Dove's *Cogewea, the Half-Blood,* Leslie Marmon Silko's *Ceremony,* Gerald Vizenor's *Bearheart: The Heirship Chronicles* and *Heirs of Columbus,* and Louise Erdrich's *Love Medicine, Tracks,* and

The Bingo Palace. In these texts, the strategic deployment of gambling metaphors helps to dramatize various tribal positions that had hitherto been examined from social, political, and economic perspectives. My reading, however, is only partly sociological. In distinguishing tribal gambling referents, plots, and scenarios, I engage some of the features that identify a tribal aesthetic in writing. This part of the book is mostly concerned with the unique artistry of Native American fiction and the storytelling traditions from which it emerges.

As the primary sources of this study would indicate, I have not limited my reading to particular genres, but have pursued certain ideas and concepts as they appear and reappear in various kinds of writing. The focus on tribal history has also required me to translate, as far as I am able, a sense of tribal experience from a variety of time periods and locations into a contemporary critical discourse. Placing a great deal of trust in its sources and the author's own judgment, this book attempts to read literature and make it speak to the immediate sociopolitical concerns of tribal and nontribal peoples. Intentionally Janus-faced, it explores the past in terms of present situations and future possibilities. In its attempts to account for the radical changes that have transpired in North America, it seeks to understand how those changes have been remembered by the original peoples and their descendants. Thus, it is from the elusive yet real qualities of Native North America itself, the unique features of the place the indigenous peoples first named, and of their original and ongoing experience with the land, each other, and the European newcomers, that the subject of this book emerges.

Part One.

Pequots

"Could Yee Blame Us 1.
for Revenging So Cruell a Murder?"

A Dialogic Critique of the Pequot War Narratives

In his 1634 promotional tract, *New England's Prospect,* William Wood describes for his readers the "Games" and "Sports of Activities" of the Native Massachusetts. Of their games, he carefully describes two, *puim,* being "not much unlike cards," and *hubbub,* or "dice," being "no other than lottery."[1] Of their sports he describes football, shooting, running, and swimming. Despite how amusing these scenes must have been to his English readers, many of whom also played sports and gambled, or the pleasure Wood may have found in describing them (as indicated by his boast that one English could beat ten Indians at football),[2] this aspect of indigenous culture is roundly condemned by the Puritan, who chastises the Indians for spending "half their days in gambling and lazing."[3] According to Wood, the Indians were so "bewitched" by gaming that they routinely gambled their most prized possessions: beaver and moose skins, kettles, wampampeag, mowhacheis, hatchets, and knives.[4] All, Wood claims, were "confiscate" by gaming. His comments would turn prophetic as the New England Indians did find themselves bereft of their goods, but not through their passion for gaming, as Wood charges, but through the progress of English imperialism. Speaking metaphorically, we might say that the Indians gambled and lost with the English, just as the English gambled and won with the Indians.

The gambling metaphor is an apt one for describing Anglo-Indian relations in this period. Although it is tempting to think of the Pequot conquest as inevitable, in 1634, when the Pequots were on relatively good terms with the English, the results of contact had yet to be determined. For many colonial observers drawn by lucrative trade in pelts and lands as yet unclaimed by other

Europeans, the conquest of the Pequots three years later may have seemed to finalize a contest that began when Dutch and English traders first infiltrated the territory in the 1620s and 1630s. By 1638, some 10,000 Pequots would lose their lives, 80 percent of an estimated 13,000-person nation.[5] Most of these died in the smallpox epidemic of 1634; over a thousand more were killed during the Anglo-Pequot War of 1636–37. A year later, the colonials would write up the articles of surrender and decree the name "Pequot" to be "outlawed forever."[6] According to the Treaty of Hartford, also known as the Tri-Partite Agreement between Hartford, Mohegan, and Narragansett, surviving Pequots were no longer to inhabit their ancient territory (a territory that was now to be left vacant for English planters), but were to be incorporated into surrounding Native communities and become Mohegans and Narragansetts.[7] By apparently acquiescing to these provisions of the treaty, the Pequots gained a measure of physical relief. With official hostilities against them at an end, surviving Pequots could begin to piece together their lives. But all of this was to be at the cost of their national title; as far as the courts were concerned, the former trading partners of the Dutch and English had ceased to exist as a separate people.

The terrible consequences of the war, combined with the belief in the predestined doom of the Indians, contributed to the myth of Pequot extinction. As mentioned in the introduction, this idea is most memorably preserved in Ishmael's reference to the celebrated tribe of Massachusetts Indians.[8] Without casting aspersions upon Melville, it is correct to say that Ishmael's statement contains two errors. The first error, ostensibly inconsequential, is the claim that the Pequots were Massachusetts Indians. Although dispersed widely throughout the northeast (indeed, throughout North America) their traditional homeland has been, and continues to be, the Pequot (now Thames) and Mystic River valleys in southeastern Connecticut. The second error has had enormous ramifications. Despite the widespread assumption that they completely disappeared in the early seventeenth century, and the fact that they had come to the brink of extinction through plague, warfare, and displacement, a Pequot community has maintained a continual presence in southern New England.

The Treaty of Hartford would have signaled the end of the Pequots had not the Pequots had other ideas about their destiny. Not content to remain among the Mohegans and Narragansetts, the Pequots entered into new agreements with colonial officials by the late 1640s, ten years after Pequot nonexistence had become a point of law. The most important of these agreements established the Indians' title to tracts of land in southeastern Connecticut. Guarded since by generations of Pequots, these tracts continue to form the basis of group rights, the continued viability of which has been recently asserted in dramatic and powerful ways. At Mashantucket, the home of the western Pequots near Ledyard, Connecticut, the expression of traditional land rights has transformed a nearly abandoned tribal territory into a state and regional power. Participants in the revival of tribal culture that began in the 1960s and later, through the development of the American Indian gambling industry, the Mashantucket Pequots have become the wealthiest Indian tribe per capita in the United States.

The principal symbol and cause of Mashantucket Pequot wealth is Foxwoods, the tribe's high-stakes gambling casino. Owned and operated by the Mashantucket Pequot Tribal Nation, the colossal facility has made the hitherto forgotten tribe a major player in local, state, and national politics. Pequot gambling profits have fueled the tribe's dramatic expansion. In 1983, when the Pequots won federal recognition, Mashantucket comprised only 214 acres. Ten years later, the tribe held over 1,200 acres in trust with the U.S. federal government and several hundred more acres in fee simple. In 1974, when the tribal council drafted its first written constitution, very few permanent structures existed on the tribe's rocky, tree-covered hills. A generation later, dozens of permanent houses, a walk-in health care facility, fire department, gym, and council center occupied the growing land base. Reflecting its new leadership role among Native American peoples, the tribe sponsors "Schemitzun," a national powwow hosted annually in Hartford; supports legal advocacy groups, like the Native American Rights Fund; and has become a powerful lobbying force for Native American issues nationally. From the dominant position the Pequots occupied in Connecticut's seventeenth-century fur trade to the booming casino sovereignty of the 1990s, it would appear that the tribe's fortunes have come full circle.

Among other far-reaching effects, the contemporary Pequot renaissance has stimulated a significant reevaluation of Native American experience. Twenty-five years of tribal collaborations with the academic community have yielded two national conferences on Native history. The first of these, held in 1987, led to the publication of *The Pequots in Southern New England: The Fall and Rise of an American Indian Nation*, the first written history of Pequot Indians authorized by a body of Pequot leaders and the first major study of the tribe published since John W. DeForest's 1851 work, *History of the Indians of Connecticut.* In the mid-1990s, the tribe donated $10 million to the Smithsonian Institution's American Indian museum project. In August of 1998, it opened its own multi-million-dollar museum and research center at Mashantucket. Affiliated as it is with the life and political fortunes of a contemporary Mashantucket community, this recent scholarship has focused on the impact of colonialism on living Native peoples.

It is with this view of Pequot survival in mind that we will examine the Pequot War narratives. In chronicling the events of that early Anglo-Indian conflict, these texts show how the dialogues that transpired across ethnic borders in seventeenth-century New England were complicated by conflicting assumptions on all sides. As Arnold Krupat suggests, cross-cultural analyses like the one proposed here involve the attempt "to mediate very different, sometimes radically different, ways of understanding the world and 'having' knowledge—as it must then attempt to mediate very different ways of speaking or writing about this 'knowledge.'"[9] The dialogic approach to literary analysis, as it was first articulated by Russian theorist Mikhail Bakhtin, is useful in this regard because it premises that no text is the exclusive construct of any single group. As Krupat explains, "The language of any single speaker, one's 'own' speech, can never be absolutely and exclusively his or her own, never some sort of inalienable private property."[10] Thus formed by people engaged in dialogue, language and the knowledge it produces can never be entirely dominated by any one group. This understanding of language has been of particular value to scholars in the field of Native American studies. For example, in his 1991 work *Forked Tongues,* David Murray applies this approach to examine the complex dialogues involving Indian and non-Indian speakers that contributed to an emergent "discourse of Indianness."[11]

Murray's interest in the role of translators in shaping these dialogues makes his work particularly relevant to this study. The fact that translators were present to mediate discussions between Pequots and Englishmen underscores the point that these groups were not speaking the same language. Murray uses an economic metaphor to describe the problems that translators would necessarily face in their efforts to make English and Indian speeches intelligible to either group. Borrowing from the work of French theorist Jacques Derrida, Murray explains that the idea of language as a fixed system of meaning assumes a restricted economy where "exchanges and substitutions are guaranteed by a universal standard."[12] In such a system, the risk of misunderstanding is minimal. However, in the multiethnic and multilinguistic setting we find in seventeenth-century New England, there were at least two basic economies of language at play, those of the Native Algonquins and those of the English and Dutch colonists. Despite their common desire to engage each other in trade, these groups placed radically different values on words, deeds, and material possessions like wampum, pelts, and lands, among other social and economic prizes. These differences often resulted in misunderstanding, confusion, and violence.

The meanings generated by the Puritans were largely guided by their experiences in England, where feudalism was being replaced by capitalism and the rise of family-oriented economic independence. As Neal Salisbury writes in *Manitou and Providence,* these economic practices, when elevated to a divine character trait through English Puritanism, helped to define their group identity: "the prospect of a colony dominated by Puritans and Puritanism that would simultaneously fulfill material and spiritual goals was a truly utopian one for thousands of English who were willing to stake their lives and fortunes."[13] The availability of resources, including Indian labor in the fur trade, forests for timber, arable lands for agricultural production, and animal populations for the fur markets—to name just a few of the things that the New World presented that could be exploited for economic, political, or spiritual gain—made immigration a good bet for those socially and economically stifled in England. The principal risk to such adventurers was embodied in the Indians who, insofar as they were perceived as wild men, savages, and heathens by the newcomers, became the targets of violence and civilizing efforts. The fact that Indians usually demonstrated a desire to negotiate with the English, to engage them in trade, and prove themselves useful friends and allies, could not alter the prejudices that cast Native Americans in an adversarial role.

In contrast, Algonquian culture in southern New England was shaped, as Salisbury writes, by continuity, abundance, and stability: "The fruit of the Indians' experience was an ethos in which relationships in the social, natural and supernatural worlds were defined in terms of reciprocity rather than domination and submission."[14] Reciprocity was achieved through a complex sequence of rituals that governed the observance of social and seasonal rhythms. Hunters, for example, were obligated to observe certain rules governing the taking of animals. One colonial writer described how the heart, left rear foot, sinews, and tongue of a killed moose were removed before the skin was prepared and the venison eaten.[15] Salisbury notes that such practices "originated in beliefs that the animals had to be respected as sources of spiritual power who could with-hold their gifts if not properly addressed and treated."[16] Games and gambling contests like the ones William Wood described fostered reciprocity by providing nonviolent means of relieving social tensions and redistributing goods.[17] Thus, the economy of eastern Algonquins called for the maintenance of equilibrium in the world shared among a variety of life forms, including other Indians and European colonists.

While all geographical locations might be said to lack an absolutely fixed standard of meaning, New England frontiers in the 1630s, with their compet-ing groups of English, Dutch, Pequot, Mohegan, Niantic, and Narragansett peoples, were likely sites for misunderstanding, misapprehension, and outright confusions to occur. The instability of linguistic play is clearly evident in the four so-called Pequot War narratives. Not only do they indicate ambiguities result-ing from dialogues that transpired between Native and immigrant speakers, but also contradictions caused by factionalism within the Puritan community itself. Thus, rather than offering a colonial monologue on Pequot extinction, the Anglo-Pequot War narratives provide a means to examine important dif-ferences not only among Anglos and Indians, but among Anglos themselves, and the effect those differences had on diplomatic, political, and trading alliances. Three of these narratives, John Underhill's *Newes from America,* John Mason's *A Brief History of the Pequot War,* and Lion Gardener's *Relation of the Pequot Warres,* were written by persons who had contact with the Pequots in war and trade. By examining the circumstances under which each was written and published, this chapter will explore the beginnings of Anglo-Indian relations in southern New England and the ways in which those relations helped to set the ground work for the discourse of Indianness that emerged in the coming centuries.[18]

A Brief History of the Anglo-Pequot War

The best single study of the Anglo-Pequot War is Alfred Cave's recent narra-tive history, *The Pequot War.* The following brief history, pieced together from Cave's, Salisbury's and Jennings's studies of early New England history, *The*

Pequots in Southern New England, and my own readings of the original sources, is here offered as a foundation for the discussion that follows. A good place to pick up the thread of history is in 1634 and Wood's *New England's Prospect,* which offers one of the first printed references to Pequots in English (the Dutch explorer Adriaen Block referred to the "Pequatoos . . . the enemies of the Wampanoos" as early as 1613).[19] Wood describes the Pequots as "a stately, warlike people, of whom I never heard any misdemeanor, but that they were just and equal in their dealings, not treacherous either to their countrymen or English, requiters of courtesies, affable towards the English."[20] Wood's characterization reflects a developing alliance between the Pequots and the leaders of the Massachusetts Bay Company that had culminated in a 1634 treaty of friendship, trade, and cooperation. Unbeknownst to Wood's English audience, however, and, perhaps, unbeknownst to Wood himself, the actual situation was far more complicated and volatile.

The 1634 agreement, initiated by the Pequots, had come in the wake of recent hostilities among the Pequots, Dutch traders, and the Pequots' trade rivals, the neighboring Narragansetts.[21] Beginning in the early 1620s, the Pequots traded wampum for European cloth, metal tools, glass beads, and other trade goods.[22] At Dutch trading posts, like The House of Good Hope at Hartford, the wampum was exchanged for pelts that would later be sold on European markets. To the Europeans, wampum was analogous to money; to the Indians, it was associated with a wider range of properties. While the Indians used wampum as an economic tool, they also believed it to hold spirit power, or *Manitou,* a force described by anthropologist Ruth Benedict as a "voltage with which the universe is believed to be charged."[23] The uses the Indians made of wampum reflect its various sacred and social uses. As well as being a medium through which commodity exchange could function on the Anglo-Algonquian frontier, wampum was also made into belts that recorded important treaty negotiations; it was also used to satisfy aggrieved parties and to end blood feuds.

To stimulate trade further, the Dutch attempted to establish a "free trade zone" in the region in the early 1630s. Apparently, the agreement reached among the Dutch, Pequots, and Narragansetts stipulated that any Native who wished to trade at Hope House would be guaranteed free passage.[24] This meant that Narragansetts could, in theory, travel through Pequot territory unmolested. Soon after the Dutch assumed this agreement to be in effect, some Pequots were blamed for killing some Narragansett traders. The Dutch responded by taking captive and later killing Totabem, a Pequot leader.[25] In retribution, the sachem's kinsmen, possibly even his own son, along with other Indian allies, are believed to have killed an Englishman, Captain John Stone, along with a Captain Norton, and their bark's crew.

The killing of Stone and the others became the ostensible cause of the war, particularly from the Bay Company's point of view. However, Stone's status among the English magistrates shows him to be something more than a simple victim of Pequot aggression. A licensed privateer known from Brazil to the Caribbean to New Netherlands and New England, John Stone was born to a wealthy and influential London family.[26] When he first arrived in New England, in the late spring of 1633, he was immediately prosecuted for piracy. According to John Winthrop's journal, Stone seized a pinnace belonging to Plymouth near the Dutch trading house at Manhattan. Drinking with the Dutch Director-General, Wouter Van Twiller, and acting upon some "reproach" the Plymouth men had supposedly made against Virginia, he took command of the vessel and threatened to sail it away. The ship was released, apparently as a result of the intervention of some Dutch seamen who persuaded Stone not to carry away the goods of their Plymouth friends.[27] In Massachusetts, the magistrates considered bringing the case before the admiralty court in England. The charges were dropped when they became "persuaded," as Winthrop writes, "that it would turn to their reproach, and that it could be no piracy."[28] A month later, Stone was again brought into court, this time for drunkenness and suspected adultery. The latter charge was never proven, and Stone was released, fined 100 pounds, and ordered to leave New England, "upon pain of death" if he should ever return.[29]

After this episode, Stone apparently set sail for Virginia, but along the way, detoured up the Connecticut River. According to what Winthrop reports having been told to him by the Pequots themselves, Stone took two Indians hostage, "bound them, and made them show him the way up the river."[30] Perhaps he was trying to reach the Dutch house at Hartford, where, as his experience at Manhattan might indicate, he would certainly be more welcome than he was among his fellow Englishmen. At some point during this ill-conceived mission, he miscalculated and was killed, along with his crew, but not by the Pequots. According to John Mason, a combatant in the war, the killers of Stone and the others were not "native" Pequots, but those who had "frequent recourse unto them, to whom they tendered some of those Goods" which had been taken from the bark.[31]

Initially, Stone's death had little bearing on Anglo-Pequot relations. However, as Massachusetts Bay sought just cause to subdue the Pequots, his timely murder provided the most available means. Thus, in the 1634 meeting with Pequot emissaries, the Bay Colony magistrates demanded that the Pequots deliver up the killers of Stone and his crew. In addition, they demanded 400 fathoms of wampum, forty beaver skins, and thirty otters skins, an amount that Cave estimates to equal one-half the colony's yearly tax income.[32] The English also demanded that the Pequots cede to the English "all their right at Connecti-cut," a condition to which, Winthrop claims, the Pequots agreed.[33] The Pequots did not produce Stone's killers; nor, according to available records, did they deny complicity in his murder. Cave speculates that they may have believed the tribute in wampum and furs was enough to settle their account with the English. In light of what transpired, Cave argues that this was a fatal mistake. Yet, before we place the demise of the Pequots on the miscalculations of their leaders, let us consider the options those leaders faced. As Cave notes, the English demand for Stone's killers was, from a Pequot perspective, an unreasonable request "which clearly they could not meet without loss of honor."[34] We might add that more than honor was at stake. Boston's demands threatened the sovereignty of the Pequot Nation by subordinating it to Massachusetts Bay, a power that had just recently established itself in the area. Under these circumstances, it is difficult to imagine Pequot leaders choosing a different course of action. Despite the best efforts of historians to uncover the truth, other important questions remain unanswered: Could the Pequots have produced Stone's killers? Would conflict have been avoided if they had? Was Stone, himself an outcast and pariah to the Puritan community, merely a surreptitious pawn in a larger struggle for territo-rial control?

Because it strains credulity to insist that the Pequots were massacred for the death of an outlaw, historians have traced the causes of the Anglo-Pequot War to a more complicated set of circumstances that includes the advent of European commerce along the eastern seaboard of North America, the land expansion policies of the new colonists, and the Puritans' ideological assump-tions about Indians. Trade policies, expansionism, and religious ideology are inseparable in their effects upon the treatment of Native peoples by European colonists. As Vine Deloria Jr. writes, "land has been the basis on which racial relations have been defined ever since the first settlers got off the boat."[35] Columbus's stated mission, Ward Churchill reminds us, was to discover wealth belonging to other peoples and to seize it for himself, his associates, and the crown of Spain. Toward this end, he instituted policies of slavery and extermination.[36] Such brutality was condoned by the church, which denied so-called pagans and heathens the rights accorded Christians. Similar attitudes among English Protestants set the groundwork for their own Indian policy. "Convinced . . . of divine right to Indian lands," writes Roy Harvey Pearce, "the Puritans discovered in the Indians themselves evidence of Satanic opposition to the very principle of divinity."[37] From these beginnings, the alleged savagery of Native peoples became, in the American mind, the chief obstacle to progress. As Pearce expresses it, "Civilization had created a savage, so as to kill him."[38]

The Puritans' exploitation of the land's human and natural resources was a continuation of policies that began in the mid-1500s, when the northeastern seaboard first became a lucrative source for timber, pelts, and other raw materials desired by European traders. The demand for these commodities underwrote early trading and settlement expeditions, including those of the Pilgrim Separatists, who, along with being religious fundamentalists, were hard-nosed businessmen. Although these enterprises eventually made many Europeans and European Americans wealthy, it impoverished the indigenous peoples, caused the massive depopulation of furbearing mammals, and led to the destruction of indigenous forests.[39] As William Cronon explains, English farmers also worked wholesale changes on the environment. As early settlement communities sought to become self-sufficient, English men and women cultivated large tracts of land for their own subsistence. Their earliest efforts to thus settle the land were aided by the results of a smallpox epidemic that had devastated the region a few years earlier. Presumably introduced to the Natives by trappers and other traders, the pox carried off entire shoreline communities; archaeologists estimate 80 to 90 percent mortality in Indian communities affected by the disease.[40] As a result, lands cleared by indigenous peoples were readily available to the newcomers. In this way, the basic land requirements of the colonists were easily satisfied.

Unfortunately for the region's surviving Natives, the fledgling European-American economy was also driven by speculation on the land's potential to generate surplus commodities, tax revenues, and rents.[41] For Native peoples, this meant that the basic material of their existence was exactly that which was most desired by the powerful invaders. Aware that their land use policies were suspect, the colonists postulated a legal construct known as *vacuum domicilium.*

Advanced by John Winthrop, John Cotton, and others who were anxious to deflect criticism and to satisfy their own minds, this theory held that people who inhabited unsubdued land, i.e., land that they used for hunting and the gathering of the spontaneous productions of nature, held no civil or legal right to their domains. Their "natural" rights were superseded by the civil rights of those who tilled the acreage and subdued the so-called "wilderness waste."[42] This doctrine was based on the willful misconception that Indians neither cultivated nor improved the lands under their dominion.

The threat *vacuum domicilium* posed to Native inhabitants was aggravated by competition for land among the colonies. The power and independence of any particular colony was dependent upon the extent and quality of the land over which it could assert jurisdiction. In *The Invasion of America,* Francis Jennings argues that this intracolonial competition for "unclaimed" land influenced the timing, prosecution, and aftermath of the Anglo-Pequot War.[43] When viewed from this perspective, the Pequots can be described as pawns in a larger chess game between Massachusetts Bay and Connecticut River colonists vying for control of the region.

The concerted efforts that English colonists made to place Indian territories under their control lends a great deal of credence to Jennings' insight that the acquisition of territory was a decisive factor in English aggression against the Pequots. By 1636, the English had claimed and placed under their collective jurisdiction a large New England territory bounded by the Connecticut River in the west, the expanding Massachusetts Bay settlement in the northeast, and Plymouth in the southeast. Within this ring, several large concentrations of indigenous peoples continued to live. Chief among these were the Wampanoags, the Narragansetts, and the Pequots. Ostensibly under the jurisdiction of Plymouth, the Wampanoags were, for the time being, relatively unmolested. The larger Narragansetts Nation had forged a strong alliance with Roger Williams in 1635 that allowed them to stave off conquest for another fifty years. The Pequots were the most remote of these groups. Buffered by the Nipmucks in the north and the Narragansetts in the east, they had had relatively little contact with the English. Moreover, the Pequots had been spared the plague that had devastated coastal villages in the 1610s, and, by the early 1630s, had become a power in the expanding wampum trade. Their own sphere of influence included eastern Long Island, a rich source of wampum-bead shells. Transporting this prized commodity to the mainland in large, seagoing canoes, the Pequots controlled a good deal of the region's wampum supply.[44] That was reason enough to draw the attention of the English, and as their territory was infiltrated by traders and settlers, control of their land base became a primary goal.

Other events contributed to the fragile coalition of Pequots and Englishmen that ended in 1636. The first of these was an epidemic of smallpox. In 1634, a Connecticut trader reported that the disease had carried as far west as any known Indian plantation.[45] Archaeologists estimate that more than 10,000 people and 80 percent of the Pequot Nation may have perished at this time.[46] The surviving group of 3,000 or 4,000 people was further weakened by a rift between Sassacus, their principal sachem, and Uncas, a rival Mohegan chief, who had married a daughter of the slain Totabem. Their disagreements, complicated by the enormous pressures bearing upon both groups, caused Uncas and his followers to declare their independence from Sassacus and become an independent Mohegan Nation. By 1635, when the English established settlement communities in Hartford and Saybrook, the Pequots were isolated and weakened. These Connecticut River settlements were largely independent of Massachusetts Bay and their mutual interests, control of the lower Connecticut River valley and the wampum trade, quickly merged. The Pequot power base was further eroded in 1636 when Uncas entered into an anti-Pequot alliance with Hartford and the Narragansett leader Miantonomi.[47] From this point on, Sassacus and his people were effectively surrounded.

The war of conquest against the Pequots began in August of 1636 when Massachusetts Bay sent punitive expeditions against Native communities at Block Island and also against Pequot settlements along the Pequot (now Thames) River. Led by John Endecott, this strike force was commissioned to take possession of Block Island and to demand tribute and other concessions from the Pequots. The Indians at Block Island were being held collectively responsible for the killing of John Oldham. In *Facing West,* Richard Drinnon describes Oldham as a "grasping, contentious man who picked quarrels with everybody."[48] He is believed to have angered a number of Narragansett sachems and might very well have been killed by them.[49] Because his boat and slain body had been discovered off the coast of Block Island, the Block Islanders, allies of the Narragansetts, were targeted. Endecott was instructed to put the men to death, but spare the women and children. According to John Underhill, about fourteen Indians were killed and several others maimed during the raid.[50] As the Indians fled, their

houses were burned, their fields were destroyed, and their corn and other possessions were confiscated by the English.

After regrouping at Saybrook, the English sailed to Pequot. According to
the commission from Massachusetts, they were to demand an additional 1,000
pounds of wampum for damages, the killers of Stone and his crew, and several
Pequot children as hostages.[51] When the Pequots failed to meet any of these
demands, they were attacked and their fields and houses in the immediate vicinity were destroyed, while their stores of corn were ransacked. The Narragansetts
reported that at least a dozen Pequots were killed in the raid.[52] Lion Gardener
would report only one Pequot death.[53] The bloodshed, destruction, and theft
instigated a violent response from the Pequots. Soon after, they set siege to the
fort at Saybrook, killing several men in the winter of 1636–37, and in April of
1637, they attacked the colonists at Wethersfield. Six English men and three
women were killed in the raid and two young women were taken captive.[54]

The Pequot attack on Wethersfield was both a reprisal against English
aggression and an attempt to uphold their obligations to Sequin, a Wangunk
sachem and Pequot ally on the Connecticut River. When the English first established Wethersfield, they agreed to allow the original Native inhabitants of the site
to remain within the new town's boundary. In April, the English abruptly broke
this "covenant," as it is described in colonial records, and drove the Natives
out.[55] After the war, Bay Colony magistrates ruled that indeed Sequin had been
unfairly treated by the colonists and should be cleared of all charges.[56] Apparently, these new refugees turned to their only source of redress, the Pequots. The
Pequots' resolve, however, only provoked the Connecticut colonists at Hartford,
who hitherto had been uninvolved in the Bay Colony's intrigues to subdue the
nation. In May of 1637, they raised a force of some ninety men under Captain
John Mason, a veteran of continental wars who had served with the English
expeditionary army in the Netherlands.[57] With an additional force of Mohegan
allies under Uncas, and another twenty men from Massachusetts Bay under John
Underhill, they destroyed Weinshauks, a Pequot town along the Mystic River,
burning it to the ground and killing as many as 700 people, including elders,
women, and children, in a single dawn raid.

Sassacus and his followers fled west with as much wampum and other
provisions as they could carry, while others fled to Narragansett and Long Island
to seek protection. Apparently, Sassacus had hoped to find refuge, if not allies,
among the Mohawks. Most of these survivors, however, were surrounded by

a new force of English soldiers in a swamp near present-day Fairfield. Sassacus and a few others escaped, only to find the Iroquois hostile to them. The others were killed or taken captive. Sassacus was subsequently beheaded by the Mohawks.

In his assessment of the war, Cave writes that Sassacus was miscast as a "savage" aggressor. Appropriating the language of gambling and play, he describes him as an inept leader who never learned how to play the game, a game that Uncas mastered and Miantonomi, the Narragansett leader, ultimately lost.[58] The "final outcome" of the war, he writes, "was loss of Algonquian autonomy," and he notes that a revisionist history of the Pequot War written from the Native American point of view "might well de-emphasize decisions made at Boston, Plymouth, Saybrook, and Hartford and focus instead on the miscalculations and blunders in Pequot, Mohegan, and Narragansett councils that paved the way for the early establishment of English hegemony in southern New England."[59] While this view may contribute to an attempt to understand the Anglo-Pequot War from an enlightened cross-cultural perspective, it comes dangerously close to blaming the victims for what can only be described as the absolute disregard for Native peoples that a great many English colonists continually demonstrated. As we will see in chapters 2 and 3, even the most politic Native leaders failed to win any lasting concessions from Englishmen bent on expropriating their territories and exploiting their resources.

Around Mystic, the mop-up operation continued. Another large band of Pequots had taken refuge at a place called Ohomowauke, or the Owl's Nest, a swamp in the upper reaches of the Mystic River, near or within the borders of present-day Mashantucket.[60] In late June of 1637, these survivors were surrounded by soldiers from Massachusetts Bay under Captain Israel Stoughton. The Pequots held out as long as they could, but with starvation threatening the weakest members of the group, they finally surrendered. One hundred prisoners are said to have been taken. The men were bound, put on a ship, and carried out to sea to be thrown overboard and drowned.[61] The women and children were claimed by the English. A letter from Captain Stoughton to Governor Winthrop describes the handling of these valued captives:

> By this pinace, you shall receive forty-eight or fifty women and children, unless there stay any here to be helpful, &c. Concerning which, there

is one, I formerly mentioned, that is the fairest and largest that I saw amongst them, to whom I have given a coate to cloathe her. It is my desire to have her for a servant, if it may stand with your good liking, else not. There is a little squaw that steward Culacut desireth, to whom he hath given a coate. Lieut. Davenport also desireth one, to wit, a small one. . . . He desireth her if it will stand with your good liking.[62]

Writing about the effects of this action two centuries later, William Apess described the emotional scarring that resulted from the Pequots having had their mothers, wives, sisters, and daughters thus claimed by the conquerors: "However much subsequent efforts were made to soothe their sorrows, in this particular, they considered the glory of their nation as having departed."[63] In the following months, more Pequots were divided up among their English and Indian conquerors. Others were put on slave ships and transported to Bermuda and the West Indies, with some being transported as far as Central America.[64] In the following year, remaining Pequots were formally divided among the Mohegans and Narragansetts, and the nation itself was officially outlawed.

The Pequot War Narratives and Their Legacy

The first study to read the Pequot War narratives as literature was Richard Slotkin's *Regeneration through Violence*. Writing in the wake of the civil rights and antiwar movements of the late 1960s, Slotkin noticed an affinity between Indian war chronicles and epics of chivalry and European quest mythologies. Informed by the use of these traditional genres in combination with the war adventure and captivity narrative, the Pequot War narratives established part of the ideological and formal groundwork for the frontier romances of the nineteenth century. The first of these narratives, published in London in 1638, was Philip Vincent's "A True Relation of the Late Battle Fought in New England, Between the English and the Savages, with the Present State of Things There." Short on details, and without reference to conflicts underway within the English–American community itself, "A True Relation" codified the story of Indian depredation and English response that would be retold countless times in the coming centuries. For Vincent, the war began when the Pequots launched an unprovoked attack against Saybrook that resulted in the killing of three men. Interestingly, Vincent does not demonize his adversaries. Unlike the satanic Pequots that would appear in later texts, Vincent's "Pequetans" are sons of Adam and made from the same "matter" and "mold" as their civilized English counterparts. Lacking the art and grace of civilization, however, they are inferior to and easily defeated by the English. As Slotkin notes, Vincent builds his narrative on the conventions of classical drama.[65] In this first narrative, Pequot history is an inevitable, tragic decline into silence and death: "a day of thanksgiving was solemnly celebrated for this happy success; the Pequetans now seeming nothing but a name."[66] In contrast to their Pequot aggressors, Vincent describes the English as a sober, devout, and industrious people with a progressive history.

The seemingly formulaic nature of Vincent's text indicates the extent to which the particular events of the conflict could be readily framed within and explained through existing narrative patterns. As Hayden White argues, no historical event is intrinsically tragic or comic. How a particular set of occurrences are configured in writing depends on the mind-set of the writer and the expectations of the audience for whom he writes, both of which are tied to particular cultural and historical experiences.[67] The tragic emplotment of Pequot history thus resulted from a confluence of England's literary heritage and the colonists' ideological assumptions about Indians, assumptions that assigned indigenous peoples to extinction.

For living Native peoples, Vincent's history reflects a disturbing disparity of power. As a result of their victory, the colonists were now assured of their peace, "by killing the barbarians, better than our English Virginians were by being killed by them." Vincent continues: "for having once terrified them, by severe execution of just revenge, they shall never hear of more harm from them, except, perhaps, the killing of a man or two at his work, upon advantage, which their sentinels and corps-du-guards may easily prevent. Nay, they shall have those brutes their servants, their slaves, either willingly or of necessity, and docible enough, if not obsequious."[68] Vincent's reference to the Virginians refers to the Powhatan uprising of 1622, an attack that resulted in the death of one-quarter of Virginia's 1,200 English residents.[69] As its reference to this conflict would indicate, Vincent's history articulates a broader British colonial perspective on the Anglo-Pequot War. A third-person narrative, it suggests how the events in New England were part of an overall pattern of conflict and expansion that resulted in the radical decline of Indian power and an attendant rise of English dominance.

Thus structured on simple binaries, "A True Relation" fails to account for conflicts among the English themselves or to include a representation of counterclaims made by the Pequots. For these, we must turn to the first narrative of the war produced by one of its chief prosecutors, Captain John Underhill's *Newes from America.* This was the first text to offer the English reading public an insider's first-hand account of the dramatic events that had recently unfolded in the New World. As the title of his book suggests, Underhill's concern was not strictly with conflict with Indians, but with a larger group of issues that concerned the colonists' domestic disputes as well.

Underhill was the son of a career soldier who, in the early seventeenth century, emigrated to the Netherlands, the European center of military science. Following in his father's footsteps, he studied military science and fought in the Thirty Years War.[70] In 1630, Underhill emigrated to New England and was soon appointed captain of the Massachusetts Bay Colony militia. Under the government of the colony, he held a number of military posts and, beginning as early as 1632, participated in raids against regional Natives. Underhill found these actions to be profitable; for his service against Indians on the Muddy River near Brookline, he was awarded 100 acres of land.[71] In 1636, Underhill sailed with Endecott to Block Island and the Pequot settlements along the Pequot River; in 1637, he led the small contingent of Massachusetts Bay soldiers in Mason's raid. In the fall of that year, his fortunes took a turn for the worse. Associated with the so-called Antinomian party, Underhill was censored, disarmed, and disenfranchised by the Bay Company magistrates.[72] He would not be reinstated until 1641, when new rumors of Indian conspiracies began to circulate.[73] Between 1642 and 1653, Underhill lived in New Netherlands, where he led attacks on Indian communities in Long Island and Westchester.[74]

As a result of his successes against the Indians, Underhill has been viewed as a prototype for other legendary Indian fighters like Kit Carson and Tom Quick.[75] Lawrence Hauptman explains that this tendency to cast Underhill in a heroic role effaces the man's violent tendencies, which could only be understood as heroic when construed as part of the larger American epic of winning the West from the savages. In his provocative essay, Hauptman suggests that Underhill can aptly be described as a sociopath suffering from what today would be diagnosed as "antisocial personality disorder."[76] As well as participating in violence against Indians, Underhill provoked authorities wherever he landed and behaved badly enough to be banished from three colonies.

In order to appreciate the context, style, and content of Underhill's narrative, it is necessary to examine his participation in the "Antinomian" movement more closely. Hauptman argues that Underhill was not a man of deep religious convictions, associated as he was at various times in his life with High Church Anglicanism, Puritanism, Antinomianism, Anabaptism, and Quakerism.[77] Nonetheless, his narrative has been construed as a response to the Antinomian Controversy and Puritan reprisals against Antinomians. Like other independent movements within the colony's jurisdiction, the Antinomians threatened the Bay Company's ability to make and enforce laws, adjudicate conflict, and otherwise dominate the settlement process. These intercolonial conflicts were aggravated by pressures from England. In 1634, the ship that brought one famous Antinomian leader to Boston, Anne Hutchinson, also delivered the king's official request for the return of an increasingly independent Bay Company's charter.[78]

Lead by Governor Henry Vane, a young man with powerful connections in England, the Reverend John Wheelwright, Thomas Hutchinson, and his wife, Anne, the Antinomians represented formidable, if marginal, interests within the Puritan community. The root cause of the controversy appears to have been the Antinomians' discontent with what they perceived to be the legalistic, text-bound teaching of the colony's ministers.[79] Contending that the community's church and government leaders were laboring under a "covenant of works" (i.e., the belief that good works and worldly success were a sign of grace), they hoped to restore a "covenant of grace" (i.e., the belief that worldly signs were no indicator of God's predestined will).[80] Openly at odds with the increasingly authoritarian practices of the church fathers, the Antinomians advanced a model of religious instruction that encouraged dialogue amongst all members of the church, including its women and children. Most radically of all, the Antinomians included Anne Hutchinson among their leaders at a time when women were allowed no official roles in the community.[81]

In response to what they perceived as a growing threat to order and stability, the magistrates charged the Hutchinson–Wheelwright party, a group they now referred to as "Antinomians," or "against the law," with heresy and sedition, two capital charges. The controversy escalated in early 1637, when Wheelwright delivered an inflammatory sermon. Outraged, the magistrates brought Wheelwright to court and subsequently found him guilty of contempt and sedition. In March of 1637, before the sentence was handed down, Underhill, along with Anne Hutchinson and other members of the group, signed a petition protesting the verdict and demanding that it be rescinded. This led to more punitive decisions against the Antinomians, who were brought into court and cross-examined by the magistrates. The well-known trial of Anne Hutchinson became the climax of this drama. By late 1637, just a few months after the conclusion of the Anglo-Pequot War, several families and persons would be banished from the colony, Underhill among them.[82]

Newes from America, published in 1638 in London, was written when Underhill took refuge in England. Slotkin identifies the main themes of the book as expressing Underhill's desire for personal and religious freedoms restricted only by the restraints of God and conscience.[83] Combining apologia with a religious allegory, promotional pamphlet, and war adventure, *Newes from America* is well suited to a dialogic critique. To apply Bakhtin's phraseology, the text is "shot through" with "shared thoughts, points of view, alien value judgments, and accents," that participate simultaneously in a variety of overlapping discourses, including those of English colonists and Pequot Indians.[84]

Heavily influenced by Underhill's recent problems with the Bay Colony's magistrates, *Newes from America* is shot through with references to the Antinomian crisis. In connecting the colony's social and religious upheavals with the timing of the war, Larzer Ziff has argued that the Anglo-Pequot War was partly instigated by the need to resolve intercolonial tensions generated by the Antinomian Controversy.[85] Taking this argument a step further, Anne Kibbey, a feminist scholar, has suggested that the war resulted from the patriarchal need to justify violence as a means of control.[86] Responding to these issues, Underhill seems to have been interested in deflecting criticism from the colony while at the same time defending his own perceived Antinomianism. In England, anti-Puritan "clamours," as Underhill refers to them, were particularly acute in 1637–38, when it was reported that "New England men usurpe over their wives and keep them in servile subjection" (6). Writing in the wake of Anne Hutchinson's trial, Underhill seems eager to recant his own error in supporting the Wheelwright-Hutchinson party by repeating what had become orthodoxy in New England, that "[husbands] are not bound to call their wives in Councell, though they are bound to take their private advice (so farre as they see it make for their advantage and their good)" (6). To illustrate this idea, Underhill describes how his own wife, "with Dalilah's flattery and with her mournful teares," proved herself to be a useful and obedient helpmate by insisting that he wear his helmet on the expeditions to Block Island and Pequot (5–6). Comments such as this one offer a subtle retraction of Underhill's Antinomianism and a defense of the magistrates' edicts.

Underhill's demonstrations of religious zeal provide the text with another element of personal defense. Whatever his spiritual beliefs may have been, it would difficult by today's standards to question Underhill's piety. In *Newes from America,* we find several demonstrations of this piety, one of which occurs in the middle of the book, just before the narration of the attack on the Pequot fort in Mystic. The passage recalls the experience of the two girls taken in the Pequot raid at Wethersfield. Underhill describes how he and the other soldiers interviewed the elder of the two. Suspecting the Pequots of sexual misconduct, they show a keen interest in knowing if she had been "solicited to uncleanness" (29). According to Underhill, she describes her heart being "much broken" by the ordeal. As a result, she is led to consider God's "just displeasure to them that had lived under so prudent means of grace . . . and had been so ungrateful" (29). Prefiguring Mary Rowlandson's captivity narrative by some forty years, her experience becomes a lesson for herself, the soldiers attending her, and the reader. As Slotkin writes, Underhill's wilderness is a place of trial; hardship and violence, rather than indicating the absence of God, are signs of his presence and love.[87] Anticipating the violence against the Pequots, Underhill's catechism continues: "better in a fierie furnace with the presence of Christ, then in a Kingly palace without him" (31). The sermon concludes six pages later with a defense of both parties to the Antinomian conflict. "Why do you stand and admire at New England," he writes to his English audience, "that there should be contentions there, and differences there, and that for the truth of Christ?" (34).

Written during a period of New England history known as the Great Migration, *Newes from America* participates in the discourse of New World promotion. In several passages, Underhill waxes eloquent on the beauty and abundance of the land. As well as referencing the "war-like proceedings" against the Indians, the book's full title encouraged prospective settlers with references to newly "discovered" places that, "as yet have very few or no Inhabitants which would yeeld special accommodation to such as will Plant there, Viz: Queenapoick, Agu-wom, Hudsons River, Long Island, Nahanticut, Martins Vineyard, Pequet, Naransett Bay, Elizabeth Islands, Piscataway, Casko with about a hundred Islands neere to Casko." Four of these places, Queenapoick, Long Island, Nahanticut, and Pequet, were newly available to English settlers as a result of the war. In the midst of his narration of the war, Underhill treats the reader to a three-and-a-half page digression that "sets forth the excellence of the whole country" (19). *Newes from America* thus shows an affinity with promotional tracts like William Wood's *New England's Prospect.* In common with Wood, who does not represent the Indians as a great danger to the colonists, Underhill minimizes the Pequot threat. Accordingly, the prosecution of the "war" in *Newes from America* reads more like a police action than a military campaign.

As a war chronicle, *Newes from America* offers dramatic accounts of Endecott's raids on Block Island and Pequot in 1636 and the destruction of Weinshauks in 1637. Underhill builds tension in his narrative by emphasizing the danger the Indians pose to the colonists. Describing how the "insolent" and "barbarous" Pequot Nation was defeated by a "few feeble instruments" and "souldiers not accustomed to warre," he creates anticipation for the glorious victory that follows (2). However, despite Underhill's insistence on the vulnerability of the English forces, he gives clear indications of their military advantage. Skins for armor, canoes for pinnaces, and arrows for musket balls and cannon shot make for poor exchanges. The military tactics of the Natives put them at a further disadvantage. As Underhill notes, the Indians preferred to divide their forces into small groups. Leading these smaller forces, Indian captains took care to minimize their own casualties while exacting them from the enemy. Ward Churchill explains that this mode of fighting was not intended to destroy an enemy but to define a territory, the traditional purpose of much Indian warfare.[88] The object of minimizing casualties was also encouraged by the practice of counting coups. For an indigenous man, a reputation for bravery in warfare could be gained by simply striking an enemy on his body or head; it was not always necessary to kill him. For a career soldier like Underhill, trained in the far more violent modes of European warfare, this style of fighting was closer to a sporting contest:

> *when wee saw wee could have no advantage against them in the open*
> *field, wee requested our Indians for to entertaine fight with them, our*
> *end was that wee might see the nature of the Indian warre: which they*

granted us and fell out; the Pequeats, Naragansetts, and the Mohigeners
changing a few arrowes together after such a manner, as I dare boldly
affirme, they might fight seven yeares and not kill seven men: they came
not neere one another, but shot remote, and not point blanke, as wee often
doe with our bullets, but at rovers, and then they gaze up in the skies to see
where the Arrow falls, and not untill its fallen doe they shoot againe, this
fight is more for pastime, then to conquer and subdue enemies. (40–41)

Considering the modes of warfare that had become customary for Europeans at this time, it is not surprising that Underhill would make such a low estimation of the Pequots' effectiveness as a fighting force. As Hauptman reminds us, the Anglo-Pequot War occurred in the midst of Europe's Thirty Years' War, a period from 1618 to 1648 when an estimated 7.5 million Germans, one-third of the total population, were killed and some 20,000 Swiss towns destroyed.[89]

Because of what they perceived to be the English militia's superhuman firepower and resiliency, properties they associated with *Manitou* as well as other material advantages, the Indians were extremely reluctant to engage colonial troops in open battle, preferring instead to launch surprise attacks and ambushes. A clear picture of what the Pequots considered to be their own vulnerability and the militia's extreme bellicosity is illustrated in Underhill's narration of the 1636 raid. It describes how five English ships bearing Endecott's men sailed unexpectedly into the heart of Pequot territory. In *Newes from America,* the ensuing negotiations and the violence that follows them are represented as a complex drama enacted by leaders of the English militia and their Indian adversaries. The action begins as the English ships are sailing along the Niantic shore. The men aboard are addressed by a "multitude" of Niantics running along the beach: "What cheere Englishmen; what cheere, what doe you come for" (9). According to Underhill, the Indians went on "cheerily" until the vessels reached the Pequot River, where their tone abruptly changed: "What Englishman, what cheere, what cheere, are you hoggerie, will you cram us—That is, are you angry, will you kill us, and doe you come to fight" (9). Through all of this, the English remained silent. This strategy contributed to the anxiety of the Indians, who became increasingly disconcerted and fearful as nightfall approached. Refusing to speak to the Indians, the English militia anchored their ships in the Pequot River, where they spent the night. Far from silent, the Indians continuously vocalized their unease. According to Underhill, "They made most dolefull, and woefull cryes all night, (so that wee could scarce rest) hollowing one to another, and giving the word from place to place, to gather their forces together, fearing the English were come to warre against them" (9).

While the Pequots' actual responses to Endecott's raid will always be the subject of speculation, Underhill's reporting of their words and deeds contributes significantly to a dialogic reading of the text. Allowing voices from a variety of ideologically invested positions to speak, *Newes from America* provides the Pequots with a space to represent their own side of the issue. The most dramatic instance of this occurs on the morning following the arrival of the English ships, when Endecott's ship is visited by a Pequot emissary. Underhill introduces this man as a "grave Senior, a man of good understanding, portly, cariage grave, and majesticall in his expressions" who demands to know why the English have come (10). The ambassador relates the execution of the Pequot sachem by the Dutch for the deaths of the Narragansett traders. "This much exasperated our spirits," the senior is reported as saying, "and made us vow revenge" (11). Pequot reprisals against Captain Stone followed shortly thereafter:

> *suddenly after came these Captains with a vessell into the River, and pretended to trade with us as the former did: wee did not discountenance them for the present, but tooke our opportunity and came aboord. The Sachems sonne succeeding this Father, was the man that came; into the Cabin of Captain Stone, and Captaine Stone having drunke more than did him good, fell backwards on the bed asleep; the Sagamore tooke his opportunitie, and having a little hatchet under his garment, therewith knockt him in the head. . . . Saith the Ambassadour to us, could yee blame us for revenging so cruell a murder: for wee distinguish not between the Dutch and English, but tooke them to be one Nation, and therefore wee doe not conceive that we wronged you, for they slew our king; and think-ing these Captaines to be of the same Nation and people, as those that slew him, made us set upon this course of revenge. (11–12)*

When the English responded that the Pequots "were able to distinguish between Dutch and English, having had sufficient experience of both nations," the ambassador insisted, "we know no difference betweene the Dutch and the Eng-lish, they are both strangers to us, we tooke them to bee all one, therefore we crave pardon, wee have not wilfully wronged the English" (12). Not wishing to debate the point, the English demanded the heads of those who had slain Stone and his men. The ambassador again responded diplomatically: "I will intreat you to give me libertie to goe ashore, and I shall informe the body of the people what your intent and resolution is: and if you will stay aboord, I will bring you a sudden answer" (13).

While the English allowed the ambassador to leave, they did not stay aboard their ships, but "suddenly after" followed. The ambassador, apparently alarmed by this action, entreated the English to "come no neerer" (13). The ambassador soon returned to inform the English that "he had inquired for the Sachem" so that the two sides might come to a "parlie: but neither of both of the Princes were at home, they were gone to Long Island" (13). Replying that they "must not be put off thus, the English threatened to "beat up the Drumme, and march through the Countrey, and spoyle [the] corne" (13). To this the ambassador replied, "if you will but stay a little while, I will steppe to the plantation and seeke for them" (13).

One of the intriguing issues raised by Underhill's representation of the Pequot ambassador involves the question of translation. Earlier in the narrative, Underhill makes reference to an Indian translator present with the company who participated in the raid on Block Island. Jill Lepore speculates that this may have been Metacom's (King Philip's) future counselor, John Sassamond, a literate Wampanoag.[90] Another possible translator of the emissary's speech is Thomas Stanton, an Englishman whom Cave characterizes as a "gifted young translator" fluent in the Algonquian dialects of southern New England.[91] Perhaps the ambassador knew English, or communicated through a universally understood sign language. Or, perhaps, for the sake of the dramatic impact, Underhill represented the Pequot position as best he could. Regardless of its sources, the voice attributed to this Pequot leader reveals a rhetorical dissonance that, in time, has challenged the interpretation of events the author sought to impose on his subject. Within a narrative conceived, in part, to refute and silence Pequot voices, the Pequots' persistent attempts to reach an understanding with the English that reflected their own sense of justice and what reciprocity demanded are revealed. As Cave notes, the ambassador's speech was shrewdly crafted to present Stone's killing in terms that the English would find constituted a justifiable act of revenge.[92] The fact that he failed to achieve this end indicates the extent to which the English refused to consider nonviolent resolutions to the conflict.

This "grave," "senior" man would not return to the scene. His place is taken by a second Pequot, who tells the English that "Mommenoteck was found, and would appear before [them] suddenly" (14). An hour later, the increasingly impatient English are visited by a third Pequot, who entreats the English to show "further patience . . . for he had assembled the body of the Pequeats together, to know who the parties were that had slaine these English men" (14). Apparently, the Pequots were willing to give up the killers, if it could be shown that they were indeed among them. According to Underhill, this last messenger also brought word from the sachem that if the English would lay down their arms and approach thirteen paces from them and meet the "heathen" prince, "he would cause his men to doe the like" so that the two groups could come to a "parlie" (14).

The complete breakdown of efforts to resolve the situation peacefully is dramatically illustrated by Underhill, who terms "insolent" the efforts of the Pequots to arrange talks, protect their food stores, organize a defense, and move the elders, women, and children to safety (15). As Drinnon writes, "the Pequots were 'insolent' only if it be insolent to resist subjugation and dispossession."[93] Unwilling to talk, and frustrated in their demands, Endecott's men attack the Pequot town: "marching into a champion field we displayed our colours, but none would come neere us, but standing remotely off did laugh at us for our patience, wee suddenly set upon our march, and firing their Wigwams, spoyling their corn, and many other necessaries that they had buried in the ground wee raked up, which the souldiers had for bootie. Thus wee spent the day burning and spoyling the Countrey" (15). It was in response to these actions that the Pequots would later lay siege to the fort at Saybrook and attack the colonists at Wethersfield. These reprisals would have tragic consequences. The following spring, Pequot towns would be targeted by a new colonial militia formed to conquer the "insolent" nation.

The destruction of Weinshauks in May of 1637 has remained a controversial issue. In Underhill's time, as well as our own, readers have wondered what, if anything, justified such an indiscriminate slaughter. *Newes from America* is informed by such questions. While Underhill speaks from a position ideologically invested in the goals of Connecticut and Massachusett Bay Colony authorities, his text represents a wider range of voices and positions. Among the many dissonant chords sounded in Underhill's text are those of the English militia's Indian allies. Underhill described their shock in the wake of the fort massacre;

"'Nach, it. Nach, it,' they cried. 'It is too furious and slaies too many men'" (43). In England, news of the slaughter was also received with disapproval, the traces of which can be found in Underhill. "It may be demanded," he wrote, "why should you be so furious (as some have said); should not Christians have more mercy and compassion?" (40). Underhill defends the militia by citing biblical precedent: "sometimes the Scripture declareth women and children must perish with their parents; some-time the case alters: but we will not dispute it now. We had sufficient light from the word of God for our proceedings" (40). Emphasizing these oppositional voices in *Newes from America* demonstrates the heterodox nature of the Anglo-Pequot War. Although the dominant Puritan faction took a very hard line in dealing with the Indians, we see differences in opinion not only between the Puritans and the Pequots, but among other groups of Indians and Englishmen as well. Underhill's text, in recording all of these voices, demonstrates the complexity of Indian-white relations in early southern New England. While Underhill seems interested in "quenching" the "clamour" of dissonant voices, his text has had the effect of preserving those voices.

Some twenty years after Vincent and Underhill published their books independently in London, two other firsthand accounts of the Anglo-Pequot War were written to resolve the jurisdictional questions raised by the war. These were John Mason's *A Brief History of the Pequot War* and Lion Gardener's *Relation of the Pequot Warres.* Both were important in establishing Connecticut's claim to the Pequots' conquered territory. Written in 1656, Mason's history first appeared as such in 1736 when Thomas Prince published the complete work with his own careful glosses and an introduction that emphasized, quite out of character with the original, the figure of Mason himself.[94] Earlier, an abridged version had appeared in the 1670s when Increase Mather and William Hubbard worked sections of Mason's history into official accounts of the King Philip's War. Written around 1660, Gardener's *Relation* did not appear to a general audience until 1832, in the midst of the removal controversy. Both were written at the behest of the General Court of Connecticut, which needed them to legitimize their claim to Pequot territory. Unlike Vincent's and Underhill's, these texts are of continuing significance to indigenous-colonial relations in southeastern Connecticut because they helped to determine which colonial government would claim jurisdiction over the Pequots and other groups affected by the war.

When Winthrop gave the order to attack Block Island in 1636, Massachusetts Bay considered Connecticut to be within its jurisdictional boundaries. Recently immigrated settlers from Massachusetts Bay then living in Connecticut River settlements at Hartford, Windsor, and Wethersfield had agreed to continue under the colony's rule as a condition of their removal.[95] Saybrook, on the other hand, was independent of Massachusetts Bay. Governed by John Winthrop Jr., this outpost at the mouth of the Connecticut River was established by a royal commission from Lords Say and Brooke. Although Massachusetts considered all of Connecticut to be within its patent boundaries, the Connecticut colonists under the younger Winthrop would eventually claim western Rhode Island to the Connecticut River Valley as their own. These overlapping claims to the territories formerly controlled by the Pequots have led some scholars to argue that Mason's raid was a preemptive strike to establish a Connecticut colony with claims to conquered Pequot territories. Francis Jennings has offered the provocative thesis that the brutal massacre of the Pequots at Mystic, and the exterminatory campaign that followed, largely resulted from intracolonial conflicts over control of the lands that comprised the Pequot and Connecticut river valleys.[96] Charles Orr, a historian who edited the first complete volume of the Pequot War narratives in the 1880s, wrote that the Connecticut General Assembly's decision to fund and to organize Mason's expedition against the Pequots was Connecticut's first sovereign act toward statehood.[97]

Whatever its intentions may have been, Hartford's bold action against the Pequots led to a legal war between Massachusetts and Connecticut. Massachusetts claimed that all the territory east of the Pequot River to the Rhode Island border was its by right of conquest. To the contrary, Connecticut claimed that its jurisdiction extended several miles east of that line, to the banks of the Pawcatuck River. Although Connecticut had de facto control of the territory, Massachusetts pressed its claims in 1646, 1647, and again in 1657. In that latter year, the Commissioners of the United Colonies heard arguments from both sides; Mason himself was the legal representative for Connecticut.[98] In 1658, the commissioners ruled in favor of Massachusetts. The restoration of Charles II, however, provided Connecticut with another opportunity to incorporate the territory. With Mason acting as chief executive, Governor John Winthrop Jr. traveled to England and petitioned the king. In 1662, he returned with a new patent that guaranteed, once and for all, Connecticut's claim to the territory east of the Pequot River to the banks of the Pawcatuck.[99]

. . . . .

In its efforts to refute the claims of Massachusetts Bay, Mason's *A Brief History of the Pequot War* emphasizes the role of the forces commissioned by Hartford and led by Mason, and minimizes the impact of the smaller contingent of bay men who also participated in the raid. Within this context, it is significant to note that both of the two prefatory letters attributed to Mason are intended for a legal audience. The first is inscribed to the General Court at Connecticut, which, Mason claims, had often requested him to address the subject of the war. Thus, at the start of his history, Mason reveals a concern for "order" and "truth," qualities he distinguishes from "vain narration" (vii). The second prefatory note follows under this heading, "To the Judicious Reader" (v); at its conclusion, Mason is careful to identify himself as a New Englander. Although "judicious" could be a generic appeal to his audience, it would seem that Mason had the person or persons judging the case in mind. Within this context we might speculate that the "Brief" of the narrative's title is not meant to convey a sense of its length, but to identify the text as part of the legal documents collected to argue the case in England. According to *Black's Law Dictionary,* a *brief* is defined as "a written statement setting out the legal contentions of a party in litigation, esp. on appeal; a document prepared by counsel as the basis for arguing a case, consisting of legal and factual arguments and the authorities in support of them."[100] A brief can also be defined as "an abstract of all documents affecting the title of real property."[101] In the case of Mason's text, all of these meanings apply.

Prepared as part of a larger group of legal documents, Mason's history explicitly links the conquest of the Pequots with the land claims of Connecticut. The second prefatory note concludes with the following statement: "In a word, the Lord was as it were pleased to say unto us, The Land of Canaan will I give unto thee tho' but a few strangers in it."[102] By way of this legal frame, *A Brief History* makes the war not a matter of contested but of well-defined meanings. It attempts to eliminate the ambiguities of cultural conflict evident in *Newes from America* and replace them with the certainty of law. Thus, Mason's narrative, unlike any other contemporary account of the conflict, concludes with an action against a Pequot settlement on the banks of the Pawcatuck River. With the boundary of the claim established, Mason once again conjoins providence and real estate: "Thus the Lord was pleased to smite our Enemies in the hinder Parts, and to give us their Land for an Inheritance: Who remembered us in our low Estate, and redeemed us out of our Enemies' hands" (21). With this invocation of the deity to defend Connecticut's right to conquered Pequot territory, Mason's history explicitly links land claims issues to violence against Indians. Claiming an island at the mouth of the Mystic River by right of conquest, Mason himself was one of the principal beneficiaries of the war; in 1650, he was awarded another 1,000 acres by Connecticut's General Assembly.[103]

Divorced of its legal context, *A Brief History* was published for a general audience in 1736. Since at least 1716, and the publication of Benjamin Church's *Entertaining Passages on the King Philip's War,* Indian war narratives had become a popular genre for Anglo-American readers eager for new and exciting texts. In addition to being a stirring war adventure, Mason's narrative was also popular because its self-righteous style evoked the original piety of New England Puritanism. Appearing near the start of the Great Awakening, it contributed to the religious revival that would sweep through Connecticut and Massachusetts. Slotkin describes this rejuvenated Mason as a symbol of past heroism and the "power lost with the faith of the fathers and their intimacy with God." For Mason, the war itself is a "chastisement of the children of darkness by agents of the Lord."[104] It is only when his actions are construed in this way that John Mason, the man who gave the order to fire the Pequot village at Mystic, can be construed as an American hero.

If the legalistic dimensions of Mason's commentary on the Pequot War delayed its appearance to a general audience by some eighty years, Lion Gardener's *Relation of the Pequot War,* a text that offers a radical critique of early colonial Indian policy, waited 170 years. Unlike the other Pequot War narratives, his narration emphasizes the intracolonial aspects of the conflict. A professional army engineer who had served in Europe under the Prince of Orange,[105] Gardener begins his account with a complaint against the Bay Colony's handling of the Pequots, and not a complaint against the Pequots themselves. While he repeats the long-held orthodoxy that hostilities between the English and Pequots commenced with the murder of Captain Stone, he is quick to note that Stone was a Virginian, and as such, a stranger to the New England community and of no concern in its affairs. Stressing the delta outpost's independence from Boston,

Gardener complains about the shortage of men and criticizes the Boston magistrates for reneging on their promise to send reinforcements and supplies. He also points out that the Pequots had paid a substantial tribute of otter, beaver, and wampum because the "English had required those Pequits that had killed a Virginian, one Capt. Stone, with his Bark's crew, in Connecticut River, for their presents."[106] As Cave points out, the presents indicate the Pequots' desire for a nonviolent resolution to the conflict.

In assigning the cause of the hostilities to Massachusetts Bay, Gardener's relation supported the idea that Mason's expedition, originating in Hartford, was a distinctly Connecticut response to Pequot aggression. Toward this end, Gardener derides Endecott's ill-conceived mission to the Pequot River in 1636. Describing the Bay Colony's militia as "well-fitted," he fears that their actions will, to his "great grief," make the vulnerable fort at Saybrook "their rendezvous or seat of war." "You come hither to raise these wasps about my ears," he tells the bay men, "and then you will take wing and flee away" (140). Making "many allegations" against the magistrate's plans to take Pequot hostages and demand tribute, he further disassociates Connecticut from the machinations of Boston. "But go they did to Pequit," he writes, "and as they came without acquainting any of us in the River with it, so they went against our will" (140). For Gardener, it was the attack on Pequot that followed in the wake of his protestations that was the principal cause of the war: "The Bay-men killed not a man, save that one Kichomiquim, an Indian Sachem of the Bay, killed a Pequoty; and thus began the war between the Indians and us in these parts" (141–42). Repeated twice, this statement actually serves to justify Pequot attacks on colonial settlements and recontextualizes Mason's Connecticut-based strike on Mystic as an act of self-defense necessitated by the Bay Company's neglect and mismanagement.

By representing Pequot aggression as acts of self-defense motivated by violence originating in Massachusetts Bay, Gardener's narration of the war was a serviceable text for Winthrop Jr. as he sought to settle the land claims issue in favor of Connecticut. We can speculate that because it offered an interpretation of the war that weakly supported, if not undermined, colonial America's belief in its own righteousness in dealing with the Native Americans on fair and equitable terms, as well as the conceit that its wars against indigenous peoples were "just cause," Gardener's *Relation* was a text worth suppressing. By emphasizing dissension among colonial leaders and casting them in an unheroic light, Gardener's narrative reveals a critical dissonance within New England itself that resisted the production of its own master narratives.

Despite its challenge to many long-held orthodoxies, it would be wrong to construe Gardener's *Relation* as a pro-Indian text. While it criticized colonial leaders and actions, it also contributed to the rumors that eventually led to the execution of Miantonomi, the Narragansett sachem who was condemned by the English in Hartford and later executed by Uncas, Hartford's Mohegan ally.[107] Toward this end, Gardener reports this extraordinary speech attributed to the ill-fated Narragansett leader:

> So are we all Indians as the English are, and say brother to one another; so must we be one as they are, otherwise we shall be all gone shortly, for you know our fathers had plenty of deer and skins, our plains were full of deer, as also our woods, and of turkies, and our coves full of fish and fowl. But these English having gotten our land, they with scythes cut down the grass, and with axes fell the trees; their cows and horses eat the grass, and their hogs spoil our clam banks, and we shall all be starved. (154)

Gardener's ability to synthesize his collective experience with Indian peoples into this succinct complaint against English settlers suggests that he was an astute observer of his Indian adversaries and counterparts. Having held the dangerous territory at the mouth of the Connecticut River for the English and knowing what it meant to be the besieged, and not the aggressor, he could more fully comprehend the sense of bewilderment and exasperation that escalated into Indian violence. However, in corroborating the charges against Miantonomi, Gardener helped to hasten the sachem's demise.

The pathos that the doomed Miantonomi evokes in readers was not lost on William T. Williams, Esq., the New London gentleman and historian who edited Gardener's narrative for publication in the Massachusetts Historical Society Manuscript Series in 1832. In an introductory essay to Gardener's *Relation,* he makes reference to Miantonomi's tragic fate and describes at length the graves of the rival chiefs in Norwich. Uncas's grave, he writes, sits on a "royal burying ground . . . appropriated to the Uncas family." This "beautiful and romantic site," as he describes it, is owned by Calvin Goddard, Esq., of Norwich.[108] According to Williams, it was well preserved and "honrably" railed in and "appropriated to its use" as a grave. Perhaps in memory of Uncas's vital service to the English, we also read that Goddard has plans to enlarge the area and mark it with an "appropriate" stone. Miantonomi's grave is in much worse repair: "But a few years since a large heap of stones, thrown together by the wandering Indians, according to the custom of their country, and as a melancholy mark of the love the Narragansetts had for their fallen chief, lay on his grave: but the despicable cupidity of some people in that vicinity has removed them to make a common stone wall, as it saved them the trouble of gathering stones for that purpose. The spot of his sepulture is, however, yet known."[109] In many ways, this passage is characteristic of writings about New England Indians in the 1820s and 1830s, a period, as Cave notes, when some writers described the American savage as a doomed and helpless primitive, an "object of pity for whom the sentimental might shed a tear."[110] Like other East Coast writers and historians of the period, Williams valorized a romantic regional past complete with Indian nations vying for ascendancy. This curatorial impulse to preserve, and thereby evoke, a legendary New England landscape serves to enlarge the context of the narrative that follows. At the same time, however, Williams' reference to the struggle between the rival chiefs effaces the progress of English imperialism by emphasizing violence among indigenous groups themselves.

Williams also expresses regret over the colonials' attempt to erase completely a Pequot presence in southern New England by outlawing the nation and renaming the Pequot River the Thames.[111] His rather mild sense of disapproval of colonial policy is reflected in other contemporary texts. Just five years earlier, Catharine Maria Sedgwick, a writer descended from the Williamses in Stockbridge, Massachusetts, published *Hope Leslie,* a novel that problematized the strategy, but not the outcome, of the Pequot War. As we will see in chapter 2, such considerations of the Pequots were part of a larger discourse on Indians that occurred during the removal controversies of the 1820s and 1830s. In this respect, Gardener's text, as it was introduced by Williams' essay, provides a discursive link between the Pequot War narratives of the early and mid-seventeenth century and the literature pertaining to Indian–white conflict produced in the early nineteenth century.

In his attempts to connect the colonial past with the present, Williams offers the reader information about living communities of Native Americans, particularly surviving groups of Mohegan, Narragansett, Niantic, and Pequot peoples. Of these he has the most favorable impression of the Mohegans:

> *Considerable exertion is making now in favor of the Mohegans. A small, but neat church, has lately been erected by charity for them, and the United States have appropriated nine-hundred dollars to build a school-master's house, and for his salary. The house for the school-master is erected and a school master hired, who also preaches to the tribe. All of the tribe are anxiously sought out, and the benevolent are trying to bring them all together to their ancient seat. There are about seventy men on their land, or perhaps a few more. They own about three thousand acres of good land in Montville, about three miles below Norwich landing. The Trading Cove brook is their northern bound; their eastern is the Thames River.*[112]

Such were the rewards for a Native people that aligned itself early and successfully with the interests of the colonists at Hartford.

Williams' report on contemporary Pequots, however, reveals a virulent strain of racism that continued to plague the surviving community:

> *There is a remnant of the Pequots still existing. They lie in the town of Groton, and amount to about forty souls, in all, or perhaps a few more or less; but do not vary much from that number. They have about eleven hundred acres of poor land reserved to them in Groton, on which they live. They are more mixed than the Mohegans with negro and white blood, yet are a distinct tribe and still retain a hatred of the Mohegans. A short time since, I had the opportunity of seeing most of the tribe together. They are more vicious, and not so decent or so good-looking a people as the Mohegans. This however may be owing to their being more mixed with other blood.*[113]

This blatantly racist description of the Pequots underscores nineteenth-century America's preoccupation with race and the moral, social, and intellectual attributes accorded skin color. While their remarkable good fortune had brought the Mohegans to be viewed as civilized and Christianized Indians, the unfortunate Pequots, having intermarried with another unfortunate people, were marked as a community of degraded savages. Although their history was now valued as spice for the region, the yet living group was abhorred for having adopted an interracial survivance. In chapter 2, we will see how miscegenation posed one insurmountable barrier to improving Anglo-Indian relations, while in chapter 3, we will explore ongoing Pequot efforts to maintain their social and political communities and territorial rights through an acculturation to writing and Christianity.

"Lost in the Deep, 2. Voiceless Obscurity"

The Pequots as Metaphor in Catharine Maria Sedgwick's HOPE LESLIE

Best known for his utopian novel, *Looking Backward,* Edward Bellamy dramatized America's negative potential in his 1879 work *The Duke of Stockbridge.* Set during Shays' Rebellion, the novel describes a post-Revolutionary society that offered no chance for a poor man. In a depressed economy where only the wealthiest thrive, debtors stand by and watch as their possessions and property are auctioned off at prices far below market value; when monies so raised fall short of amounts owed, the poor are summarily thrown into prison. With this policy strictly enforced, the jails of his fictional town are filled to capacity. According to those who profit from his misfortune, the poor man has only himself to blame; his own bad habits are surely the cause of his troubles. This attitude is dramatized in a scene in which two young men are publicly whipped for playing cards. The cards, decorated with "heathenish" designs, are confiscated by the court. "How plainly do they typify," expounds a minister, "ill-gotten riches and bleeding hearts, violence and the grave."[1]

As this passage indicates, the American bourgeoisie identified gambling as a sign of class degeneracy. The deserving upper class practiced proper thrift and industry; the unregenerate lower class gambled. Bellamy well understood the irony of this situation and exploited it for dramatic impact. A similar distinction between those whose cultural practices and attitudes marked them as the most productive kind of citizens and those who lacked some intrinsic quality essential for taking on the rights and responsibilities of citizenship is treated with considerably less irony in Catharine Maria Sedgwick's *Hope Leslie; or, Early Times in the Massachusetts.* First published in 1827, Sedgwick's novel, as significantly informed by Stockbridge history as Bellamy's, takes as its subject Indian-white relations in the aftermath of the Anglo-Pequot War. In contrast to *The Duke of Stockbridge, Hope Leslie* describes a heroic frontier gentry beset by a variety of dissident factions, including Indians, Catholics, and Anglican cavaliers, who threaten the settlement with violence, anarchy, and sinfulness. The novel also provides an implicit commentary on the history of land encroachment and forced land cession that reduced the Native population to a state of debt peonage. It is this history that Sedgwick's narrative attempts to efface.

As is typical with historical novels, *Hope Leslie* is informed by the issues of its day. In 1827, the most significant of these involved Indian removal. Removal called for lands occupied by Indian nations east of the Mississippi to be exchanged for western lands. The most vocal supporters of removal were southern politicians like Andrew Jackson, who saw the opening of new lands for settlement and commerce as necessary for the social and economic development of the old Southwest. As the leader of the new Democrats, Jackson also sought the dismantling of the Bank of the United States, a federalist institution his supporters saw as an obstacle to commercial expansion. Jackson's Democrats were opposed by those who supported Indian land rights and those who were protective of their privileged social and economic status. Sympathetic to the concerns of this latter group, *Hope Leslie* implicitly supported the removalist policies of the southern states and their advocates at the same time that it upheld the gentry's traditional claim to power and the class distinctions it sought to enforce.

As the country moved toward removal, novels like James Fenimore Cooper's *Last of the Mohicans,* Lydia Maria Child's *Hobomok,* and Sedgwick's *Hope Leslie* transformed the history of Indian-white relations into a consumable, middle-class literature. For American writers and critics who sought to produce a unique national literature with indigenous, American roots, the history of Indian-white relations, as it had been written by Anglo-American writers and digested by Anglo-American readers, provided a basic source material.[2] Thus, while Sedgwick's novel was highly original, it was not the first Anglo-American text to exploit the dramatic and symbolic potential of the Anglo-Pequot War. As the appearance of Lion Gardener's *Relation of the Pequot Warres,* in the 1830s, indicates, that conflict had continued to be very much a part of the national consciousness throughout the antebellum period. Over time, the presumed and virtual extinction of the Pequots became both a literary device and a moral barometer that Indians and non-Indians alike employed to dramatize various concerns. It was during this period, when the remnants of the Pequot Nation had either been scattered throughout the Americas or survived in small communities in their home territory, that the word *Pequot* emerged as a sign identifying a variety of social, religious, and political positions on the question of Indian rights.

The late eighteenth and early nineteenth centuries saw individuals as diverse as Timothy Dwight, Elias Boudinot, William Apess, and Herman Melville incorporate the Pequot sign into their writings. A review of these references distinguishes four basic attitudes toward the meaning of that sign. In one formulation, *Pequot* was synonymous with "savage" and symbolized the Indian as chief obstacle to progress. The Pequot thus served as a metaphor for the eventual and necessary extinction of all Indians.

In a second formulation, the brutal massacre of the Pequots was figured as a moral crime. Adopted by advocates of tribal rights, this position cast a critical eye upon the white treatment of Indians and sought a reform of Indian policy. Among Native leaders, the presumed extinction of the Pequots served as a rallying cry against incursions by white settlers.

In a third formulation, the Pequots were not entirely extinct, but survived as a degraded, mixed-blood people. A spiritually and intellectually benighted race, such Pequots were, as William T. Williams represented them, symbolic of those Indians who willfully refused to receive the benefits of Christian civilization.

Opposing this last formulation was a fourth, in which surviving Pequots are model citizens. As we shall see in chapter 3, William Apess, a self-defined Pequot, used this approach to call attention to the injustices Indian peoples suffered and the need for the government, the courts, and the public at large to extend civil rights to Indians.

Writing from the first position, Timothy Dwight made references to the Anglo-Pequot War in *Greenfield Hill,* a long poem published in 1794 that celebrated the history of Fairfield, Connecticut, the site of the famous swamp fight. For Dwight, as it would for Sedgwick, the tragic overtones of the Pequots' violent demise served primarily to dramatize the triumph of Anglo-American civilization over indigenous American savagery. Dwight renders his Pequots as savage but formidable enemies whose defeat is a necessary step in the establishment of the town. Thus, he describes how the "sluggish wigwams," "clusters wild," and "snaky paths" of the Indians give way to the gardens, lawns, homes, and churches of the English.[3] As a Yankee farmer laboriously turns the soil, memories of the war are released. The poet recalls the terror of an Indian raid and the depredations of the child-murdering savages. John Stone himself is referred to as a "guiltless offering at th' infernal shrine" of savagery; in this way, the Pequots' presumed victims are canonized.[4] The poet also sheds a tear over the demise of the Pequots, a tear that "steals, impassion'd, o'er a nation's doom."[5] But Pequot doom is necessary if Fairfield is to become an English-American town.

In other texts, sympathy for the Pequots was connected to policy reform movements. In an 1816 study on Indian history and culture, *A Star in the West; or, a Humble Attempt to Discover the Ten Lost Tribes of Israel,* Elias Boudinot used the Anglo-Pequot War to openly criticize the attitudes that had shaped American Indian policy. Boudinot was a president of the American Bible Society and a strong defender of Native rights. In his text, Pequot extinction was plotted ironically. Rather than dramatizing the superiority of white America, the presumed triumph over savagery is refigured as a moral defeat. Taking up the argument that American Indians were descended from the Ten Lost Tribes of Israel, his book contributed to what Roy Harvey Pearce describes as a "grass-roots revivalist movement" to secure for the Indians a safe place within the United States.[6] It was with this purpose in mind that Boudinot recalled for the reader the massacre of Pequots at Mystic and Fairfield. In this revisionist history, the Pequot War narratives are characterized as "cold-blooded accounts of indiscriminate butchery."[7] Intending thus to provoke the reader's shame and regret, Boudinot employed Pequot history to condemn violence against Indians.

Indians likewise remembered the devastation of the Anglo-Pequot War and were doubtless moved by the example. In a speech attributed to the Shawnee leader Tecumseh, the speaker calls upon his audience to remember many once-powerful nations, including the Pequot, Narragansett, and Wampanoag, that had fallen before the avarice and oppression of the whites: "Have we not courage enough remaining to defend our country and maintain our ancient independence? Will we calmly suffer the white intruders and tyrants to enslave us?"[8] For Native leaders fighting to resist colonial incursions, the demise of the eastern nations helped to galvanize resistance to territorial encroachments. Pequot extinction thus demonstrated the urgency for a united Indian response to the invaders.

Participating in the historical conversation on the Anglo-Pequot War, Sedgwick's novel incorporates to one degree or another each of these perspectives. Like *A Star in the West,* it decries the indiscriminate slaughter of Indians. Sensitive to the perspectives of Indians, it allows Native characters to speak out against oppression and injustice. Despite these sympathetic gestures, the novel ultimately validates the Puritan conquest, and thus has most in common with Dwight's *Greenfield Hill.* While it laments the demise of the Pequots, it represents Indians as the principal threat to progress. In *Hope Leslie,* this threat is contained by an English family and its loyal servants. The counterparts to a family of Pequots, this group embodies the principles of an ideal community.

Sedgwick's novel, set in the wake of the Anglo-Pequot War and during the wave of English settlement that subsequently flooded the Connecticut River Valley, made its own argument in favor of removal. One of the most popular frontier romances, it explored the removal issue through an extended dialogue between imagined Anglo and Pequot voices. The principal characters in the text are two young women, Hope Leslie, an Anglo-American woman, and Magawisca, a Pequot princess. Countervailing popular stereotypes that fitted women to ineffective and subordinate roles (the helpmate, captive, or camp-drudge), Sedgwick assigns the important work of civilizing the frontier to both figures. While Hope serves as the prototype for a politically active American woman, Magawisca performs the functions of the mythical Indian princess. The adventures of these idealistic, intelligent, and outspoken young women provided a dramatic context to reevaluate the colonial legacy for a contemporary audience.

Although Sedgwick's allegory on the settlement process drew heavily from seventeenth-century sources, her thinking was undoubtedly informed by the history of Stockbridge. Formally incorporated in 1739 as an Indian town, Stockbridge was not conquered from the Indians, but gradually traded from them. Over a period of about fifty years, the original Mohican inhabitants of the town were systematically divested of their holdings and compelled to move west; what had been effected by force in the 1630s and 1670s against the Pequots, Wampanoags, and Narragansetts was here accomplished by legal process. Although grossly inequitable, most real-estate transactions that placed Indian territory in Anglo hands were entirely within the law.[9] Sedgwick's grandmother and great-grandfather greatly benefited from this process. The family's future comfort, including the luxury in which Sedgwick herself was raised, resulted from its great success in appropriating Mohican territory for its own use. The history of this appropriation provides an important context for reading the novel.

The history of Stockbridge can be traced to the history of Mohican peoples residing in the Housatonic River Valley. By the early 1720s, English settlements along the Connecticut River were pressing upon the eastern edge of the Berkshire Hills. On the western side of these hills, sixty miles west of Springfield, several communities of Housatonic Mohicans had settled. Pushed west by the Dutch and English in the Hudson River Valley, north by English settlers in the lower Housatonic, and held south by the Mohawks, this indigenous community would be the last of the Mohicans to enjoy its traditional sovereignty and independence. Yet through adroit diplomacy and strong leadership, the Mohicans staved off final displacement for many years. By cooperating with the English they became the Stockbridge Indians and gained a legal right to the town that was designed, at least in theory, for their primary use and habitation.

By the time Stockbridge was founded, the Mohicans already had had a great deal of experience in dealing with the Europeans. On the eve of contact, they occupied a large territory along the Hudson River north to Lake Champlain. In 1609, they met and traded with Henry Hudson and thus became involved in the fur trade.[10] For the Mohicans, competition for trade contributed to hostilities and warfare with other indigenous peoples. In 1628, contentions between the Dutch and Indians put them in a war against the Mohawks. On the losing end of the conflict, the Mohicans found their power to be greatly diminished.[11] The Mohawks now controlled Mohican territory west of the Hudson River, and the Mohicans themselves were forced to pay tribute to the Iroquois. Around this time, the Housatonic Mohicans also developed a trade alliance with the English at Springfield.[12] In 1662, John Pynchon established the first English trading post among them.[13] By 1675, hostilities between the Dutch, English, Mohawks, and Mohicans had officially ceased. Now allied with both the English at Albany and Springfield, the Mohicans remained neutral throughout the King Philip's War.

Despite the relative security of their diplomatic position, the Mohicans were increasingly threatened by disease, alcohol, and territorial expropriation. The fur trade, an ostensible benefit to Natives, contributed to these problems by disrupting traditional lifestyles, stimulating intertribal conflict, and absorbing Natives into the commercial economy. In pre–fur trade culture, animals were killed in relatively smaller numbers, as they were needed, for food, clothing, and ceremonial purposes. With the advent of a commercial economy, furbearing mammals were slaughtered en masse, a practice that both eroded traditional culture and undermined the Indians' long-term economic health. As animal populations diminished, intertribal tensions increased among Native peoples in search of the increasingly scarce commodity. This process left Indians vulnerable to land speculators, who profited from the collapse of fur markets.

Other dangers resulted from business practices that were intentionally exploitative. As one Hudson River Mohican explained, in the early 1720s, alcohol consumption was not an innocent byproduct of Indian–white contact, but a means to an end: "When our people come from hunting to the town or plantations and acquaint the traders and people that we want powder and shot and clothing, they first give us a large cup of rum. And after we get the taste of it crave for more so that . . . all the beaver and peltry we have hunted goes from drink, and we are left destitute either of clothing or ammunition."[14] As they became more involved in the colonial economy, the Mohicans had less control of their role within it. In an effort to regain a measure of self-determination, the Mohicans of the upper Housatonic staked their survival on the acceptance of an English mission and schoolhouse.

The beginnings of Stockbridge can be traced to the spring of 1734, when Konkapot and Umpachenee, two headmen of the upper Housatonic Mohicans, found themselves in Springfield to receive military commissions from the English in the wars against French Canada. They were there approached by two clergymen, Stephen Williams and Samuel Hopkins, who told them that the English were concerned about their poor state and desired to help them. The answer to the Mohicans' problems, the Englishmen claimed, was to accept a mission to teach them the gospel and to provide them with a proper Christian education.[15] Konkapot, and perhaps Umpachenee as well, promised to give this matter full consideration. Upon returning to the village, they gathered the community to weigh the issue. Four days later, and after much debate, the mission was accepted. Soon after, John Sergeant, a young tutor from Yale, was appointed to run the mission and Timothy Woodbridge, a great-grandson of John Elliot, was appointed to run the school.[16] Their work was generously funded by Isaac Hollis, a London clergyman who had agreed to underwrite the long-term training and education of twelve Indian boys. Later, an Indian girls school was established.[17] Within his first two years, Sergeant baptized dozens of new Christians. This was a considerable achievement for any English minister and indicates the degree to which the Mohicans accepted and trusted Sergeant. As the chief liaison between the Indians and the English, the minister dominated the early period of Stockbridge history.

From the beginning of this enterprise, the English concern for Mohican souls was connected to the acquisition of Mohican territory. In the decade preceding the establishment of the mission, Anglo-Indian relations were characterized by a flurry of land sales. In the late 1720s, one Englishman is said to have purchased more than 3,000 acres from a Mohican for thirty pounds and a suit of clothes.[18] It was at about this time that Colonel John Stoddard, a major landholder in the Connecticut River Valley, is believed to have convinced the Mohicans to relinquish their claims to two future townships for 460 pounds, three barrels of cider, and thirty quarts of rum.[19] The Indians retained two settlements for themselves, one at Skatehook, in the lower township, and another at Whanatakook, the site of future Stockbridge.[20]

All of this occurred as increasing numbers of English settlers entered the region. In order to avoid another era of frontier violence (western Massachusetts had yet to recover from the destruction of the Anglo-Algonquin Wars of the 1670s), and to control the settlement process, Stoddard and his friends sought to effect a nonviolent takeover of the region that would ensure their own prosperity. It is in this context that in 1735, just a year after the Mohicans had decided to accept the mission, Williams approached them with a new proposal that would establish Stockbridge, a town of six square miles. The Indians would be required to relinquish their other claims in the area, but the concentration of their scattered holdings and the gathering of their people at a single location would encourage the work of the mission, and hence, the successful integration of the Indians into the English-American community. This new township would be incorporated like any other Massachusetts town, and the Indians themselves, as freeholders, would run the town board. Initially, many Mohicans were suspicious of this land-swap offer. Umpachenee, in particular, is said to have questioned the motives of the English and expressed concern that future generations of Americans would not recognize the Indians' title to the land.[21] Stoddard insisted that the English were only concerned for the Indians' welfare. Apparently persuaded that it was the best course open to them, the Housatonic Mohicans accepted the plan and were henceforth known as the Stockbridge Indians.

Unlike the efforts of many of its Jesuit counterparts in Canada, the Stockbridge Mission did not carry on its work in wilderness isolation. The task of civilizing the Indians was also to be accomplished by a select group of four English families chosen by Sergeant and Colonel Stoddard.[22] These model pioneers,

led by Ephraim Williams, Catharine Maria's great-grandfather, were to build
a town for both themselves and the Indians. Initially, this was to be a reciprocal arrangement; the Indians would benefit from the instruction and example of
these model English, and the English, including Sergeant, would benefit from
generous land grants. Aware that they provided a buffer between the English and
French-allied Indians to the north, the Housatonic Mohicans parlayed their
manpower and lands for a place in the town's government.

As the Indians sought to adapt to the new conditions of their existence,
education became a central concern. Indian boys were soon taught to speak,
read, and write English. One of the first of these was Konkapot's son. Sent to the
New Haven Day School, he, like other Indian boys, was groomed for a leadership
role in the emerging male-dominated English town.[23] The secular features of
English culture, particularly its household structure, work patterns, and modes
of resource management, were taught to Indian boys and girls apprenticed to
English families. Mohawk children also were enrolled at the mission school.

As the work of the mission progressed, pressure on the Indians to relinquish their remaining lands intensified. As new deals were struck, they continually found themselves losing both numbers and land while the English were
rapidly increasing in both. Within fifteen years, Ephraim Williams had parlayed
his original 150-acre homestead into 1,500 acres of the finest real estate in the
area. Most of this was acquired in 1744, when Indian lands were formally separated from those of the English.[24] This early experiment with allotment produced
growing resentment among the Indians, intensified apostasy among those who
had been converted, and effected a slow but continuous exodus westward.

Colonial warfare provided another factor that contributed to the gradual
decline of a Mohican presence in Stockbridge. The Indians fought for the town
in both the French and Indian and Revolutionary Wars. Cooper's *Last of the
Mohicans* is partly inspired by their service with Robert Rogers, the leader of a
popular guerilla force in the Seven Years' War.[25] The Stockbridges also fought
and died for American liberty in the Revolution. Ken Mynter reports that the
Stockbridges fought at Bunker Hill and the Battle of White Plains. During the
bitter winter of 1777–78, the Stockbridges and the Oneidas delivered over 300
bushels of corn by snowshoe and pack basket to Washington's army at Valley
Forge.[26] In recognition of their service, General Washington ordered that the
gift of an ox and a ration of whiskey be presented to them.[27]

While the Stockbridges no doubt appreciated the general's good will, they were looking for more substantial rewards. They had fought for the Americans partly in the hope that their services would be compensated with protection of their traditional land rights. They also expected that land deals struck before the war would be honored. Not only did the Stockbridges lose men to the fighting, but upon their return, the survivors found their country increasingly overrun with settlers and promises to pay for lands formerly ceded reneged upon.[28] To redress these grievances, the Stockbridges petitioned the Continental Congress, then sitting in Manhattan: "We having taken an active part in the War, suffered very greatly by it in blood and interest, trusting in the good people of this island to do us justice with regard to our lands, we thought we deserved better treatment."[29] This petition fell on deaf ears. Virtually expropriated of their entire territory, the Stockbridges finally relinquished the town to the Americans.

In 1785, a year before Shays' Rebellion began, the last large group of Indian migrants is said to have headed west to Brotherton, in Oneida territory. In *Hope Leslie*, Sedgwick makes reference to this final exodus: "Within the memory of the present generation the remnant of the tribe migrated to the west; and even now some of their families make a summer pilgrimage to this, their Jerusalem, and are regarded with a melancholy interest by the present occupants of the soil."[30]

. . . . .

One of the most successful players in early Stockbridge history was Abigail Williams, Ephraim Williams' daughter and Catharine Maria Sedgwick's grandmother. Williams became Sergeant's bride in 1739, the same year Stockbridge was incorporated. Although she lacked her husband's missionary zeal, she shared her father's desire to create an Anglo-American town. When Sergeant died in 1749, she inherited his large holdings. Soon Ephraim was inviting his friends from Springfield and Northampton to settle in Stockbridge. Eighteen months later, Abigail married Brigadier General Joseph Dwight of Brookfield, and the "Dwight-Williams Ring," as it came to be known, was complete. The group hired their relatives and friends to manage the town's Indians affairs and appropriated the Hollis fund for its own use. These actions helped to ruin the fragile coalition of Indians and Englishmen that Sergeant had established. Within a few years, the Hollis fund was bankrupt, the school had become the

Dwight's private residence, and the Mohawk students had returned to New York. Subsequent efforts to revive the mission by Jonathan Edwards, Sergeant's replacement, failed.[31] Stockbridge was becoming an exclusively Anglo town.

The success of the Dwight-Williams ring would be enjoyed for generations to come. Descended from Dwights on their mother's side, the Sedgwick children were among the most privileged youth in Stockbridge. A visitor to the town in the 1830s remarked that the region seemed to be entirely inhabited by Sedgwicks and their belongings.[32] That Sedgwick had her hometown in mind as she wrote *Hope Leslie* is evidenced by several references that locate Stockbridge as the site of Springfield, the novel's imagined frontier community. Both towns were built on a riverbank where the wigwams gave place to the "clumsy, but more convenient dwellings" of the English (17). Both Ephraim Williams and William Fletcher, the novel's model pioneer, lived on large riverside estates, located, in Axtell's phrasing, on "a proud eminence overlooking the native village,"[33] or in Sedgwick's, "on a gentle eminence that commanded an extensive view of the bountiful [river]" (17).

An Indian monument constitutes another feature common to both places. According to Stockbridge lore, the Indians kept a large pile of stones on a mountain overlooking the village. Each time they passed this way, another stone was added to the heap. This act is said to have been an expression of "gratitude to the Great Spirit, for preserving them to look down upon the valley again."[34] In *Hope Leslie,* we read about another such mountain "crowned with a pyramidal pile of stones." But, around these are found the relics of savage, Indian sacrifices (100).

The differing explanations for the existence of this rock pile indicate something of the ideological assumptions that fostered the English takeover of Indian land. As Hope's sacrifice pyramid indicates, the English believed that Indian claims to the land were null and void by the uses they made of it. In the early seventeenth century, the theory of Indian misuse was codified in the doctrine of *vacuum domicilium,* as discussed in chapter 1. The traces of this doctrine, as well as the beliefs that sustained it, are evident in an early passage of *Hope Leslie.* In the second chapter, the narrator describes how the first settlers followed the course of the Indians, "and planted themselves on the borders of the rivers—the natural gardens of the earth, where the soil is mellowed and enriched by the annual overflowing of the streams, and prepared by the unassisted processes of nature to yield to the indolent Indian his scanty supply of maize and other esculents. The wigwams which constituted the village, or, to use the graphic aboriginal designation, the 'smoke' of the native gave place to the clumsy, but more convenient dwellings of the pilgrims" (16–17).

This passage enforces the prevalent misconception that Indians did no work and survived only on what "unassisted" nature yielded them. When the novel credits Indians with doing work, it derides their purposes. On the next page, the Indians are credited with having cleared the meadows of large trees. But lest the reader confuse this operation with proper work, it is added that the area was then "consecrated" for "revels." The rest was left a "Savage, howling wilderness" (18). Hope seems genuinely distressed that this land has been seen and enjoyed only by savages who "have their summer home in them" (100). In this way, the noble savage is conflated with the privilege of European nobility. Ironically, however, Sedgwick was herself a member of the privileged class.

The doctrine of *vacuum domicilium* is also advanced by Everell Fletcher, the novel's young hero. Upon his return from school in England, Everell informs a fellow traveler aboard ship that the Puritans "have acquired [the land] either by purchase of the natives, or by lawful conquest, which gives us the right to the *vacuum domicilium*" (126). In this way, *Hope Leslie* categorically denies the land claims of Native peoples. Although it criticizes particular actions against the Indians, for example, the massacre of the Pequots or Winthrop's rude treatment of the Narragansett sachem, Miantonomi, the novel reinforces English land claims. At the same time, it denies the legitimacy of other colonial groups vying for a place in an emerging New England. Thus, figures like Antinomian Anne Hutchinson and Anglican trader Thomas Morton, both early threats to the authority of the Puritan state, are portrayed as "deluded" (19) and "crazy" (199).

Significantly, *Hope Leslie* also criticizes colonial magistrates like Governor Winthrop. It is remarked that William Fletcher first removed to the western province to escape the oppressive rule of the Boston magistrates, who, the narrator writes, imposed "those shackles on others from which they had just released themselves at such a price" (16). Governor Winthrop himself is portrayed as a rigid and vain individual. Unlike the "noble pilgrims," whose sacrifices restored religious and civil liberties to the oppressed and trampled (73), he is described as wealthy before he immigrated (144). Subject to this patriarch's undisputed rule, Madame Winthrop is compared to a horse "easy on the bit"

(145). The height of Winthrop's arrogance is demonstrated when he decides to marry the "lawless" Hope to Sir Philip Gardiner, a man whom, Fletcher notes, is old enough to be her father (154). The foolishness of Winthrop's plan is demonstrated when Gardiner's villainy is revealed.

While these portrayals suggest that *Hope Leslie* is not a simple paean to the Puritans, it unequivocally supports the larger claims of Anglo-American society. This is most evident in Hope's relationship to Magawisca, the novel's Indian protagonist and Hope's dark twin. A would-be spokesperson for Indian rights, Magawisca is presented as a model Indian. The narrator is quick to comment, however, that Magawisca has "no prototype among the aborigines of this country" (6); she is a representation of the "possible," not the "actual." Thus, although marked by the "peculiarities of her race," her countenance is beautiful, "even to an European eye" (23). Magawisca's physical beauty is matched by her rare gifts of mind and spirit. As the apparent embodiment of natural virtue, she has the moral ground to advance a pro-Indian version of the Anglo-Pequot War. In chapter 4 of the novel, she describes for Everell the extreme violence and cruelty of the English attack on the Pequots. Everell is suitably humbled by her report. At the conclusion of her narration, he expresses his sympathy and admiration for her people and seems convinced, as the narrator would convince the reader, that the Pequots were not the savage, predatory villains of the Puritan chronicles, but a wronged people who were exterminated, "not by superior natural force, but by the adventitious circumstances of arms, skill, and knowledge" (54). Significantly, this chapter's epigram is John Robinson's famous lament on the Wessagusset killings of the 1620s: "It would have been happy if they had converted some before they had killed any" (41).

Despite their reasonability, Magawisca's claims are undermined by the actions of other Indians. Even as she relates the conquest from a Pequot point of view, her father is preparing to wreck havoc on the Fletcher household. Although she has promised to protect the family, she does not alert the family members to his scheme. The effect of her oratory on Everell also has dangerous consequences. In sympathizing with her and the plight of her people, he is becoming increasingly susceptible to her charms. During an all-night vigil to guard against Indian attack, the pair apparently forget the purpose of their watch and are only roused from their "romantic abstraction" by Digby, an older servant who wisely remains suspicious of the Indian girl (54). In this way, Everell seems in danger of forgetting Magawisca's place. Dana Nelson suggests that Sedgwick here equivocates on both the authority and the effect of Magawisca's commentary.[35] Although Magawisca is the most noble kind of Indian, she is never completely trustworthy, nor the equal of her English counterparts. Rating lower on the social scale than a household servant, she does not sleep in the house proper, but in a shed adjoining the kitchen. Despite her obvious virtues, great pains are taken to ensure that she and Everell do not become romantically involved, as an Anglo-Indian relationship of this kind would undermine the distinctions of race and caste upon which *Hope Leslie* constructs its social vision.

Yet Magawisca's role as protector of the English is vital to its survival. For practical purposes, then, the most noble feature of Magawisca is her fidelity to her surrogate family. Her chief duty seems to be protecting the Fletchers from her vengeful Indian father. Mononotto eventually captures Everell and condemns him to death. But Magawisca, motivated by virtue and love, throws herself before his sword, and thereby loses an arm for the saintly young Englishman. In choosing to protect the invaders at the expense of herself and her people, Magawisca demonstrates the dilemma of the Indian Princess.

Rayna Green traces this legendary figure to British folk ballads of the sixteenth century. In these popular songs, a young British man travels to faraway lands, where he is captured by a foreign king and sentenced to death. Before the sentence can be executed, however, he is saved by the king's daughter. In some versions she becomes a Christian and marries the young man.[36]

On American soil, the basic plot of these ballads provided a ready framework to narratize the experiences of the early colonists. As Green argues, the story of John Smith's legendary rescue by Pocahontas was likely influenced, if not outright borrowed, from a ballad. Significantly, Pocahontas becomes an Englishwoman and dies on English soil. Having committed herself to helping the English, and marrying one of their kind, she is forever separated from her original community. In being good, that is, in being a princess, she must defy her own father, exile herself from his kingdom, and even risk death itself. In the process, she legitimizes the conquests of the white men whom she aids.[37]

The parallels in *Hope Leslie* are evident. Having fallen in love with Everell, Magawisca must save him from her own father. She is mutilated in the process of doing so. Yet unlike her seventeenth-century counterpart, Magawisca is not allowed to marry her white lover, or to become an English lady. As Green argues, once the princess becomes a prospective wife and sexual partner, she can no longer be good; as a sexual being, she is a threat to the colonials. Magawisca's budding romance with Everell is dangerous for two reasons: First, it distracts him from his duties to his community, and, second, marriage to an Indian woman would upset the novel's ethnic and class hierarchies. For Native women, the implications of this psychosexual patterning were quite disturbing. Valued for the sacrifices they made on behalf of the European–American male, Indian women were otherwise expendable and dangerous.[38]

The novel's treatment of Indian men is likewise complicated by negative assumptions about the assumed racial and cultural traits of Indians. Echoing Puritan portrayals of Native leaders, Sassacus, the principal sachem of the conquered Pequots, is described by a fellow Pequot as a "strange tree in our forests" who "struck his root deep, and lifted his tall head above our loftiest branches, and cast his shadow over us" (26). Claiming responsibility for killing Sassacus, he brings his scalp to the English for a reward. William Fletcher is disgusted by this trade in dead Indians, lamenting that "motives of mistaken policy should tempt his brethren to depart from the plainest principles of their religion" (26). Although the text again equivocates on who is to blame for the scalp trade—the violent tendencies of the savages or the policies of the Puritans that encouraged those tendencies—the high ground is given to Fletcher, who occupies the moral center of text.

The Mohawk warriors who aid Magawisca's father, Mononotto, and participate in the raid on Springfield are among the most negatively stereotyped characters in the text. Described as "insatiate bloodhounds" (74) driven by an insane urge to kill, they take pleasure in murdering innocent persons. This tendency is demonstrated during the attack on the Fletcher household. Having just slain the good Mrs. Fletcher, they turn their attention to her infant son:

The savage . . . had tossed the infant boy to the ground; he fell quite unharmed on the turn of Mononotto's feet. There raising his head, and looking up into the chieftain's face, he probably perceived a gleam of mercy, for with the quick instinct of infancy, that with unerring sagacity directs its appeal, he clasped the naked leg of the savage with one arm, and stretched the other towards him with a piteous supplication, that no words could have expressed.

Mononotto's heart melted within him; he stooped to raise the sweet

supliant, when one of the Mohawks fiercely seized him, tossed him wildly
around his head, and dashed him on the doorstone. (65)

Such rhetoric helped to displace accounts of English soldiers' treatment of Indian babies. While it reinforces the novel's basic assertion that Indian men are fundamentally violent and cruel, this passage also functions to distinguish Mononotto from the considerably more barbaric Mohawk warriors. Noble, articulate, and somewhat rational, he is portrayed as a devoted father and leader. The justice of his cause, however, is overshadowed by his means of redress. Like his Mohawk associates, he becomes a stereotype of the vengeful Indian warrior, who participates in the indiscriminate killing of English settlers. He is only prevented from doing so by his more noble daughter, whom he inadvertently mutilates.

Oneco, Mononotto's son, does not reveal the violent tendencies of his father. Nonetheless, his devotion to Hope's little sister, Faith Leslie, is just as threatening. Oneco is shown to be a gentle suitor and loving husband of Hope's sister, but their marriage is as much a product of Faith's weakness and vulnerability as it is of Oneco's strength and virtue. Unlike the more grown and mature Hope, who enters the novel with a mental and verbal aptitude equal to that of the adults around her, Faith is introduced as a "pretty petted child, wayward and bashful" (29). These traits are dramatized by her initial reaction to Mr. Fletcher, her surrogate father; literally avoiding his touch, she figuratively repels assimilation into his household. Soon after, she is captured by the Indians. When she reappears as the wife of Oneco, she seems to have been assimilated completely into his culture. According to Magawisca, the young and impressionable Faith retains no mark of her former society. She has lost the ability to speak English and has difficulty recognizing her own sister.

The debasement of Faith's position is dramatized by the melodramatic manner with which Hope receives the news that her sister has married an Indian. According to the narrator, Hope "shuddered as if a knife had been plunged into her bosom" (188). This response reflects the negative associations that often attended the representation in white texts of marriages between Indian men and white women. It is important to note that Sedgwick balances Hope's blatantly racist outburst, "God forbid . . . my sister married to an Indian!," with Magawisca's indignant response: "'Yes—an Indian, in whose veins runs the blood of the strongest, the fleetest of the children of the forest, who never turned their backs on friends or enemies, and whose souls have returned to the Great Spirit, stainless as they came from him'" (188). As Nelson writes, "Magawisca's reciprocal scorn is fully authorized by her version of the massacre at Mystic."[39] Her statement also prepares the reader for the revelation that Faith is happy in her new state and will not be reassimilated into the Anglo world.

In *The Land before Her,* Annette Kolodny suggests that Sedgwick was influenced by Thomas E. Seaver's *A Narrative of the Life of Mrs. Mary Jemison,* a text that made imaginatively possible a "white heroine whose romantic attachment to an Indian included a happy accommodation to life in the woods."[40] As Kolodny notes, Jemison's biography was one of the most popular books published in 1820s America. According to one source, it was the unrivaled best-seller of 1824.[41] Like *Hope Leslie,* Seaver's text describes intercultural contact and conflict, places a woman at the center of a frontier drama, and treats the subject of Indian-white marriages. The real-life story of someone who had been acculturated into an indigenous community, it provides a nonfiction analogue to Faith Leslie's untold story.

In her portrayal of Faith, Sedgwick also drew from the history of her own famous ancestor, Eunice Williams. Like Jemison, Williams became an Indian captive in the eighteenth-century border wars between the British and French colonies. She would later become a lifelong member of the Kahnawake Mohawks, her adopting community. The story of her capture, as told by her father, the Reverend John Williams, in his 1707 text, *The Redeemed Captive,* was the most famous captivity narrative ever published in New England. John Demos reports that, appearing in six editions in the eighteenth century and five more in the nineteenth, it became a "revered part of the literary canon of 'Puritanism.'"[42] John Williams had little to say about his daughter's experience among the Indians. But what he did say reflects the horror that Hope Leslie experienced at seeing her sister assimilated into Native society, married to an Indian, and converted to Catholicism. Informed by the trials of the Williams' family, *Hope Leslie* reflects the trauma of war and captivity that had become part of New England's cultural memory.

Contrary to the sentiments expressed by most mainstream American writers, the experiences of Mary Jemison and Eunice Williams indicate that while the acculturation process was difficult, it did not prohibit one from leading a long, productive, and happy life. While the Williams despaired at having their daughter, sister, and cousin remain an unredeemed captive, Eunice adjusted well to her new life as a French Indian. Unfortunately, Eunice Williams left no written record of her experiences among the Iroquois. We must then turn to Mary Jemison's life story to gain insight into the lives of European-American women acculturated into Native society. Despite Seaver's anti-Indian bias, her biography can be read as a challenge to the negative stereotyping of Native American culture that pervades Sedgwick's text.

Born in Ireland, Mary Jemison emigrated to America at a young age. Her parents settled their large family on a farm in western Pennsylvania in the late 1750s. During the French and Indian War, the farm was attacked and Mary and her family were taken captive by Shawnee Indians. Her parents and some of her siblings were summarily killed by the attackers, while Jemison herself, then only about fourteen years old, was spared, but not returned to the whites. Soon after, she was adopted into a Seneca family, and within a few years of her capture, was married to a Delaware known as Sheninjee.

The process by which Mary Jemison was married into her adopting community offers important contrasts to the experience of Sedgwick's fictional Faith Leslie. As noted above, Faith's youth and waywardness make her a prime candidate for assimilation into Indian culture. This process is effected by Oneco, her captor/suitor, who begins to provide for Faith as soon as she is separated from her English family. As the captives are marched through Indian country, he courts his child-bride, making "a bed and pillow for his little favorite, fit for the repose of a wood nymph" (76). She receives his attentions "as passively as the young bird takes foods from its mother" (76). Given their mutual affection, and Faith's dependent state, it is no surprise that the couple are later married by a French Jesuit.

Mary Jemison's marriage to Sheninjee is effected in quite a different manner. Unlike Faith, who is cared for by her future Indian husband, Mary Jemison is assimilated into the Indian community by other women. Having adopted her to replace a brother killed in battle, these "sisters" teach her the language and lifestyle of the Seneca. As she becomes part of the community, Mary is given a new Indian name. Among the Seneca she will be known as *Dickewamis*, a word she translates to mean "pretty girl," "handsome girl," or "pleasant, good thing."[43] It is only after a substantial apprenticeship that Jemison is married into the community. Marriage, in this process, is the consummation, not the starting point, of acculturation.

While Mary Jemison represents accommodation to Indian society in positive terms, *Hope Leslie* insists on the degradation of the white Indian. This attitude informs Hope's brief reunion with Faith. In this scene, the limits of Hope's virtue are tested. Disgusted by the appearance of her sister, she must be commanded by Magawisca to take Faith's hand. Once activated, Hope does everything in her power to win her sister back to civilization. Initially, her pleas have no effect, partly because Faith no longer comprehends English. The apparent victim of brainwashing, she is described as "pale" and "spiritless;" her "vacancy" of expression is only redeemed by its "gentleness and modesty" (229). This passage confirms the widespread belief that only persons captured by the Indians when they were very young, or who were of low rank and breeding, could be assimilated into Indian culture.[44] In *Hope Leslie,* no white person of discerning mind and sound judgment would ever choose to live among the Indians. As Mrs. Fletcher expresses it to Magawisca, civilized life is far easier than the Indian's "wild, wandering ways" (24). The Pequot princess has no response to this comment, and in general, cannot defend her people against what the text assumes to be the obvious lack of her culture.

Despite their unquestioned belief in the superiority of Christian civilization, and their theories about the qualities of those who assimilated into Indian society, whites often had difficulty coming to terms with the apparent success of the Indians at transforming white captives into loyal members of the tribe. As Axtell, Demos, and others have noted, a large number of whites adopted into indigenous communities decidedly favored Indian society.[45] Mary Jemison helps the reader to understand why.

As she explains, the lives of Seneca women had distinct advantages over those of their white counterparts: "Notwithstanding the Indian women have all the fuel and bread to procure, and the cooking to perform, their task is probably not harder than that of white women, who have those articles provided for them; and their cares certainly are not half so numerous, nor as great. In the summer season, we planted, tended and harvested our corn, and generally had all our children with us; but had no master to oversee or drive us, so that we could work as leisurely as we pleased" (84).

As well as not finding the rhythms of Indian life exceptionally burdensome, Jemison enjoyed a much higher status within her adopted culture than she would have among the colonists. Traditional Iroquois culture is matriarchal and therefore places women at the center of community life.[46] Her responsibilities as a clan mother, as well as the lack of restrictions placed on members of her sex, would generally work to her benefit. It was as a Seneca woman, and not an Irish female immigrant, that Mary Jemison was able to gain title to Gardeau, a large and rich tract of land along the Genessee River.

Jemison's characterization of the lifestyle of Indian women contradicts representations in Anglo texts of the Indian women's situation. These representations can be traced to the earliest days of colonization. In early seventeenth century New England, William Wood reported that Native women were driven to seek asylum from their tyrannical Indian husbands at the doorsteps of colonial houses.[47] Thomas Jefferson, writing a century-and-a-half later, would similarly claim that Indian women were submitted to unjust drudgery: "It is civilization alone which replaces women in the enjoyment of their natural equality. That first teaches us to subdue the selfish passions, and to respect those rights in others which we value in ourselves."[48] For this Enlightenment thinker, the "natural" state of women was to be kept "stationary and unexposed to danger" so that they might produce more offspring.[49] The mobility apparently imposed upon Native women, and the access to abortive herbs they enjoyed, inhibit their childbearing ability and, in Jefferson's strained logic, constitute further evidence of their oppressed condition. Jemison's description of her life among the Seneca provides one of the first printed challenges to this long-held orthodoxy.

Mary's attachment to her Indian family and her concern for her mixed-blood children constituted other important factors that convinced her to stay among the Indians. At several points in her story, she has the opportunity to return to the white settlements. It was at these critical junctures that she decided to remain a Seneca. Her reasons indicate how effective the adoption process could be. "My family was there," she informs Seaver, "and there I had many friends to whom I was warmly attached in consideration of the favors, affections and friendship with which they had uniformly treated me, from the time of my adoption" (83). Sheninjee's death provides Mary with her best opportunity to return to the settlements. At that time, responding to pressure from white negotiators, the headmen favor her being returned to the English. Not wishing to return, Mary describes how she hid in the woods until the men went away. Soon after, she marries her second Indian husband, Hiokatoo, and bears six children, each of whom she names after a member of her original Irish family. In this way,

Mary Jemison applied her Seneca training: as the Seneca physically adopted her to replace a slain brother, she symbolically replaced her Irish parents and siblings by naming her Indian children after them. In these and many other ways, Seaver's text demonstrates itself to be no simple captivity narrative, but a story of cross-cultural awareness and understanding.

Unfortunately for Mary's children, tolerance of difference did not characterize the response of the immigrants to the indigenous peoples or their mixed-blood children. Despite their English names, Mary knew that her family would undoubtedly fare worse among the whites. This awareness provided her with another important reason to remain among the Seneca: "One reason for my resolving to stay . . . was that I had got a large family of Indian children, that I must take with me; and that if I should be so fortunate as to find my relatives, they would despise them, if not myself; and treat us as enemies; or, at least with a degree of cold indifference, which I thought I could not endure" (120). By this time, experience had taught Mary Jemison that a return to white society would automatically entail a loss of status and freedom for both herself and her children. As her story progresses, we see that her place among the Seneca was increasingly one that she assumed for herself.

In *Hope Leslie,* it seems only natural that Indians should accept their inferiority and relinquish both territorial claims and personal independence to the whites, or suffer the consequences. Having been born into a savage state, they must necessarily enter a civilized one at its lowest level. It is further assumed that Indians must remain at that level. Questions of racial status aside, as much is demanded by the social hierarchy constructed in the text. The basic unit of social organization in *Hope Leslie* is the household. Like the feudal English manor, these households are not composed of blood relatives only. Supporting the nuclear family is a host of servants. The Fletcher household is attended by three servants, Master Craddock, Digby, and Jennett. A live-in tutor, Craddock is referred to as Hope's "aegis-bearer," Digby is introduced as Mr. Fletcher's "confidential domestic," and Jennett is described as a "middle-aged serving woman." None of these characters has a first name, families of their own, or any life whatsoever outside of the Fletcher household. Appended to this group are Magawisca and Oneco. Despised and untrusted by the other servants, they occupy the periphery of the household; hence, Magawisca sleeps in the shed adjoining the kitchen. Just as the white servants are locked into their positions, so are the Indians.

A comparison to Bellamy's *The Duke of Stockbridge* highlights Sedgwick's class bias. As noted earlier, a number of references locate post-revolutionary Stockbridge as the central site of the novel. While Catharine Maria was born too late to know about Shays' Rebellion firsthand, there can be no doubt that she grew up hearing stories about the dramatic events with which her father had so recently been involved. Given the deep class and ethnic antagonisms that pervade the novel, it is not unreasonable to assume that some of these stories described how the Shaysites, under cover of darkness, crept "Indian-like" into the town and lurked about the homes.[50] In *Hope Leslie,* the new settlement is led by William Fletcher, a wise and noble patriarch. In *The Duke of Stockbridge,* Bellamy lampoons Sedgwick's father as an arrogant and violent champion of the ruling classes. The very institutions and groups that Sedgwick defends, Bellamy criticizes.

Led by the Revolutionary War veteran, Captain Daniel Shays, the rebels were mainly composed of impoverished soldiers who found themselves without money or jobs upon their return home. Some of these men had farmed their own land before they went off to fight; in the depressed post-war economy, they were unable to earn a living. With no help forthcoming from the government for which they had fought, and relief being denied them in the local courts, they organized, armed, and marched to the courthouses and jails, where they demanded reform and released their friends. Eventually, they would march on Boston, only to be routed by a state-raised militia. While they were put down, the Shaysites did win important concessions from the legislature, including the fair appraisal of real estate and personal property for the payment of debts and a reduction in the cost of court fees.[51]

True to his socialist ideals, Bellamy memorializes the heroism of the rebels while offering a cogent analysis of class warfare on the Massachusetts frontier. In his imaginative retelling of those events from the early nationalist period, the often crude but basically good rebels are opposed by an overbearing and moneygrubbing Stockbridge elite. This latter coterie of large land owners, merchants, judges, clergy, and lawyers, is championed by Theodore Sedgwick, a character based on Catharine Maria's father, a prominent federalist of the same name. In the course of the novel, Sedgwick leads the charge against the rebels, who are finally dispersed, defeated, and killed.

Among the characters in *The Duke of Stockbridge* are several Stockbridge

Mohicans, including Abe Konkapot, a Revolutionary War captain; Jehoiachim Naunumpetix, "the Indian tithing man;" and two Indian selectmen, Johannes Metoxin and Joseph Sanquesquot.[52] Of these, only Konkapot plays an important role in the text. Although of secondary importance to the novel's Anglo characters, he proves himself to be a dependable friend and ally to Hamlin Perez, the rebel leader. Thus, the Shaysites and the Indians are linked: from the rebel's point of view, as brothers in arms against the oppressive ruling classes, from the gentry's point of view, as ruffians who are no better than the savages and heathens with whom they are allied.

For the New England gentry in the early nineteenth century, it was such class and ethnic antagonisms, rather than Indian–white conflict specifically, that presented the greater problem. As the presidential election of 1828 drew near, an emerging democratic movement under Andrew Jackson threatened to wrest power away from the Federalist aristocracy. Led by businessmen, farmers, and entrepreneurs without allegiance to the eastern elite, these new Democrats were on the verge of gaining control over the next generation of American politics. In this environment, the old guard was becoming increasingly marginalized. *Hope Leslie,* informed by conservative federalist politics, insists on the continuing centrality of that gentry, as well as the social distinctions, embodied in its most polished and active women, it sought to enforce. Indians had no place in the world they established, even if, as the history of the Stockbridges would indicate, their resources and goodwill provided the basic material for it.

These attitudes are neatly summarized in the novel's conclusion, when Hope, Everell, and Magawisca meet for the last time. The trio has just fled the jail where Magawisca awaited sentencing on charges of conspiracy. Hope arranged her escape to honor Everell's wishes and pay off the debt they owe the Pequot woman for the sacrifices she had made on their behalf. As Magawisca prepares to flee west, Hope entreats her to someday return:

> *The present difference of the English with the Indians, is but a vapor*
> *that has, even now, nearly passed away. Go, for a short time, where you*
> *may be concealed from those who are not yet prepared to do you justice,*
> *and then—I will answer for it—every heart and every voice will unite to*
> *recall you; you shall be welcomed with the honour due to you from all, and*
> *always cherished with the devotion due from us.*
> *. . . Promise us that you will return and dwell with us. (330)*

Hope's generous offer is unequivocally rejected. Sensible to the wrongs committed against her people, Magawisca blames their exile on the English. As a result of English cruelty, she insists, the Indians will not be consoled and can never forgive: "The law of vengeance is written on our hearts—you say you have a written rule of forgiveness—it may be better—if ye would be guided by it—it is not for us—the Indian and the white man can no more mingle and become one, than day and night" (330). Hope is saddened by this response. Magawisca's noble mind, she believes, will be wasted in the "hideous solitudes" of the forest (332). If only she could be persuaded to return to the white settlements and "enjoy the brighter light of Christian revelation—a revelation," she claims, that is "so much higher, nobler, and fuller, than that which proceeds from the voice of nature" (332).

Despite Hope's protestations, the Pequot woman willfully removes herself forever from Hope and Everell's sight. Bringing her dialogue with the English to a close, Magawisca's speech indicates some of the complex factors that contributed to the ongoing failure of Indian-white relations in the early nineteenth century. From the novel's perspective, those relations were failing for two basic reasons: On the one hand, because the Indians were justifiably outraged by the injuries they had suffered at the hands of brutal, white colonists; on the other, because the Indians had not been converted to Christianity. The irony that resulted because the Indians had very little reason or incentive to emulate Christians was resolved in favor of the colonists who believed unquestionably in the superiority of their own culture; although wronged, Magawisca had ultimately failed to see the light.

It is no surprise, then, that Sedgwick's savages, noble or otherwise, tragically depart the scene: "The little remnant of the Pequot race . . . began their pilgrimage to the far western forests. That which remains untold of their story is lost in the deep, voiceless obscurity of the unknown regions" (339). Resistance to the assumptions that inform this conclusion would soon be expressed by William Apess, a self-defined Pequot who would champion the cause of the New England Algonquins throughout the late 1820s and 1830s.

Part Two.

Crossbloods

Land, Literacy, and the Lord 3.

Pequot Tribal Advocacy in the Eighteenth and Nineteenth Centuries

"This here Jesus, he and his wife Mary, and they had a little boy with them, they traveled all over the world. They made mountains and trees, they made trees, they made springs everywhere, *teeqaade toolol* . . . This here Jesus he was a great man; he was *the best gambler* in the whole United States! [emphasis added]"[1] The preceding quote is attributed to a Pit River/Klamath storyteller. In *Other Destinies,* Louis Owens offers it as an example of how Native Americans incorporate European myth into their own "highly syncretic oral tradition."[2] In this case, the speaker mixes indigenous stories with Christian ones to express a tribal perspective in the postcontact environment. In the revised story, the biblical trio of Joseph, Mary, and the baby Jesus is replaced by Jesus, Mary, and their unnamed son. Rather than New Testament miracles, they perform acts of creation like those described in Native American myth. By thus making Christian icons and symbols serve a new, tribal purpose, the Pit River/Klamath story is instructive. It suggests that rather than eroding tribal values, European languages, concepts, and signs can be adapted by Native peoples to express traditional attitudes and identities. This concept is crucial for understanding how Indian spokespeople in eighteenth- and nineteenth-century New England acculturated the dominant discourses of their times, including the language of colonial courts, Protestant missionaries, and American Revolutionary politics, in their struggles to preserve territorial boundaries and gain civil rights.

As the eighteenth century wore on, Indian communities throughout the northeast found themselves besieged by a growing English settlement community. Continuously subjected to the premises of *vacuum domicilium,* they fought an uphill battle to maintain the few tracts of land that remained in their hands. The battlefields of this period were the state assemblies and courts, the weapons, the language of those bodies. In the restricted economy of those times, Indians placed claims upon lands Anglos had appropriated for farming, grazing, and timber. While the settlers considered these territories to be their own, Indians sent formal protests to state legislatures that identified those lands as reserved for them by prior agreement. In this environment, writing was a necessary weapon and one of the only ones available to Native peoples who sought to remain in possession of their territories.

A written record of the Pequots' efforts to defend their land base is preserved in Connecticut's *Indian Papers,* a collection of handwritten documents that detail more than a hundred years of land claims controversies. In the mid-1970s, these documents were brought to light by contemporary Mashantucket Pequots eager to reassert traditional tribal land rights. Many of these texts refer to an eighteenth-century boundary dispute and show how the processes that were divesting the Stockbridge Indians of their territories in the Massachusetts Berkshires were at work on other tribal lands as well. These records reveal that, between the 1720s and 1760s, the Mashantucket Pequots lost more than half of what once had been described as a 1,700-acre tract near the headwaters of the Mystic River. Much like their Stockbridge contemporaries, the Pequots protested this appropriation, the record of which can be found in tribal memorials and petitions presented to the state courts. Offering us a route back into the lives of New England Indians, these texts indicate the complex and often contradictory influences that inform early Indian advocacy texts. The *Indian Papers* also demonstrate the extent to which the missionaries' zeal, when combined with Native efforts to acquire literacy, led to the emergence of a tribal rhetoric on civil rights. In the nineteenth century, an established tradition of tribal discourse would influence the writing of William Apess, a self-defined Pequot and Christian Indian who applied evangelical methods to his own written and spoken efforts to advance the social, political, and economic claims of Indians.

The beginnings of Indian literacy in New England can be traced to the Harvard Indian School in the mid-seventeenth century. The school's mission was to train promising young Indian proselytes to propagate the gospel among their own tribes.[3] In the later seventeenth century, John Eliot adapted the English alphabet to create a phonetic writing in Massachusetts; it thus became possible for the Natives to read and write in their own language. Eliot's intention was to Christianize the Indians. Toward that end, he produced Bibles and prayer books in Massachusetts. However, surviving Massachusetts documents show that the Indians mostly used their new skill to record transactions involving land.[4] As Kathleen Bragdon writes, among seventeenth- and eighteenth-century Wampanoags, literacy did not so much mean a break with tradition as a way to "contain" and "confine" the new in ways that were compatible with the old.[5] While they recognized the value of written records, Indians in this period continued to commit religious and legal texts to memory.

The beginnings of Pequot tribal advocacy can be traced to the decades following the Anglo-Pequot War. Despite the provision of the Treaty of Hartford that outlawed the Pequots forever, reconstituted Pequot communities in southern New England soon began to take shape. Over time, surviving Pequots were able to reestablish themselves in recognized Pequot communities with a degree of political sovereignty and territorial control. While the Treaty of Hartford initially allowed these survivors little room to negotiate with the English, by the mid-1640s, settlers in the conquered territory desired a cooperative relationship with them. At this time, conflicts among the Mohegans, Narragansetts, and eastern Niantics, along with the changing needs of colonists who wished to settle the region, made it possible for the Pequots to assume an important intermediary role in the region's politics.

It is during this period that a young man by the name of Robin Cassacinamon would emerge as the leader of the Nameag Pequots, a group that would later become known as the Mashantucket Pequots. John Winthrop Jr., then governor of Connecticut, described the Nameag Pequots as a "people which live very near the English, and do wholly adhere to them, and are apt to fall into English employment."[6] That Cassacinamon was a useful and trusted person is evident in a report written by Roger Williams in 1638, which mentions that the young Pequot man was one of a party that traveled to Boston to help negotiate the release of a Pequot woman Uncas sought to marry. Kevin McBride reports that this woman eventually moved to Mohegan and Cassacinamon received a reward of ten fathoms of wampum.[7] Eight years later, in 1646, colonial records place Cassacinamon as a servant in the Winthrop household at the newly established Pequot Plantation in Nameag, the future site of New London. It is unclear as to whether or not his residence there was voluntary, but his close association with

the Winthrops was instrumental in the establishment at Nameag of both an English plantation and an independent Pequot community.

In the colony's first years, the Pequots under Cassacinamon are reported
to have housed colonists and hunted for them. More important, they provided
a buffer between the English and other Indian groups. Winthrop considered
it of "great concernment to have [Pequot Plantation] planted, to be a curb to
the [Mohegan] Indians," noting that friendly Pequots would "easily discover
any Indian plotts."[8] In this period, Anglo-Pequot relations appear to have made
a 180-degree turnaround. Like the Mohegans during the time of the war, the
Nameag Pequots had become English allies against other more threatening Indians. The Pequots also found themselves a curb against the Massachusetts Bay
Colony and its claim to possess the territory east of the Pequot River. With the
Pequots under its jurisdiction, Connecticut could demonstrate its own right to
the conquered territory. Thus, in 1650, when Winthrop allowed the Pequots to
resettle a 500-acre plot at Noank, an area east of the Pequot River and on the
western side of Mystic Harbor, just a mile or two from the site of the fort massacre, he was strengthening Connecticut's claim to the disputed area.

The Cassacinamon-Winthrop alliance provided an opportunity for an
autonomous Pequot tribe to reestablish itself under the auspices of the colony's
governor; the decree that outlawed the name of the Pequots forever was effectively overturned. Soon, another provision of the Treaty of Hartford fell by the
wayside. Supported by the colonials, Nameag provided a home for those Pequots
who wished to be free of the Mohegans and Narragansetts; it was thus possible
for Pequot captives of neighboring tribal nations to return to their homeland. In
an important test of their newfound independence from Mohegan, the Pequots,
in 1646, extended a hunt into conquered Pequot territory controlled by Uncas,
who retaliated by raiding Pequot villages at Nameag.[9] To his surprise, the Mohegan sachem was formally chastised by the Commissioners of the United Colonies
in New Haven, who now favored a semiautonomous Pequot community under its
control.[10]

As the seventeenth century wore on, Cassacinamon's reputation for leadership and diplomacy grew among Indians and Englishmen alike. Playing an
important intermediary role in the region's politics, he fostered cooperation
across tribal lines and helped to maintain peaceful relations among the tribes
and the colonists. His effectiveness as a mediator is demonstrated in a report

that described his successful efforts to diffuse a potentially violent encounter between the English and Indians. In 1669, he organized a gathering, or dance, of Pequots, Mohegans, and Niantics at Noank. Both Uncas, the Mohegan sachem, and Ninegret, the Niantic sachem, attended. Predictably, this show of inter-tribal solidarity fed English paranoia about Indian conspiracies. John Mason was especially surprised: "Ninegrates and Unckas beeing togeather at the dans at Robins town is and was a matter of wonderment to mee yt thaye who durst not looke each uppon other this 20 years but at the missell of a gun or at the pile of an arrow."[11]

Sensing unrest among the Indians, the English were quick to respond. A militia was sent to Noank to seize Ninigret and break up the gathering. This led to a standoff with weapons drawn on both sides. Cassacinamon adroitly diffused the situation. Afraid that English blood might be shed, and that Pequot and other Indians who had had no part in the violence would be punished, he paid off the militia commander with wampum. "Wampum was like the grass," he is reported to have said, "when it was gon it would come againe but if men be once kild they will live no more."[12] Apparently this offer was accepted and the English returned home satisfied of the Indians' loyalty.

Cassacinamon's most lasting achievement was the negotiation of a 1666 agreement that allotted the Nameag Pequots an inland tract of roughly 1,700 acres. This site, known as Mashantucket, a Pequot-Mohegan place name that has been translated to mean "much-wooded land," became the official home of the western Pequots in 1712, the year the general assembly, under protest from the tribe, allotted their Noank holdings to English settlers.[13] As the cession of Nameag to white settlers indicates, even Native communities on good terms with the English were unable to protect lands coveted by the English. The move to Mashantucket did not bring an end to Anglo-Pequot boundary disputes. The agreements that Cassacinamon made with the English in the late seventeenth century became the source of new controversies in the early eighteenth century.

According to the *Indian Papers,* it was in 1721 when a second Robin Cassacinamon, now spelled "Cassinnamint," would complain to Connecticut's general assembly of English encroachments and building on Mashantucket. Believed to be the first Robin's son, he recalled the much-contested removal from Noank, "where wee & our Father's Liv'd & improv'd Many Years (& thought it was our own & had a good right to ye same)" and offered a detailed account of the present situation at Mashantucket.[14] It is not known if Cassin-namint was literate. The document ends with the inscription, "Robin Cassin-namint", under which appears a flourish in ink and the words "his marke." It is quite possible, even likely, that Cassinnamint attached his mark to a document someone else had prepared. Given the gaps in the historical record, it is difficult to ascertain to what degree eighteenth-century Pequots were engaged in the production of the documents that represented them, or to what degree the words of the 1721 petition reflect what the Pequot leader may actually have said.

Despite these questions regarding its authorship, Cassinnamint's 1721 petition offers an intriguing glimpse into the lives of Pequots during a critical time in their history. Mashantucket had been their home for some two generations and was the chief means of their survival as a community. In his address to the court, Cassinnamint reminds his English listeners of their long-standing promise to uphold the tribe's territorial rights: "Your Honrs took Care of us & ordered some Gentlemen to lay out Mashantuxit where our Predices-sors Anciently dwelt And Improved by Planting both Corn & Orchards; & our Orchards are of a great worth & Value to us by Reason of our Grandfathers & fathers Planted them & the Apples are a great Relief to us." Cassinnamint's references to the agricultural practices of his people demonstrate his aware-ness that English courts tied civil property rights to land use practices. If they were to succeed, the Pequots needed to show that they "improved" their land in ways that whites understood the term. As the occasion of the petition indicates, the situation had degenerated to the point where the Indians had effectively lost control of a significant portion of the territory. According to the petition, "ye Town of Groaton" had "lotted out" what Cassinnamint describes as "ye best of our Lands, . . . including our Orchards, by fencing in of our sd lands (& Building likewise) which is to our great Wrong & Diassatisfaction."

As the argument builds, the sachem's appeal to justice takes on an increas-ingly acerbic tone, as in the following passage where he chides the English for their bad faith gestures: "the English in ye time of ye War Called us brethren & Esteemed us to be Rational Creatures but behold now they make us as Goats by moving us from place to place to Clear Rough Land & make it profitable for 'em." In reminding the court that Pequot soldiers had served in the state's militia in its wars against the Wampanoags, Narragansetts, and French and Indians, Cassin-namint offers his strongest criticism of the English. The Pequots were willing to commit their men to the fighting, but expected that their valuable services would be repaid with certain guarantees and protections. Like the Stockbridges, they found that promises to uphold land agreements were forgotten as settlers continued to chip away at the territory. To add force to his argument, he reminds the English that it was the Indians who first improved the territory; the land that white squatters found ready for farming and livestock grazing was prepared by Indians who first used it for living space, agriculture, and hunting. Perhaps feeling that he had gone too far in his criticisms, or perhaps as a convention of petition writing, Cassinnamint ends on a polite and pious note. On "Behalf of himself and his people," he "humbly prays that the assembly will be pleased to do them justice."

The controversy reflected in Cassinnamint's 1721 petition would not be officially resolved until the 1760s, when the courts ceded over 650 acres of Mashantucket to white settlers. Subsequent papers indicate that by 1730, roughly half of the original allotment was being used by Englishmen for grazing and other purposes. English houses also were beginning to appear on the tract. Through their overseers, James Avery and John Morgan, the Pequots protested these developments and sought the removal of these new squatters. On the other side of the question the state maintained that fee had never been passed to the Indians, that as grantors of the property, it had simply allowed the Indians to use it.

In response to additional Pequot memorials, the general assembly, in 1731, prohibited the appropriation of additional territory and appointed a committee to study the problem. A year later, the committee reported that half the territory was sufficient for the Indians' use and that the English should be allowed to improve upon the remainder. As a concession to the Indians, it also recommended that the disputed area be divided and fenced into fifty-acre lots, ten acres of which would be reserved for the Pequots to secure fire wood.

In protest, the Pequots, in 1741, had Morgan draft another petition on behalf of the tribe's claim to the territory. It begins with a reminder to the magistrates of the sacrifices the Pequots had made on their behalf and includes a reference to the original 1666 agreement that established Mashantucket as an officially recognized Pequot territory:

[The Mashantucket Pequots] ever since the conquest of them have been true and faithful to ye English and Served them Against the Common Enemy with their Dearst Lives in many Remarkable Instances as in the

*Naragansit wars and in all ye attempts by ye English mad upon Canada
and that as volunteers & upon free cost That they had in Reward for
their faithfull Servises Set out to them in sd Groton a tract of Land Called
Mashuntuxit Containing about 1700 acres for them to Live upon and in
that ye same is very broken and uneven tis but just for them to Improve for
planting.*[15]

Having thus recalled the tribe's historical claim to Mashantucket, the Pequots
criticized the court-ordered study that found half the territory to be sufficient for
their needs. They also pointed out that the settlers had violated the terms of the
1732 ruling by building houses on the territory, clearing all or most of the timber
from several of the fifty-acre plots, appropriating Indian corn fields for English
farming, and allowing the cattle to roam freely. A month later another petition
additionally requested that Avery be dismissed from service. The Pequots suspected Avery and his relatives of having an interest in the appropriated lands,
and desired to have Joseph Rose of Preston, their "good and faithful friend,"
appointed in his place.[16] The unusual spelling found in this document suggests
that it was not written by Morgan; frustrated in their efforts to redress their
grievance through established channels, the Pequots desperately sought a reli-
able spokesman.

As these petitions indicate, the written word was a necessary element of
tribal advocacy. Unfortunately for the Pequots, literacy among the Indians of
southeastern Connecticut was in its infancy. The infringement on tribal lands
fed the Indians' desire to master this mode of communication, as it was partly as
a means to contest land encroachments that indigenous peoples first sought to
master the art of writing. For the most part, however, the English had no interest
in teaching the Indians to write for that purpose. Having invested a great deal of
time, effort, and money in training the Indians to read and study the Bible, they
saw writing as an important part of the Christianization process. In this context, writing was perceived as a means by which Indians could demonstrate their
piety.

The tension between writing as a tool to advance legal and political rights
and writing as a means to assimilate and control the Native population, that is, to
Christianize and civilize it, is clearly demonstrated in a report to the state legislature in 1734. This document, signed by George Griswold and John Parsons, is
both a request to establish a mission and school among the Niantic Indians and

to secure the Indians' land claims. According to the memorialists, the Indians seem "disrous of Larning and to be brought out of darkness to ye knowlege of ye gosple."[17] The writer is quick to note, however, that the Niantics relate the acceptance of a mission to the protection of their territorial sovereignty: "Their Chief told us yt they would not be Concerned with one religion—or have a School unless ye English would deal honestly with them respecting their Land."

A 1735 memorial from the Mashantucket Pequots to the governor expresses a similar concern. Complaining that the "Chefest Desire of the English is to Deprive us of the Privelidg of our land and drive us off to our utter ruin," the memorialists indicate the interrelationship between religion, literacy, and land claims: "It makes us Conserned for our Childrn what will be Com of them for thay are about having the gospell Preched to them, and are a Learning to read and all our young men And woman that are Cappell of Lerning of it and thare is Some of our young men wold be Glad to bild housen upon it and Live as the Englis do Cold they have a Sufficiancy of the Produse of the Land."[18] These documents show that the Indians actively sought to acquire literacy. A reluctance to accept a mission, or the absence of missionaries they found acceptable, contributed to their difficulties in acquiring the new skills. Yet, as encroachments continued, the need for effective group advocacy in the courts became a matter of increasing importance. It was in this context that two congregational ministers, John Owen and Andrew Crosswell, were accepted as teachers and advocates to the Mashantucket Pequots in 1741.

Owen and Crosswell's appearance at Mashantucket coincided with both the religious revival known as the Great Awakening and the complications of an ongoing land claims controversy that resulted in the attempted dismissal of one of the Pequots' two court-appointed overseers. A year after they were appointed to run a mission and schoolhouse at Mashantucket, Owen and Crosswell drafted two memorials to the legislature, one on behalf of the Pequots and another on behalf of the mission they sought to establish. The Pequot memorial, "interpreted" by the ministers, is, like its immediate predecessor, a complaint against Avery and the state-appointed committee. However, in tone, diction, and argument, this memorial is a great deal more diplomatic and conciliatory. Neither Avery nor the committee is mentioned by name. Simply referred to as the "honest men" the state has appointed to "take care of us & our lands from time to time," the memorialists tactfully note that they are doing a bad job: "they live a great way from us & know very little of our affairs." Morgan's own service to the tribe is praised, and the Pequots request that he continue to be recognized as their representative.

Also new to this document is the extreme humility with which the Pequots approach the bench. In a long introduction to their complaint, the memorialists lament the impoverishment of their spiritual condition:

> Yt of late we have been much concern'd about our souls, & know wt we may do to please ye Great God, who we are Sensible is very angry with us for our wickedness and drunkenness our Sabbath breaking & idleness—some of us we hope have believed on the Lord Jesue Christ. But our knowledg is but very little we want to learn to read the Bible and to have our Children learn to read it too, & therby learn to know more of the Great God & what He would have us to do in this world yt we may live with him in the next.[19]

While the deterioration of conditions at Mashantucket and the level to which negative stereotypes had been internalized by the community undoubtedly inform this passage, its wording indicates the extent to which Owen and Crosswell's portrait of the Pequots was influenced by powerful negative assumptions whites made about un-Christianized Indians. As they sought to raise money for the mission, Owen and Crosswell emphasized what they perceived to be the tribe's poor condition. The 1742 memorial also demonstrates the extent to which the acceptance of Christianity, a religion that Indians partly adopted to advance their standing in colonial society, required Indians to humble themselves to their colonial overlords. It would seem that the immediate effect of accepting a mission was not to raise the Pequots' standing with the state courts, but to lower further their estimation among the magistrates.

A request for funding to maintain a schoolmaster, probably Crosswell, also distinguishes the 1742 memorial. For this generation of Pequot leadership, literacy had become a major goal. According to the ministers' own report to the assembly, more than thirty members of the tribe were inclined to learn to read and had taken "uncommon pains to attain knowlege."[20] In the 1750s, similar efforts by Native peoples throughout the state led to the passing of an act for the "well Ordering and Governing [of] the Indians and securing their Interests and Lands."[21] Accordingly, Indian children bound out to white families were to be taught to read: "Every Person in this Colony that hath taken, or shall hereafter take any Indian Children of this, or the neighboring Governments into the Care of their Families, are herby ordered to use their utmost Endeavours to Teach them to read English; and also to Instruct them in the Principles of the Christian Faith, by Catechising them." The by-product of Native efforts to establish and maintain tribal rights and English efforts to Christianize and assimilate the Indian population, laws such as this one contributed to the emergence of a Native ministry active in proselytizing, teaching, and advocating the rights of the indigenous community. The most prominent of these ministers was Samson Occom, a Mohegan who attended Eleazor Wheelock's Indian school in Lebanon, Connecticut. Occom's missionary efforts among regional Indians contributed to the development of a distinct Indiantown community at Mashantucket devoted to the principles of Christianity and the practice of English-American style agriculture.

During this period, the Mohegans were likewise embroiled in an ongoing land claims controversy with whites settlers. Occom, as a Mohegan and a Christian, found himself in a precarious position between two opposing parties. As Dana Nelson writes, "If Occom's evangelical interest in the spiritual condition of Native peoples was a continuous thread in his life, so too was his concern for their economic and political security."[22] Speculating on his motives, Nelson argues that his conversion to Christianity made sense as part of a "complex and calculated response to dwindling Mohegan populations, political power, and entitlements." As well as being a "private decision," conversion was a "politically strategic choice."[23] As a Mohegan, Occom sought to use his education not only to bring fellow Indians the Christian religion but also to defend their interests in land. However, as a Christian, he was expected to focus his efforts on the tasks set for him by white ministers like Wheelock, who disallowed him involvement in economic and political affairs, particularly tribal land controversies. In the 1760s, the courts decided the Mohegan land case in favor of the state, a ruling that Occom would describe as having serious consequences for the future security of the tribe. To add insult to injury, Occom would be formally chastised for his efforts to defend Mohegan land rights and threatened with revocation of his ministerial license if he did not apologize for his activism on behalf of his people.[24]

The Pequots, whose own concessions to the dominant culture ultimately failed to secure Mashantucket's shrinking boundaries, also found literacy and the promises of missionaries a dubious hedge against territorial expropriations.

Events leading up to the state's formal cession of 656 acres of Mashantucket in 1761 indicate the apparent futility of their efforts. Ten years after Owen and Crosswell's arrival at Mashantucket in the early 1740s, we find the Pequots again drafting memorials to the general assembly. In 1751, Joseph Wyouke, and other Pequot Indians, requested that the court establish yet another committee to reexamine the issue for the stated purpose of removing the squatters.[25] By now, however, the settlers had strengthened their hold on the disputed acreage by selling portions of it to other colonists, a fact that gave the courts added incentive to rule in favor of the colonists. Thus, in 1761, a court-appointed committee finally decided the question in favor of the settlers. The language of the report, however, belies its true intentions. According to the committee, the disagreement between the two parties is largely the result of the "unhappy tenure of their lands" which will have a "tendency" to "create broils and contentions."[26] It is advised, therefore, that the Pequots be granted the sole use and improvement of 989 acres, that, yet free of legal "incumbrances . . . would be a better estate to them than the whole under the present tenure." Of course, under this ruling, what the Pequots considered to be their estate would be reduced by nearly half. The Pequots did not fail to note the dubiousness of this resolution. Shortly after the general assembly adopted the committee's recommendation, the Pequots drafted a memorial that bitterly protested this decision, claiming that the committee had "not considered, nor Determined nor found any facts from which any Conclusion with Certainty can arise that the English Proprietors had an Equitable Right in the Lands proposed to be confirmed to them."[27] As with its predecessors, this argument fell on deaf ears.

Despite their inability to convince the courts of the justice of their claims, the Pequots refused to drop the issue. A 1773 document underwritten by Daniel Quotcheats, Simon Quotcheatts, and Samson Panquenuse complains that the proprietors had concealed and secreted the boundaries of the 989 acres and sixty-eight rods established in the 1761 agreement and allowed the encroachments to continue.[28] In 1785, the Pequots would again complain that they found themselves "Interrupted in the Possession of Our lands by your People round about Cutting & Destroying our Timber & Crowding their improvements in upon our Lands."[29] These memorials apparently went unheeded by the courts. Eventually, with the loss of the land came the loss of hope among the Christian Pequots of Mashantucket that they could continue to live in their traditional homeland with any degree of security and comfort. Thus, in the late 1780s, a significant portion of the Indiantown community immigrated to Brotherton in New York, joining along the way with other regional Natives who had likewise been dispossessed of their lands. These "Yankee Indians," as they came to be known, eventually settled in Wisconsin, where their descendents continue to live to this day.[30]

With the migration to Brotherton, Mashantucket lost a great many able men and women, some of whom were literate. Many of those who stayed behind were too old or too weak to complete the journey. Others were disabled war veterans.[31] Despite its reduced population, Mashantucket continued to be recognized as the home base of a distinct Pequot community. Acting upon its role as overseer to the tribe, the state provided a limited degree of assistance, albeit at the Pequots' expense. According to a report drafted by overseer Samuel Mott, in 1804, monies collected to pay for the Pequots' medical, clothing, and funeral expenses were obtained from "the strips of land" the proprietors had gotten from their tract.[32] This suggests that ceded lands had been sold by the state. Some of the profits from those sales had then been reserved for the maintenance of the tribe.

Reduced to just a fraction of their former numbers, and poorer for the loss of the land, the remaining Pequots at Mashantucket survived as best they could. In time, the loss of tribal members to Brotherton led to the introduction of new groups into the community. Throughout this period, Pequots intermarried with members of neighboring Mohegan, Narragansett, Niantic, and Montauk communities. Others intermarried with peoples of European background, including those of Anglo, French-Canadian, and Irish descent. African-Americans comprised another significant portion of the reconstituted group. At Mashantucket and elsewhere, black men compensated for the dearth of marriage partners precipitated by colonial warfare, the loss of men to the fisheries, and the move to New York. This development near the turn of the century led to the emergence of a distinct African-Algonquian community with roots in both indigenous North American and African-American cultures. The outlines of a modern Pequot identity had begun to take shape.

With a Pequot presence in southern New England reduced to an all-time low, it is remarkable that one of the most prolific tribal writers of the Removal Period would claim Pequot ancestry. William Apess was born in 1798 near

Colrain, Massachusetts. Roughly ten years younger than James Fenimore Cooper and Catharine Maria Sedgwick, he was one of the most original writers of his generation. Beginning in 1829, his publishing career spanned an almost ten-year period that coincided with the height of the removal debate. His known works include two editions of his autobiography, *A Son of the Forest* (1829 and 1831); a book of Pequot conversion narratives, *The Experiences of Five Christian Indians of the Pequot Tribe* (1833) together with the polemical "Indian Looking-Glass for the White Man"; a defense of the so-called Mashpee Revolt, *Indian Nullification of the Unconstitutional Laws of Massachusetts Relative to the Marshpee Tribe; or, The Pretended Riot Explained* (1835); and his culminating work, *Eulogy on King Philip* (1836).

In the opening pages of *A Son of the Forest,* Apess claims to be the grandson of a granddaughter of King Philip, the Wampanoag leader. He describes his grandfather as a white man. The child of this union, William's father, "on attaining a sufficient age to act for himself," joined the "Pequot tribe, to which he was maternally connected."[33] This suggests that Apess's Wampanoag grandmother was also related to the Pequots and would have been, according to Apess's reconstruction of his family tree, an intertribal person of mixed Pequot-Wampanoag ancestry. Because this self-definition seems unlikely, researchers have questioned Apess's genealogy, speculating that he was either mistaken about his background or deliberately conflated the Pequots and Wampanoags for effect. As O'Connell points out, it is "almost completely mysterious" how Apess came to identify himself as Pequot.[34]

In her reading of *Eulogy on King Philip,* Anne Marie Dannenberg notes that Apess carefully manipulated his own self-definition, variously identifying himself as "Pequot, (pan)Indian, colored, Christian, male, (first)American, and embodiment of the Enlightenment notion of the 'universal' human."[35] Gerald Vizenor calls attention to the way Apess transcended the racialisms of his time to fashion a "crossblood" identity not based on theories of racial difference and biological determinism but on the stories, imagination, and memories of tribal peoples. Describing Apess as a "despised other [who] learned to write his name and stories over the racial borders in a crossblood remembrance,"[36] he characterizes Apess's work as a crossblood literature of survivance in the comic mode, a "trickster discourse" that contests the dominant culture's tragic monologue on the extinction of the tribes.[37]

Despite the uncertainty that arises from our inability to either prove or disprove Apess's claim to Pequot ancestry, there can be no doubt that he was associated with the Mashantucket Pequots in the early nineteenth century and identified himself as a member of that community. In his second book, *The Experiences of Five Christian Indians of the Pequot Tribe*, Apess includes his own conversion experience among those of three Mashantucket Pequot women: Sally George, Hannah Caleb, and Ann Wampy. Apess identifies George, known throughout the region as Aunt Sally, as his father's relative. A principal leader of the Mashantucket Pequots at that time, she is credited with inspiring his own religious calling. "My aunt could not read," he reports, "but she could almost preach and, in her feeble manner, endeavor to give me much instruction" (40). Apess claims to have spent a winter with Aunt Sally. Along with other Indians from Ledyard, Stonington, Rhode Island, and elsewhere, African-Americans, and African-Algonquins, he attended prayer meetings and social gatherings at Mashantucket. Although Apess provides no details about what was said at these meetings, it is very likely that along with spiritual enlightenment, he received knowledge about secular matters, including the outcome of the land claims controversy that had resulted in the Pequot exodus to Brotherton.

While Aunt Sally connects Apess to the Mashantucket Pequot community, Hannah Caleb provides the textual link that connects him to Mashantucket Pequot history. In all of Apess's work, Caleb's narration offers the only specific reference to eighteenth-century land claims controversies involving the Pequots. Caleb was in a unique position to comment on tribal boundary disputes. Upon the death of her mother, the six-year-old Hannah was sent to live in the home of James Avery, the state-appointed overseer whom the tribe petitioned to have dismissed in 1741. Caleb's narrative, appearing in Apess's book, makes reference to those times, as well as to the land claims controversy itself, and thus establishes Apess's connection to an earlier generation of Pequot tribal advocates.

Having lived through the controversies that resulted in the 1761 cession, Caleb developed a rather cynical attitude toward Christianity and white Christians. As she observed, Christians seemed to behave completely at variance with their own stated principles:

> *They openly professed to love one another, as Christians, and every people of all nations whom God hath made—and yet they would backbite each*

other, and quarrel with one another, and would not so much as eat and
drink together, nor worship God together. And not only so, the poor Indi-
ans, the poor Indians, the people to whom I was wedded by the common
ties of nature, were set at naught by those noble professors of grace, merely
because we were Indians—and I had to bear a part with them, being of
the same coin, when in fact, with the same abilities, with a white skin, I
should have been looked upon with honor and respect. (145).

Caleb's aversion to white Christians was increased by the theft of Indian lands. This is evident in the one reference she makes to the division of Mashantucket in the eighteenth century. As she explains, the anti-Christian feelings that she and other Pequots experienced were "more peculiar 70 years ago than now—what their feelings would be now, if the Indians owned as much land as they did then, I cannot say. I leave the man of avarice to judge" (145). Insofar as Apess can be credited with editing and transcribing Caleb's experience for publication, it seems likely that his own views were influenced by that same controversy. The themes that pervade her narrative—racism, Christianity, and land claims—are the same ones that Apess addressed. Caleb's application of Christian piety and biblical allusion to the tribe's social and economic issues similarly anticipates Apess's style.

Following in the footsteps of an earlier generation of Christian Indian advocates, Apess became a spokesman for tribal self-determination and land rights. Reflecting the complaints earlier Pequot petitioners had made against their court-appointed overseers, his "Indian Looking-Glass for the Whiteman" exposes the conflict of interests that interfered with the white overseer's ability to uphold his responsibilities to the tribes: "They are much imposed upon by their neighbors, who have no principle. They would think it no crime to go upon Indian lands and cut and carry off their most valuable timber, or anything else they chose; and I doubt not but they think it clear gain. Another reason is because they have no education to take care of themselves; if they had, I would risk them to take care of their own property" (155–56). By stripping bare the self-interest that lay behind the overseer system, he showed readers how the impoverishment of tribal groups was a direct result of paternalistic polices that, rather than helping Indians, contributed to their degradation. Turning the language of caring against the courts, he argued for the Indians' civil right to manage their own resources.

In his efforts to undermine hierarchical notions that assigned Indians to the lowest level of the socioeconomic pyramid, Apess exploited the symbolic potential of his own experience as a tribal person to adeptly counter the stereotypes that justified white mistreatment of Indians. The drunken Indian was among the most destructive of these stereotypes. In order to expose the social realities that lay behind the image, he related an incident from his childhood in which his grandmother nearly beat him to death in an alcoholic rage. As Apess explains in *The Experiences of Five Christian Indians,* his grandmother made baskets and brooms for sale to white people. After a day of selling her wares she "fomented herself with the fiery waters of earth." In this fit of intoxication, Apess writes, she "raged most bitterly and in the meantime fell to beating me most cruelly, calling for whips, at the same time, of unnatural size to beat me with; and asking me, at the same time, question after question, if I hated her. And I would say yes at every question; and the reason why was because I knew not other form of words" (120). As Barry O'Connell suggests, the question, "Do you hate me?" offers a route back into the inner life of Apess's grandmother and the internalized self-hatred of impoverished regional Natives whose survival depended on a people who despised and oppressed them.[38] Apess exonerates his grandmother's bad behavior: "Not a wit of blame belongs to [my grandmother,]" he writes. "My sufferings certainly were through the white man's measure; for they most certainly brought spirituous liquors first " (121). Echoing Mohican complaints against traders who plied Indian fur suppliers with rum, Apess shows how alcohol abuse was not an unlucky by-product of colonization, but a tool to manipulate, control, and destroy Native peoples. While whites used such incidents to justify the paternalistic polices of state and church officials, Apess called attention to the social and economic conditions that eroded Indian families and contributed to the abuse of Indian children.

Emphasizing the theme of learned self-hatred, Apess demonstrated how the mythology that had grown up around colonial history prevented Indians from developing positive individual and group identities. As a result of the beating he sustained from his grandmother, Apess was bound out to the Furmans, an apparently kind and generous Baptist couple who introduced him to Christianity. He lived with them for six years. Initially, the boy was more secure in his new white family than he was in his own Indian one. This engendered a strong attachment to white people and a general fear of Indians.

One day, he accompanied the family as they went out to gather berries. Along the way, they fell into a company of white women on the same errand. "Their complexion was, to say the least, as dark as that of the natives. This circumstance filled my mind with terror, and I broke from the party with my utmost speed, and I could not muster courage enough to look behind until I had reached home" (11). As Apess explains, the great fear he had of the Indians was the result of the many stories he had been told about their cruelty to the whites, "how they were in the habit of killing and scalping men, women, and children" (11). "But whites did not tell me," he continues, "that they were in a great majority of instances the aggressors—that they had imbrued their hands in the lifeblood of my brethren, driven them from their once peaceful and happy homes—that they introduced among them the fatal and exterminating diseases of civilized life" (11). By contesting the colonial version of history with a more truthful, tribal one, Apess attempted to overturn the savagery/civilization paradigm. As well as undermining popular assumptions about the racial characteristics of whites and Indians, the anecdote calls attention to the ways settlers continually manipulated language and memory to assimilate and control the surviving Native population.

Eventually, Apess would learn to use the colonizer's language as a tool of liberation. Combining the language of history, law, politics, and Christianity, he became an effective advocate for New England Indian rights. Apess preserved a dramatic record of his advocacy work in his longest book, *Indian Nullification of the Unconstitutional Laws of Massachusetts Relative to the Marshpee Tribe; or, the Pretended Riot Explained*, published in 1835. Detailing his efforts to advance Indian self-determination in Massachusetts, it offers a case study of the challenges and pitfalls that beset Native activists. As an itinerant minister, Apess boldly challenged the status quo. In Plymouth, he dared to lecture a white congregation on the "civil and religious rights of the Indians" (173). Later that same year, he delivered the "word" to another white congregation at Falmouth. This audience was less than receptive to his message: "Some, who apparently thought that charity was due to themselves but not to the red men, did not relish the discourse; but such as knew that all men have rights and feelings, and which those of others to be respected as well as their own, spoke favorably of it" (173). Over time, the politically charged nature of his public speeches became increasingly controversial, particularly at Mashpee, where he found the tribe embroiled in an ongoing dispute with their court-appointed overseer. Phineas Fish, the minister appointed to Mashpee, complained that Apess's addresses were not the proper subject for preaching in a Christian meeting house. Apess's response, that it was "proper to do good in any way" and that "a variety was not amiss" (172), indicates the extent to which his religious and political interests had merged.

The so-called Mashpee Revolt, as it was characterized by white newspapers overreacting to rumors of Indian hostility, was the result of fifty years of conflict between Mashpee leaders and their overseers. Apess became involved in the controversy in early 1833. In May of that year, he was officially adopted into the tribe. Now functioning as the Mashpee's official spokesperson, he drafted a resolution stating that "we, as a tribe, will rule ourselves, and have the right to do so; for all men are born free and equal, says the Constitution of the country" (175). The resolution also forbid any white man "to cut or carry off any wood or hay or any other article" without permission from the tribe and promised to remove anyone who did so by force (175). Some whites quickly challenged the tribe's edict, but were prevented from removing wood from Mashpee by a group led by Apess. A few days later, Apess was arrested with two others, and not released until he had posted a $200 bond. To the dismay of those who supported the overseers, bail was paid by a white man sympathetic to the Indians.[39]

Not surprisingly, Apess gained more enemies than friends for taking an open political stance on tribal issues. Despite his formal adoption into the Mashpee community, he was branded an outsider with no legitimate authority to speak for the tribe. In an effort to limit Mashpee self-determination, whites employed the familiar strategy of imposing outside control over tribal membership. Among other attempts to discredit and discourage Apess, his opponents floated the charge that he was a "gambler in lotteries and had begged money from the Indians to buy tickets with" (242). Fortunately for Apess and the tribe, the Mashpee cause was taken up by William Lloyd Garrison, who wrote editorials for the *Liberator* in support of the Mashpee's efforts to achieve self-government, and Benjamin Franklin Hallet, an attorney who brought the tribe's case before the courts and legislature.[40] In March of 1834, the issue was resolved, at least for the time being, when the Senate and House of Representatives of the State of Massachusetts incorporated Mashpee as an Indian district. The Indians would elect their own selectmen, who would be responsible for the management of all tribal property and were empowered to make any laws necessary to carry out their duties.[41]

In Apess's last published text, *Eulogy on King Philip,* the unique combination of tribal protest literature, Christian evangelicalism, and the language of American political idealism and the rights of man reached its highest expression. Since the 1670s, King Philip had been one of the most prominent American figures. With few exceptions, early portrayals of Philip presented him as an indigenous devil or beast that the Puritans needed to exorcise from the Promised Land, hence, Cotton Mather's famous description of Philip as the "great leviathan" sent to the English for a "thanksgiving feast."[42] With the decline of Puritanism and the appearance of secular Indian war chronicles like Benjamin Church's *Entertaining Passages,* the hunt for Philip and his eventual killing dramatized the emergence of the American frontiersman and his superiority over the Indian.

In the early nineteenth century, Philip's reputation would continue to improve. As Easterners no longer viewed Indians as a serious threat, but instead, as the victims of land-grubbing speculators and frontiersmen, Philip became the sympathetic subject of popular fiction and drama.[43] A good example of the rehabilitated Philip is found in Washington Irving's 1825 *Sketchbook* piece, "Philip of Pokanoket." Irving describes the Indian sachem as "alive to the softer feelings of connubial love and paternal tenderness, and to the generous sentiment of friendship." For Irving, Philip was a "patriot attached to his native soil—a prince true to his subjects, and indignant of their wrongs—a soldier, daring in battle, firm in adversity, patient of fatigue [etc.]."[44] We might have expected such extravagant praise, written in the midst of the removal controversy, to support a pro-Indian position on removal. Instead, Philip's positive traits served to underscore the Indians' tragic fate. True to the form of the noble savage, Irving's Philip ends up a "wanderer" and "fugitive" in his native land. He finishes his life "like a lonely bark foundering amid darkness and tempest—without a pitying eye to weep his fall, or a friend to record his struggle."[45] The sympathy this portrait generated, as well as the indictment of Puritanism it suggested, are mitigated by the savagery of Indian life. In the piece that proceeded "Philip of Pokanoket," Irving describes Indians as living in a state of "perpetual hostility and risk." This unfortunate fact, Irving contends, is the natural consequence of a savage aptitude: "Peril and adventure are congenial to his nature; or rather seem necessary to arouse his faculties and to give interest to his existence."[46]

The tragic potential of Philip's life was also exploited by John Augustus Stone, a struggling actor and dramatist who responded to the call for new plays with Indian protagonists. First appearing in December of 1829, his five-act tragedy, *Metamora; or, Last of the Wampanoags,* became one of the most popular dramas of the nineteenth-century American stage and far outlived its creator. In the play, Philip, here identified as "Metamora," is portrayed as a devoted father and husband. As the English encroachments on Wampanoag territory continue, and pressure to sell his lands and remove to a western territory increases, his militancy is aroused: "When our fires are no longer red, in the high places of our fathers, when the bones of our kindred make fruitful the fields of the stranger, which he has planted amidst the ashes of our wigwams, when we are hunted back like the wounded elk for toward the going down of the sun, our hatchets broken, our bows unstrung and war whoop hushed, then will the stranger spare, for we will be too small for his eye to see."[47]

As noble and praiseworthy as these words might have sounded to the audience, and despite the apparent justice of his cause, Philip is a heathen and categorically doomed to fail. Like Irving's stereotypical Indian, his savage aptitude constitutes a tragic flaw. As David Murray explains, the script eventually transforms Indian anger and white unease into a nonthreatening and emotionally satisfying narrative that creates an aesthetic, not moral, sensation.[48] This treatment of a figurative Philip had real consequences for living Native peoples. As Jill Lepore points out in *The Name of War,* the inevitability of Philip's defeat helped to make removal of Cherokee and other Indians nations acceptable to the American public.[49]

Apess's own story of Philip sounds a radically different theme. As his reference to Philip in the opening pages of *A Son of the Forest* indicates, he placed the Wampanoag leader at the head of a living tradition in which Apess, as a Pequot Indian, participated. For most white readers with even a casual awareness of the Pequot War, it would be absurd to think there was a yet-living Pequot who was also related to King Philip. It was commonly assumed that the Pequots had been extinct for some 200 years, and Philip's people for almost as long. When Apess first announced himself to the American reading public as a descendant of Philip, "one of the principal chiefs of the Pequot tribe, so well known in that part of American history called King Philip's Wars," he was contesting the emplotment of Indian extinction that governed mainstream representations of Indians.[50] Apess's genealogy thus brought regional history alive by making it quite literally present. As both a member of the Pequot tribe of Indians and a descendant of Philip, his own life demonstrated the historical effects of the Puritan conquest on living Native peoples.

Eliding the Pequot and King Philip's War was already a common practice among non-Indian writers. As a Pequot, Apess employed this conflation to contest the ideological assumptions that fostered the government's removalist policies. In this way, Apess refused the normalization of extinction by "contending," as Dannenberg writes, "that institutional racism—rather than so-called natural processes—threatened the Indian, and by urging political intervention to alter the supposed destiny of indigenous peoples in America."[51] In order to replace the figurative and extinct Pequots of Dwight, Sedgwick, Boudinot, and others, or the degraded Pequots of William T. Williams, Apess offered actual, living Pequots who themselves embodied the highest ideals of Christian, civilized peoples.

For Apess, Philip symbolized the historic and ongoing struggles of the Indians of southern New England. Rather than being lost to time and history, the "noble traits that marked the wild man's course" were remembered by New England's tribal community: "I appeal to the lovers of liberty. But these few remaining descendants who now remain as the monument of the cruelty of those who came to improve our race and correct our errors—and as the immortal Washington lives endeared in time—even such is the immortal Philip honored, as held in memory by the degraded but yet grateful descendants who appreciate his character" (277). With this reference to Washington, Apess identifies Philip as a political leader analogous to the nation's founding father. In this way he emphasized the often-overlooked political structures of Native communities. Having thus established Philip's place in the history of Indian peoples, Apess replaced the figurative Philip of his white counterparts with one based on actual experience. Toward this end, Apess recounts for the reader in precise detail the various land sales, encroachments, and hostile acts that finally exasperated Philip and drove him to pursue a violent course. Much of the blame is placed on the courts of the "pretended pious," where "it would be a strange thing," writes Apess, "for poor unfortunate Indians to find justice . . . in those days, or even since" (291). No other nineteenth-century account of King Philip's War would have as much historical specificity. In fact, Apess's erudition and skill are unmatched by any but the most sophisticated contemporary scholars on New England Indian history.

As others have noted, Apess was not content to merely set the record straight. Having established Philip's connection to a living Native community, he

argued for change in the policies that had hitherto governed Indian-white relations: "I say, then, a different course must be pursued, and different laws must
be enacted, and all men must operate under one general law. And while you ask
yourselves, 'What do they, the Indians, want?' you have only to look at the unjust
laws made for them and say, 'They want what I want,' in order to make men of
them, good and wholesome citizens . . . this work must begin here first, in New
England" (310).

Commenting on this passage, Dannenberg notes the important questions
that Apess raises regarding the very strained relationship in America between
truth and politics: "As an Indian, as a Pequot . . . Apess was well aware that
both law and history are ideologically invested cultural products. Yet he knew
that without consensual truth, there would be little hope for implementation of
'one general law' for all." As throughout his other writing, Apess's *Eulogy on King
Philip* "reminds us that past and present stand in dynamic relation."[52]

One of the most prolific Indian writers of the early nineteenth century,
William Apess is also one of the most gifted American writers of any age. His
work is surprisingly at home in our own time. His insight into the devastating
effects of the reservation system, his activism among New England Indian peoples, and his ability to transform a colonial language into a unique tribal discourse
pre-figure the work of later Native American writers and activists. His methods
and insights also provide a new context to reread the writing of his immediate
contemporaries, including fiction writers like James Fenimore Cooper, Catharine Maria Sedgwick, and Lydia Maria Child, as well as later writers, like Henry
David Thoreau and Herman Melville, both of whom made their own contribu-
tions to the discourse of Indianness.

Did any of these writers read Apess's books? During his own lifetime,
Apess was read by literate Indians, mixed-bloods, blacks, and whites, as well as
publishers, printers, editorialists, abolitionists, lawyers, ministers, and judges.
Working within the boundaries that separated Indian, white, and black peoples
in New England, he gained a degree of notoriety, if only for a short period of
time. Then, as now, Apess's words opened their audiences to a dynamic tradition
of tribal advocacy. This tradition reaches back to the early seventeenth century
and the settlement of New England by English colonists and continues through
to this day. The many voices that contributed to that tradition include those of
Pequots like the unnamed emissary aboard Endecott's ship, Robin Cassinnamint, Hannah Caleb, and Sally George; Mohegans like Samson Occom; Nar-

ragansetts like Miantonomi, and Wampanoags like Philip. As Helen Jaskoski writes in the preface to *Early Native American Writing*, each of these figures demonstrated a "profound faith in the possibility of language to overcome ignorance and hostility."[53] Struggling against incredible odds, none found it easy to play a language game dominated by colonial rules and interests. Yet, each took a turn, and thus allowed for the possibility that the game could be taken up by a future generation.

. . . . .

The limited effectiveness of Pequot tribal advocates in the antebellum period is demonstrated by their inability to prevent the further cessions of Mashantucket that occurred some fifteen years after Apess's death. Although the rhetoric of savagery had been softened at this time, it had yet to be substantially revised. Thus, nationwide, indigenous peoples continued to be blamed for the demise of their communities even as white land greed caused the further impoverishment of those communities.

The irony of this situation is demonstrated in John W. DeForest's *History of the Indians of Connecticut from the Earliest Known Period to 1850*. First published in 1851, DeForest's history was (and, in some ways, continues to be) the most comprehensive treatment of its subject ever written. Like other salvage anthropologies of the period, it condemns white treatment of Indians even as it argues Indians out of existence. While DeForest's turgid prose denounces the violence against the Pequots, it ultimately supports the removal of Indians generally. Comparing the bayonetting of eighty-five patriots by the soldiers of Benedict Arnold, an act that occurred just a few miles from the site of the Pequot fort massacre, to Mason's raid on Mystic in 1637, DeForest points out the biases that inured colonists to the violence their militias committed against indigenous peoples:

> What then would have been said, had the English surrounded the village of New London by night, had they set fire to its houses, cut down those of the inhabitants who attempted to fly, and driven back the others, indiscriminately of age or sex, to perish in the flames? When would our historians have ceased to record it, or our orators have forgotten to make it the subject of their indignant comments? Yet surely there is not such

a difference between a barbarous and a civilized community, that the extermination, the complete, bloody and sudden extermination, of the one may be looked upon almost with insensibility, while that of the other would be regarded as a master-piece of atrocity.[54]

In a later passage, DeForest writes that the Pequots have "received little from us except injustice and the most pitiless neglect."[55] This statement introduces an examination of Pequot history from 1683 to 1849 and the history of encroachments, legal suits, and court decisions that resulted in the appropriation of Pequot territory by white settlers.

Although a seemingly pro-Indian moralizing pervades DeForest's text, and the author demonstrates sympathy for the plight of the Pequots, as well as describes the efforts of Pequot leaders to stave off complete removal from their territories, he ultimately represents them as barbarous, ignorant, simple, lazy, drunken, and improvident. Predictably, at the end of this definitive treatise on Connecticut Indian history, DeForest informs the reader that the Indians are ultimately responsible for their own demise: "Had they never been deprived of a foot of land otherwise than by fair and liberal purchase, and had not a single act of violence ever been committed upon them, they would still have consumed away with nearly the same rapidity, and would still ultimately have perished. Their own barbarism has destroyed them; they are in a great measure guilty of their own destruction."[56]

This condemnatory impulse contradicts the great bulk of DeForest's study, which is openly critical of the colonials' Indian policies. In consequence of the prevailing discourse on savagism, *History of the Indians of Connecticut* assigned its subject to extinction even as it meticulously detailed white America's relentless efforts to destroy Indians. Although DeForest was aware of a tradition of tribal advocacy in Connecticut, he ultimately chose to reject that tradition in favor of an orthodox colonial position on removal.

DeForest's belief in the inability of Indians to know what was best for them is reflected in the Connecticut legislature's misguided paternalism. In 1854 and 1855, the Connecticut General Assembly passed two laws that materially affected the tribes residing within state borders. The first, "An Act for the Preservation of Indians, and the Preservation of their Property," was initiated by tribal complaints against the abuses of their state-appointed overseers. The act provided for the appointment of overseers by the county court, limited their term to one year, prohibited suits against Indians, prohibited the sale of alcohol to Indians, and voided all conveyances of Indian land. At the same time, however, it also permitted the transfer of land when "such sale or exchange would be beneficial to the owner of such estate, and not injurious to the interests of the tribe."[57] The "owner of such estate," was, according to the legislature, the state itself.

In 1855, the general assembly passed a second act, which provided for the sale of the majority of the Mashantucket Reservation without the consent of the tribe. On 1 January 1856, 800 acres of the Mashantucket Pequot Reservation were sold at public auction. A mere 180 acres were left to the Pequots. The proceeds from this sale, $8,091.17, were deposited in the tribe's account. For several generations after, this money was used to help pay for the Indians' housing, medical care, and funeral expenses.[58] In effect, the state was providing for the tribe by selling its resources, thus further divesting the Pequots of the means to provide for themselves. The tribe did not consent to the sale of its lands, nor did it sit idly by as the state acted. As Jack Campisi has shown, documentary evidence proves that Mashantucket Pequot leaders actively protested this latest assault on their territory.[59] One-hundred twenty years would elapse before conditions favored the reversal of this trend and the Indians at Mashantucket could reclaim a portion of their once-large territory.

Fashioning a Tribal Utopia 4.

Pequot Self-Representation in the Contemporary Period

On Pequot Avenue in the West Mystic section of Groton, Connecticut, a landscaped center island offers mute testimony to the dramatic changes that have occurred in the state's Indian policy. For more than a century, a nine-foot bronze statue of John Mason dominated this quiet corner of town. Dedicated in 1889 to commemorate the English victory in the Pequot War, the decisive battle of which had been fought just a few miles away, it recalled civilization's heroic triumph over savagery. On a plaque attached to the statue's supporting base appeared the following inscription: "Erected in A.D. 1889 By the State of Connecticut To Commemorate the Heroic Achievements of Major John Mason and His Comrades Who Near This Spot in 1637 Overthrew the Pequot Indians and Preserved the Settlements from Destruction." Caught up in the tide of pro-Indian activism, the monument became the focus of controversy in the 1980s, when a leader of the eastern Paucatuck Pequots called for its removal.[1] In 1992, the quincentennial of Columbus's voyage of discovery and the year the Mashantucket Pequots opened their high-stakes gambling facility, a seven-member panel composed of local residents, the town historian, two Pequots, and a tenth-generation descendant of John Mason, recommended that the town honor the Pequots' request.[2]

A few miles north, rising out of the hills of Mashantucket, a new monument to the Pequot War stands, Foxwoods Resort Casino. Owned and operated by the Mashantucket Pequot Tribal Nation, the sprawling complex is recognized as one of the most profitable gambling operations in the world. No longer the poorest of the region's poor, tribal members comprise one of the wealthiest communities per capita in the United States; no longer the refuge of a poor and despised people, Mashantucket has become the home base of a major economic power.

The dramatic changes at Mashantucket have resulted from contemporary Pequots' success at mastering their own self-representation during a time when the political climate favored tribal growth and renewal. In the courts, the media, and the academy, a new generation of Pequot leaders has succeeded in establishing a tribal identity that catalyzed the community's aspirations for long-term prosperity and self-determination. Simply put, the tribe's success is a victory of self-representation. The tribe's logo is the most visible sign of Mashantucket's modern identity. Affixed to buildings, uniforms, vehicles, and printed documents, this ubiquitous blue, white, and black disk identifies the tribe's property and products. In this way, it functions like any other corporate logo. Yet unlike other such trademarks, the Pequot logo symbolizes more than three centuries of indigenous experience by incorporating several key signs that image the tribe's history: a tree standing atop a domed knoll with its branches spread aloft and its roots thickly planted in the ground, a fox, and a flourish like those produced by quill pens. Together, with the land at its base, the tree represents Mashantucket itself. The fox represents the fox clan from which, Pequot tradition holds, the tribe's core members are descended. With the tree at its back, the fox illustrates the war of attrition the Pequots have fought against encroachment. The clan, it would seem, has been driven to the very last piece of its territory. The flourish in the ground beneath the tree is a stylized version of the sachem's mark that Robin Cassacinamon is said to have affixed to treaties and petitions in the late seventeenth and early eighteenth centuries. In those times, a sachem's mark functioned like an official signature or seal. It is likely that such a mark appeared on the 1666 agreement that established Mashantucket as an official Pequot territory. Appearing on the logo, the sachem's mark identifies the property of Cassacinamon's heirs and signifies the tribe's resistance to colonial domination.

As the logo illustrates, contemporary Pequots have produced images that reflect a sense of their own cultural and historical identity. The logo also serves the need of the community to be identifiable to others as a distinct tribal entity. As well as signaling a cultural and historical difference, the logo designates a legal and political difference. Tribal corporations, unlike private corporations, enjoy limited sovereignty over state law, one result of which is that the profits from tribally owned businesses like the casino are nontaxable. As a result of this and other legal differences, state and federal governments do not grant Indian tribes the right to declare sovereign status; self-definitions must be verified by Congress. In 1983, the Mashantucket Pequots were granted that verification and became a federally recognized tribal nation within the state of Connecticut. This agreement with the federal government, officially known as the Mashantucket Pequot Land Claims Settlement Act, entitled the tribe to restitution for lands ceded in violation of federal intercourse and trade acts and access to federal and state development funds. Since 1638, the Pequots had been under the jurisdiction of the state assembly at Hartford; now, due to a remarkable collaboration of politicians, lawyers, academics, and tribal leaders, they could negotiate with the state in federally mediated courts on a theoretically equal par.

The passing of the act soon allowed the reservation's boundaries to expand for the first time in some 320 years. As we have seen, Mashantucket continued to shrink from Cassinnamint's time to the mid-nineteenth century, when all but about 200 acres of the original 1,700-acre allotment were still in Pequot hands. In state censuses taken in 1900 and 1910, the tribe numbered only a few dozen people. By the 1940s, only a single family continued to live at Mashantucket. The state expected them to be the reserve's last Indian inhabitants and plans were being made to add Mashantucket to a state park. In the 1960s and 1970s, however, a new generation of Mashantucket Pequot leaders asserted their own rights to the territory. Inspired by the activism of Native peoples throughout the United States, they reestablished a tribal presence at Mashantucket. Later, a surprising implementation of federal gaming laws by American Indian tribes nationally provided the legal foundation for the extraordinary rebirth and resurrection of Mashantucket that occurred in the 1980s.

Without recalling the long and complicated history of the contemporary American Indian movement, it is important to note its effect on "forgotten" tribes like the Pequots. In the late 1960s, Vine Deloria Jr. argued that the apparent "invisibility" of eastern tribes was their greatest asset: "No one believes they exist, yet back in the statutes and treaties lies the key to their eventual success."[3] This statement would prove to be prophetic. As a result of tribal activism nationwide and new federal laws that encouraged tribal initiatives, Indian peoples in the northeast found both incentive and opportunity to strengthen their political, social, and economic resources. Connecticut's five state-recognized tribes, the

Schaghticokes, Paugussets, Mohegans, Paucatuck Pequots, and Mashantucket Pequots, all participated in this period of activism by lobbying for changes in the state's Indian policy.

In Connecticut, the tribes' first concern was reclaiming control of the reservations. Since 1941, the state's Department of Welfare had controlled Indian affairs and administered state policy. Under this arrangement, tribes were required to petition the welfare commissioner for approval to hold gatherings on reservations and to build new homes. The state chose the building sites and assumed ownership of the homes when the original inhabitants died or abandoned them. Tribal members were forbidden to conduct any type of business on a reservation.[4] Under this system, tribal people had no effective control over the policies that governed reservations and very little incentive, and practically no means, to revitalize tribal traditions. The state simply sought to provide for the minimal preservation of existing tribes and had no policies to encourage their development and growth.

Concerned about the survival and growth of their cultural traditions and the return of reservation lands formerly ceded, leaders of the Schaghticoke Tribe in eastern Connecticut began lobbying for changes in the state's Indian policy.[5] Their petition was for greater access to the reservation where they hoped to sponsor tribal socials and meetings. When Welfare resisted these efforts, the tribe decided to appeal directly to the legislature. Because a new Indian affairs policy would apply to Native peoples throughout the state, Connecticut's other four recognized tribes became involved in the process.

Encouraged by the state's apparent willingness to listen, Connecticut's tribal leaders introduced two bills to the legislature. The first of these, introduced in 1971, called for the creation of a new state commission that would have sole responsibility over Indian affairs.[6] This bill was approved by the legislature but vetoed by the governor, who claimed the cost of creating a separate council—$25,000—was unwarranted.[7] The second bill, introduced in 1973, was part of a compromise that established an Indian affairs council to serve as a liaison between the tribes and the state's Department of Environmental Protection. This council would be composed of one representative from each of the five tribes and three non-Indian advisors appointed by the governor. Under this new arrangement, reservations would be reserved for the use of each tribe and maintained "for the exclusive benefit" of the Indians who resided there. Tribal members were now free to hunt and fish on reservation lands without a license. Homes could be passed on to heirs who were members of the tribe. Tribal membership and eligibility requirements were established by the council.[8] Although the state maintained much of its control, the new legislation provided the Indians with greater access to their lands, and with it, an opportunity to strengthen their social and political bonds.

Soon after the agreement was put into effect, Mashantucket became the home base of a revitalized Pequot community. The availability of state and federal housing grants allowed tribal members to build quality homes while economic seed monies provided them with funding for several development projects. In this early period of growth, the tribe produced maple syrup, raised livestock, built a hydroponic greenhouse to grow vegetables, sold reservation timber, and established a sand and gravel pit. Profits, however, were slow in materializing. Despite its hard work, the tribe was limited by the realities of the market place. While emergent Pequot entrepreneurs were gaining valuable experience, not one of their ventures generated enough income to sustain its own operation, much less sustainable economic growth for the tribe. In each case, the Pequots found themselves in competition with well-established non-Indian producers of the same products. The Pequots' only real capital was Mashantucket itself, a poor resource by most standards. Over the centuries, small portions of it had been used for grazing, agriculture, and timber. The rest, composed of rocky, wooded hills and swamp, had no apparent use value. As subsequent events illustrate, the availability of exploitable natural resources was less important than the land's status under the law. At the same time that the Pequots were struggling to raise money, Indian tribes in Maine and Florida were establishing high-stakes bingo facilities on federally recognized tribal lands. The popular game was generating profits rarely seen in Indian country. It soon became obvious to tribal councils throughout the United States that gambling was the best available means to stimulate their dormant economies.

In addition to being a requirement for gaming, federal recognition provided tribes with an opportunity to reclaim territories formerly lost to state auctions and cessions. The tribes had never relinquished their claims to lost acreage and still sought to reclaim some, if not all, of their original allotments. It was with this goal in mind that Native American Rights Fund attorneys filed suits to reclaim tribal lands in Maine, Massachusetts, New York, Rhode Island,

and Connecticut. In each of these states, claims were made on lands that had been sold or auctioned by the states after 1790, the year Congress passed the Intercourse and Trade Acts. According to the acts, the federal government must approve all transfers of Indian lands to non-Indians by public treaty.[9] In states with governments that existed long before the establishment of the federal government, this rule was often ignored, as with Connecticut's auction of 800 acres of Mashantucket in the 1850s.

In 1975, a federal judge ruled that the trade acts established a trust relationship between all the tribes and the federal government.[10] As a result, it was now possible for unrecognized tribes to press their land claims in federal courts. Encouraged by the new ruling, the Mashantucket Pequot Tribal Council in 1976 brought suits against Town of Ledyard residents. The tribe's action placed a cloud on property titles of lands purchased at the state auction; with a claim pending, property holders could neither sell nor subdivide the land. Because the tribe had a strong case against the sale, and because the acreage they sought to reclaim was mostly swamp and woods, the parties reached an out-of-court settlement. According to the state-sponsored agreement, the tribe could buy the land at current market prices as long as it agreed not to sue for anyone's private residence.

Because the teeth of the suit had been provided by federal legislation, and because the Pequots had had no relationship with the federal government, the outcome of the land claims suit depended upon the outcome of the tribe's petition for federal recognition; the Pequots could not sue under federal law if they were not a federally recognized tribe. Although the tribe's standing within the state had never been questioned, Congress had had few or no dealings with eastern Indian groups like the Pequots. In western areas, this situation was reversed, as the federal government had established jurisdiction over Indian lands long before states existed. In these areas, Indian relations were handled by the Department of the Interior's Bureau of Indian Affairs, another agency with which the Pequots had had no dealings. Although tribes could legally petition Congress directly for federal recognition, potential applicants were expected to apply through Interior's Branch of Acknowledgement and Research (BAR). Because all of the parties involved in the suit—the tribe, town residents, and the state—desired a speedy resolution to the issue, the Pequots decided to bring their petition directly to Congress, a rarely used legal process that bypassed Bureau of Indian Affairs policies.

In addition to expediting the process, the decision to circumvent BAR procedures gave the Pequot petition its best chance to succeed. Intended to establish one standard for all tribal contexts, BAR's policy sets forth several criteria, all of which must be met, in order to establish the basis for recognition. As Jack Campisi explains, "the group must show that it has been identified as 'American Indian' throughout its history; that it constitutes a separate, identifiable Indian community with a leadership that has maintained influence over its members throughout the tribe's history; that its members can trace descent to some known tribe or tribes; that they are not members of other tribes; and that they have never been terminated by Congress."[11]

For Native American peoples residing along the eastern seaboard, these criteria are often extremely difficult to meet. Since the early seventeenth century, aggressive settlement communities backed by powerful militia and the courts continually worked to eliminate tribal sovereignty, drastically reduce (if not eradicate altogether) the Native population, undermine group leadership, and impoverish the survivors, who, by and large, were treated as surplus labor and reduced to a condition of debt peonage. While BAR's criteria may have been established in the spirit of objectivity and fairness, it is ill-suited to testing tribalism as it currently exists in the northeast. By insisting on one set of rules for all cases, not only does BAR fail to account for the variety of local contexts and experiences that shape tribalism, but for the oppression, sanctioned by state and federal governments, that has abrogated tribal sovereignty and compromised Indian self-determination. From the perspective of tribal leaders and advocates, the definitions of tribal identity established by BAR are primarily means to protect federal interests, not to advance Indian rights.

The dangers that potentially awaited the Pequot suit had recently defeated another New England Indian community's bid for federal recognition. In August of 1976, the Mashpee Wampanoag Tribal Council of Mashpee, Cape Cod, sued in federal court for the repossession of about 16,000 acres of land, three-quarters of Mashpee, that had been earmarked for development. The defendants in the case, officially designated *New Seabury et al.,* included the New Seabury Corporation (a large development company), the Town of Mashpee (representing over 100 individual landowners), and local insurance companies and businesses.[12] Before a land claims could proceed, however, the court had first to determine if the Mashpees in fact constituted an Indian tribe.

At the outset of the hearing, it would seem that history favored the plaintiffs. Mashpee had been known since the mid-seventeenth century as Cape Cod's Indian town. Until the 1960s, the town's government had been run by Indians or people related to Indians. While these facts alone gave powerful evidence that Mashpee was the home site of an Indian tribe, the application of federal guidelines cast this view into doubt. Originally a "praying" town settled in the 1660s by Christian Indians who had survived plague and warfare in other parts of Cape Cod and Massachusetts, Mashpee had not existed as a distinct Indian community prior to contact. The town's official founder, Richard Bourne, was an English farmer. Although the Mashpees could trace their descent to known tribes, they were a composite of members of other tribes. The status of the land itself provided another stumbling block. From Mashpee's founding to the mid-nineteenth century, tribal members held their lands in common. By 1870, however, all lands held by Indian proprietors had been transferred to fee simple; plots could now be bought and sold by their individual Indian owners.[13] In effect, Mashpee had been "terminated" as an exclusive Indian town when the land was transferred to individual ownership.

The Mashpee's bid for tribal status was further undermined by their apparent lack of Indian blood. The Mashpees, like the Pequots, are a mixed people with few obvious signifiers of Indianness. As James Clifford reports, intermarriages with whites, blacks, Hessian deserters from the British Army during the Revolutionary War, and Cape Verde Islanders have contributed to the dilution of the town's original indigenous bloodlines. While Native lifeways permeate Mashpee life, Christianity has been the official religion for some 300 years. By the turn of the eighteenth century, English had replaced Massachusetts as the common language. Contemporary Mashpee, working as businessmen, schoolteachers, fishermen, domestic workers, and small contractors, are fully integrated into the economic life of Cape Cod.[14] In such an environment, the dividing line between tribal and nontribal culture can be difficult to establish.

With thousands of acres of prime waterfront real estate at stake, both sides put their cases before the court. Along with Mashpees who testified on their own behalf, the lawyers for the plaintiffs brought to the stand several expert witnesses, including James Axtell, Jack Campisi, William Sturtevant, and Vine Deloria Jr., who supported the Mashpee's claim to tribal status. The defense, with its own group of experts, argued that contemporary Mashpees more closely resembled an ethnic group than an Indian tribe. After forty days of testimony, the judge instructed the jury to determine if the Mashpees constituted an Indian tribe on six dates pertinent to the land claims. In essence, the jurors were asked to decide if a tribe in Mashpee existed continuously from 1790 to the time of the trial. When the jury determined that a tribe existed in Mashpee on only two of the six dates, the land claims suit was effectively defeated.[15] Such are the dangers of an adversarial system of justice. As Clifford writes, "the need to make a clear case to counterbalance an opposing one discourages opinions of 'yes, but,' 'it depends on how you look at it' kind."[16] Cases involving groups like the Pequots and Mashpees demand flexible, open-ended solutions that take into account both the historical circumstances that compromise Native peoples' ability to maintain distinctive communities and the often subtle differences that distinguish tribal from nontribal cultures. Cases that hinge on court-established definitions of tribes will invariably place Indians at a disadvantage.

The success of the Pequots' own land claims suit and bid for federal recognition partly resulted from the tribe's ability to avoid such legal traps. Rather than being opposed by state and local governments, the tribe received unprecedented support from Connecticut's governor and legislators. Their most active supporter was Sam Gjdenson, the representative from New London County and the chairman of the House Committee on Interior and Insular Affairs, which sat to hear the Pequots' petition. The out-of-court settlement with town residents and the state demonstrated to the federal government that the state had, as Gjdenson contended in the midst of the hearings, continuously recognized Mashantucket as the home base of a distinct Pequot community, even when its boundary was disputed. Building on this consensus, the tribal chairman effectively linked the tribe's land claims to Mashantucket's long history. Speaking before the congressional committee, Skip Hayward recalled the cessions of 1761 and 1855. "My people have never consented to the forced sales of their land," he told the legislators, "nor has the passing of years diminished our sense of injustice. Many times we have sought legal counsel, only to be told that we could not obtain legal assistance because we could not afford the attorney's fees. Were it not for the fact that our present tribal attorneys are representing us without charge, we could not maintain the pending federal court action."[17] Concluding his statement with an excerpt from Cassinnamint's 1721 petition, Hayward struck an impressive note on Capitol Hill. On the committee's recommendation, the Land Claims Settlement Act was passed by the House and Senate. The act provided a $900,000 fund to buy back tribal land, extinguished all tribal claims to other land, extended federal recognition, and allowed the tribe to place in trust any of its land.[18]

While the tribe had succeeded with Congress, its petition did not sail through the legislative process uncontested. Despite congressional approval, the Department of the Interior insisted on enforcing Branch of Acknowledgement and Research's guidelines. According to Interior's William M. Coldiron, the department's representative during the hearings, until the Pequots satisfied BAR's guidelines, Interior could not determine if the Pequots constituted a tribe.[19] Acting on Coldiron's objections, President Reagan promptly vetoed the act. According to the president, the federal government was being asked to provide a disproportional amount of the settlement award and that the Pequots had failed to submit a petition of recognition through BAR.[20] Unwilling to relinquish its claim, the tribe, with Campisi, its lawyers, and Connecticut's congressional delegation, lobbied the White House. To appease the executive, the state agreed to contribute more to the settlement fund and the tribe agreed to submit the materials requested by BAR. This compromise was accepted; on 18 October 18 1983, the Mashantucket Pequot Land Claims Settlement Act was signed into law.[21]

As the terms of the settlement indicated, the tribe's story had yet to be told. Mindful of Bureau of Indian Affairs' policies, the Pequots, with the help of Lawrence M. Hauptman, a professor of history at the State University of New York at New Paltz, James D. Wherry, the tribe's socioeconomic development specialist, and Campisi, organized a national conference on Pequot history and culture. Convened in October of 1987, this event brought together some of the most prominent scholars in the field of American Indian studies in the northeast: Alvin M. Josephy Jr., whose many works on American Indians include *The Patriot Chiefs* and *Red Power;* William S. Simmons, a professor of anthropology at the University of California Berkeley and the author of two seminal studies on New England Indians, *Cautantowwit's House* and *Spirit of the New England Tribes;* and Neal Salisbury, a professor of history at Smith College and the author of *Manitou and Providence.* Their papers, along with those of the principal organizers and other conference participants, Robert L. Bee, Lynn Ceci, Dena F. Dincauze, Kevin A. McBride, and William Starna, were published three years later as *The Pequots in Southern New England: The Fall and Rise of an American Indian Nation.*

In this volume of some 250 pages, the history of the Pequot Indians was retold for the first time in several generations. Beginning with the prehistory of southern New England, the book explores Indian culture on the eve of contact, the circumstances that led to the Anglo-Pequot War, the conquest of the Pequots, the years of diaspora and survival, and the reemergence of the Mashantucket, or western, branch of the group in the 1970s. The first written history of Pequot Indians authorized by a body of Pequot leaders, it is also the first to avoid the removalist and extinctionist language of its predecessors. In this volume, Pequot history is an ongoing, progressive, and in Vizenor's sense of the term, "comic" tribal narrative.

Vizenor's concept is best illustrated in his 1991 novel, *Heirs of Columbus.* The heirs referred to in the title are a community of tribal crossbloods who trace their origins to the mythical child of Christopher Columbus, the European explorer, and Samana, a New World shaman. As their genealogy suggests, Vizenor's fictional heirs reflect tribal realities in the postcontact world. The agonistic survivors of "that wild premier union with the fur trade and written languages," "a brush with lethal pathogens," "the deceptions of missionaries, the phraseologies of treaties, and the levies of a dominant consumer culture,"[22] crossbloods embody a tribal response to "racialism, colonial duplicities, sentimental monogenism, and generic cultures."[23] For Vizenor, crossblood culture is "comic and communal," not "tragic and sacrificial."[24] This definition emphasizes both the historical context within which tribal communities have emerged and the ability of those communities to survive in an oppressive colonialist regime. Not contained by facile binary structures like "savage and civilized," "Indian and white," "traditional and modern," "full-blood and mixed-blood," crossbloods are the products and producers of an open-ended and ongoing negotiation with their total environment. As a metaphorical counterpart to living tribal communities, Vizenor's heirs have a cross-cultural inheritance that assimilates the European explorer into a preexisting indigenous culture. Thus, in the heirs' stories, Columbus is referred to as "an obscure crossblood who bore the signature of survivance and ascended the culture of death in the old world."[25] In this way, the order of domination is reversed; Columbus is a tribal discovery to be exploited by a tribal community.

High-stakes reservation gambling is just one outcome of this Columbian exchange. The facility owned and operated by the heirs is named, appropriately enough, the Santa Maria Casino. A replica of Columbus's ship, the casino caravel symbolizes the appropriations of an expropriated people. Nearby, a replica of the *Niña* serves as a floating restaurant, and the *Pinta,* a tax-free market. Taken together, the heirs and their simulated fleet serve as metaphors for a contemporary and crossblood tribal experience. The legitimate tribal descendants of European colonists as well as indigenous North American peoples, they symbolically transform European inventions and histories into tribal ventures and traditions. Although Vizenor's comic portrayal is an extremely optimistic view of the ways that indigenous peoples may respond to colonialism, it serves the need to expand the limits of self-definition, and with it, the limits of action and response available to tribal peoples.

In many ways, the Mashantucket Pequots provide a real-life counterpart to Vizenor's fictional heirs. Like the heirs, they have advanced counternarratives of Pequot survival and resistance that contest the dominant culture's monologue that their time had and/or would come to an end. They have survived lethal pathogens, the duplicities of the fur trade, dubious court rulings, the work of missionaries, and abject poverty. Despite the radical reconfiguration of Pequot society that has occurred since the early seventeenth century, the tribe has maintained a strong communal ethos based on ties of kinship and an inherited claim to the land. For these and other reasons, the Pequots view themselves as a distinct and sovereign tribal people even as they become university educated, technologically advanced, and economically powerful.

As a result of its crossblood survivance, the tribe's apparent lack of Indianness has made it the object of intense scrutiny. Today's Pequots, living in one of the most densely populated regions of North America, are interracial, intercultural, and traditionally working class. In many respects they are indistinguishable from non-Native Americans. Although they are descended from Pequot and other northeast Indian peoples, particularly the Narragansett, the tribe is heavily intermarried with African-American, French-Canadian, Irish, Scottish, and English peoples. As long as the community remained invisible, unrecognized, and powerless, it mattered little that they were "mixed-blood" and "black" Indians. Pequot anonymity, however, is a thing of the past, and many outsiders feel that the apparent lack of "Indian" blood and visible Indianness delegitimizes other tribal claims, including the right to own and operate a high-stakes gambling facility. This anti-Pequot sentiment has partly resulted from white jealousy of the tribe's financial success. Donald Trump, a non-

Indian casino owner threatened by the tribal games, stated publicly that the Pequots are not Indian because, he concluded, they don't look like Indians.

As a result of the backlash the tribe's successful casino, development, and land-reacquisition ventures have generated, the Mashantucket Pequots have frequently been called upon to prove their Indianness. As Richard Hayward pointed out in a television interview, the tribe is often judged against racially determined stereotypes: "[People] don't understand why we're black, white, red, yellow. You know, 'Why, you're not Indian; you don't look Indian.' What does an Indian look like? You gotta look like the guy on the nickel. You know, and you've got to have blue black straight hair, and your nose has got to be shaped just so, and your lips have got to be just so. You've got to look like the part or you're not one of the original natives."[26]

As the reference to "the guy on the nickel" indicates, the Pequots are often measured against manufactured images that have little or no basis in actual experience. Nonetheless, because of the authority invested in such images, their proliferation through printing presses, doctored studio photographs, movies and television, and the relative absence of indigenous peoples, they have gained more authority than the self-representation of indigenous peoples themselves.

Popular assumptions about Native American identity are reflected in the government's language of blood quantum. Within the dominant culture, Indians have tended to be defined as either "full-bloods" or "mixed-bloods." While full-bloods are regarded as authentic Indians, they are commonly viewed as the remnants of a primitive and vanishing race. Mixed-bloods are placed in limbo, not fully Indian, not fully white, and belonging to neither culture. Black Indians, like the majority of the Pequots, are often simply thought of as black people whose Indianness is erased by darker skin tones and African phenotype. Biological classifications such as these emphasize genetically inherited qualities that deny tribal peoples the right to change and adapt to new conditions, appropriate European-American inventions for their own purposes, or determine the membership of their own communities.

Among the Pequots, the need to counteract racial definitions and categories has demanded new, tribal ways of identifying Indianness. In the 1980s, the tribe offered striking testimony of its self-definitions in a Connecticut Public Television documentary, *The New Pequots.* By allowing the Pequots to speak directly into the camera, the film offers a direct and seemingly unmediated representation of the tribe. In this way, the film effectively explodes the myths and stereotypes generated, reproduced, and manipulated by the dominant culture. Vizenor has described this process as "socioacupuncture," a "ritual striptease" that "reverses the documents, deflates data, dissolves historical time, releases the pressure in captured images, and exposes the pale inventors of the tribes."[27]

The first "pale inventors" of the Pequots were the Puritans who chronicled the tribe's alleged savagery and necessary demise. By revealing the savagery of the Puritans, the film attempts to reverse the familiar story. Toward this end, the attack on the Pequots at Weinshauks is retold by Hayward himself. Standing before the bronze statue of the armed and triumphant John Mason before it was removed from its place on Pequot Avenue, the tribal chairman poignantly describes the massacre and its aftermath. With Hayward facing off against his people's ancient nemesis, the positions of these adversaries have been reversed; the savagery of Mason is now the focus of a Pequot gaze, and it is the Pequot who speaks for the silenced Puritan. In 1656, Mason concluded his history of the Pequot War with the following observation: "Thus we may see, How the Face of God is set against them that do Evil, to cut off Remembrance of them from Earth."[28] Over 300 years later, the Pequots have been anything but unremembered and Mason himself has been the focus of censure and judgment.

In its effort to overturn colonial narratives that assume Pequot extinction, *The New Pequots* focuses primarily on the tribe's history in the wake of the Anglo-Pequot War. Thus, after recalling the violence of the 1630s, the film describes the territorial disputes that occurred over the next three centuries. Toward this end, it recalls the cessions of 1761 and 1855 that reduced Mashantucket to less than 200 acres. This section of the film concludes with a discussion of the passing of the Land Claims Settlement Act. Employing what had become a familiar strategy of the tribe, a recollection of the Pequot past is recontextualized in light of recent Pequot successes and gains.

While clearing up Mashantucket's legal history is important, the documentary's main theme is the Pequots' unique cultural inheritance and ancestral tie to the land. Toward this end, it recalls the life of Elizabeth George, Chairman Hayward's grandmother. George, with her half-sister, Martha Langevin Ellal, headed the only Indian family to maintain a residence at Mashantucket in the middle decades of the twentieth century. A lack of housing and employment on and near the reservation had long since led to a dispersal of the reserve's tribal inhabitants. By the late 1960s, persons with Mashantucket Pequot ancestry were living in Groton, New London, Stonington, and Rhode Island, while others had relocated to other areas of the northeast, including New York City. During these years, Mashantucket's borders continued to be defended by the sisters. Trespassers were driven off the reservation at gunpoint and every effort was made to resist the implementation of state law on the territory.[29] Despite the lack of public assistance, they preserved Mashantucket's unique status under the law, land base, and Native identity. In the documentary, this struggle is recorded in the memories of George's children and grandchildren. Through their testimony, she becomes a recognizable Indian presence. George's photograph, shot by Curtiss Moussie, a professional photographer who had befriended the tribal woman, reinforces their words. Shown with her high cheekbones and long, Indian-style braids, George embodies the tribe's Indianness.

In addition to being a visual indicator of Mashantucket Pequot identity, George represents a tribal belonging to the land. "She would always tell us," recalls her daughter, Theresa Hayward, "'don't ever give up your land, hold on to the land.'" This theme is developed by Sue Whipple, George's granddaughter, who recalls this moment on the eve of her grandmother's death: "'She had a little flower garden right here where that rock is, and she picked up a handful of dirt in her hand. It was just meant for me not to realize; 'What is she doing with that? Something's going to happen to her.' It didn't ever come to my mind, I just looked at her funny, because she picked up a handful of dirt. And she said, 'This is beautiful. I love the feel of it.'" Visibly moved by this recollection, Whipple provides one of the most poignant moments in the film.

George's admonition, "hold on to the land," would become a rallying cry for a new generation of Mashantucket Pequot leaders. According to Hayward, the regrouping of the tribe was an extension of his grandmother's communal ethos: "She wanted everybody to come back home. And, after she passed away we started doing that. We had to reach out to everybody, and bring everybody back, everybody that belonged here, so that they would have a chance to see and feel the land, and do something with it, so that it wouldn't be taken away. And that's what we started out doing, from her words, 'Don't ever let go of the land, hold on to it.'" Inspired by George's legacy, contemporary Pequot leadership has sought to provide a home for anyone with a verifiable claim to Mashantucket Pequot ancestry. Contemporary tribal membership is based on two state rolls taken in

1900 and 1910. Any person who can prove at least one-sixteenth ancestry from any one of a dozen or so women on those lists is eligible for membership in the tribe. This policy lead to a dramatic increase in the tribe's population. More recently, the tribe has accepted applicants with less than one-sixteenth ancestry. This has further increased its rolls.

As a result of the state, federal, and tribal collaborations that culminated in the passing of the Mashantucket Pequot Land Claims Settlement Act, three distinct subgroups of the Pequot community currently coexist at Mashantucket. The largest of these groups is composed of the tribe's "black" Indians, those Pequots of African-Algonquian descent. Another group of "white" Indians is heavily intermarried with European peoples, particularly French, Irish, and Scottish immigrants. A third group, and the reservation's smallest, is composed of persons with a mostly indigenous inheritance. These distinctions have caused friction within the community. As improving conditions made it possible for more families to return to the reservation, many people were forced to coexist with their dark- and light-skinned relatives for the first time. "There's no denying it," Hayward comments in the film, "there were racial feelings between different families." Yet all of these people are at least second cousins, and the decision to unite everyone who belongs regardless of race or ethnicity has been a central feature of the community's new success.

As a result of its commitment to extending tribal membership to all with a verifiable claim to Mashantucket Pequot ancestry, the tribal council has created a thriving crossblood community. In one of the last and most impressive moments in the documentary, the camera follows a group of Mashantucket Pequot students as they disembark a school bus. The group is composed of dark- and light-skinned children. A voice from behind the camera asks, "Who's related to who?" They answer in unison, "We're all related; we're all cousins." For these children, as for their parents, Pequot identity will be a complex negotiation of social, political, and economic ties, all of which will be inextricably bound up with their experience in the land. Like the adults of their community, they will choose among past traditions and future possibilities as they define their own Indianness. As Clifford suggests, this will be an "ongoing process, politically contested and historically unfinished."[30]

The Mashantucket Pequot Museum and Research Center, an unequivocal masterpiece of tribal self-representation, brings together the tribe's history in interactive audio and visual presentations, dioramas, artifacts, printed words, and films. First opened to the public in August of 1998, it functions as a further development of the tribe's previous efforts to tell its story. Toward this end, the museum's displays build upon the strategies and mediums of self-representation employed by the tribe since the early 1970s. In addition to providing a dramatic and detailed narrative presentation of Mashantucket Pequot history and culture, the museum devotes considerable space to natural history, New England Indian history, and indigenous experience in general. Appropriating the technologies and aesthetics of the museum, it continues the advocacy traditions the tribe had formerly established in print, video, and oral testimony.

Designed to offer an effective lesson in tribal history, the route through the museum is didactic and chronological. At its beginning and end, the journey is marked by displays that frame the presentation in terms of contemporary Pequot existence. In the museum's first exhibit, visitors are greeted with a wall-sized photograph of the contemporary tribe. Glass cases display a mixture of traditional and contemporary artifacts: a basketball jersey from the tribe's youth league; traditional tribal regalia; a scale model of the *Sassacus,* the highspeed ferry built and owned by the tribe; a wooden ball club and eagle feather presented to the tribe by John Echohawk of the Native American Rights Fund at the museum's dedication. Photographs of current tribal development projects, a scale model of the reservation and its surrounding area, printed explanations, and a sound wash featuring voices of tribal members further establish a sense of the tribe's present.

Drawing the visitor's attention away from the casino, that fetishized symbol of contemporary Pequot power, and away from narrowly focused questions about contemporary Pequot identity, the museum's 85,000 square feet of permanent exhibits offer a detailed history of the land's history. Introductions aside, the visitor's journey properly begins when he descends an escalator through the blue ice of a simulated glacier, the entrance way to Life in a Cold Climate, an exhibit on the Ice Age. At the ground zero of the museum's time line, a series of interactive videos and permanent displays educates the visitor on the Wisconsin glacier and its role in shaping the land. A series of full-scale re-creations—a woolly mammoth in snow, a pack of dire wolves, wax figures of humans engaged in a caribou hunt—provides vivid illustrations of the land's earliest period of human habitation. Through the work of contemporary Native American artists, the creation stories of the Navajo, Kiowa, Lakota, Mohawk, Ojibway, and other indigenous peoples are recounted. In an adjoining room, a video of a Cayuga elder retelling the earth diver myth plays continuously. Calling attention to the museum's appropriation of what James Clifford refers to as "majority anthropological traditions" and other western sciences, a series of displays explains the methods of geologists, archaeologists, and paleobiologists, who disclose and interpret the clues to the land's past.[31]

The museum's most elaborate gallery, and its centerpiece, is a life-size recreation of a Pequot village on the eve of contact. In this large, open space, among a simulated forest complete with a waterfall, tidal stream, and natural sounds, the visitor wanders among more than thirty wax figures—children, adolescents, adults, and elders—engaged in such common activities as farming, hunting, house building, food preparation, healing, and leisure. Among them are three figures playing *hubbub,* the New England Indian dice game described by William Wood. The distinct poses of the simulated villagers lend added verisimilitude to the scene. Because the figures are not behind glass, but placed just a few feet, if not inches, from the main path, the setting is intimate. Dressed in traditional clothing before the introduction of European cloth, the tattooed bodies, naked from the waist up and dressed in animal skins, take on a palpable quality. Portraying a peaceful and self-contained world, this idyllic and romanticized space represents Native life in the period before European contact.

Native culture is further detailed in a series of supporting side galleries. In the Daily Life Gallery, the visitor views a video featuring a contemporary Mashpee man building a dugout canoe, an exhibit on the construction of wigwams, and printed explanations to accompany an exhibit on collecting wild plants. In the Pequot Society Gallery, the visitor learns about the languages, customs, and spiritual traditions of Indians. In a series of interactive audio and video displays, Native stories, as told in their original languages with subtitles and illustrations, are sampled. The final adjoining gallery, Arrival of the Europeans, features a single figure of a Dutch trader. Bearded and dressed in European-style clothing, with a musket resting across his knees and trade beads offered in an outstretched hand, this striking figure is considerably out of place in the museum's simulated Native environment. Juxtaposed to the inhabitants of the Pequot village, the ersatz Dutchman is an obviously alien presence in a Native American world.

Having re-created a virtual landscape of Native life in New England in precontact times, "white culture, commerce, and power arrive," as Clifford suggests in his reading of museums in the Pacific Northwest, "in medias res."[32] The museum's next series of displays offers a time line, films, interactive audio and visual presentations, printed explanations, and more wax figures that educate the visitor on the background and causes of the Anglo-Pequot War. A short film shown continuously in an adjoining gallery provides a detailed explanation of the uses of wampum in the seventeenth-century fur trade. In Pequot War Theater, *The Witness* plays continuously. A film re-creation of the conflict, it condenses the two-year war into roughly thirty minutes of screen time. Twin theaters ensure that all visitors will have an opportunity to view the film.

On the wide screen, the wax figures in the Pequot village seemingly come to life. Among the historical personages portrayed in the film are John Endecott, John Mason, Uncas, and the Pequot emissary aboard Endecott's boat. The film's climax presents a dramatic depiction of the destruction of Weinshauks. At this point, the politics of the museum are at their most oppositional. Bringing the region's history of colonization and exploitation to the forefront, the film offers what Clifford refers to as an "informing and shaming" discourse. The sort of contemplative stance that is common to most museum experiences is challenged here by an "unsettling melange of aesthetic, cultural, political, and historical messages" that implicates majority audiences, by virtue of their white Christian European background, in the violence the film portrays.[33]

As *The Witness* dramatically illustrates, the Mashantucket Pequot Museum is not simply an exercise in display, but a facility designed to illicit emotional as well as intellectual responses from its visitor. In a gesture that reminds the audience of the cultural tradition being cinematically recalled, the movie is framed as a lesson in storytelling. In the first and final scenes of the drama, an elder Pequot man, dressed in a mixture of late seventeenth century European and Native American clothing styles, relates the history of the war to a child, who is now entrusted to remember the story and pass it on to future generations. The telling and retelling of the story constitutes the basis of Pequot identity. As Clifford suggests, this tribal museum display, in emphasizing an open-ended history, salvages a message of hope and pride from tragedy.[34]

The museum's final series of galleries, Life on the Reservation, covers the period from the conclusion of the Pequot War to the present day. It features a dozen more wax figures of Pequots in various stages of assimilation. Among those represented are Robin Cassacinamon, who appears to be examining a printed document. In William Apess Theater, a Comanche actor portrays the Native minister. Filmed on location at the Mashpee Meeting House in Mashpee, Cape Cod, he reads excerpts from and discourses upon the narratives of Ann Wampy, Hannah Caleb, and Sally George, as they appeared in Apess's *Five Christian Indians of the Pequot Tribe.* In the Federal Recognition Theater, the visitor views a short documentary film that features interviews with lawyers, anthropologists, tribal members, and congressmen involved in the recognition hearings. Among the artifacts included in this section are such traditional markers of Indianness as handmade baskets. Also featured are modern artifacts, like the Smith Corona typewriter that Richard Hayward used to prepare documents to support the land claims suit and federal recognition bid. In a final exhibit, *A Tribal Portrait,* enlarged black-and-white photographs of current tribal members and a voice wash bring the visitor full circle. While these exhibits are undeniably anticlimactic, they are, in political terms, the most important ones featured in the museum. As John Bodinger de Uriarte points out, the tradition represented by the exhibits "legitimizes contemporary practices by imagining them as unbroken continuities, both distant and time-honored."[35] It is by establishing continuity within the radical changes that have marked the last 350 years of Pequot experience that the museum fully achieves its didactic purposes.

Since the early 1970s, the refashioning of a tribal community at Mashantucket has resulted from a dynamic and open-ended process. American Indian activism throughout the United States, changes in federal and state Indian policies, greater public awareness of Native issues, and strong leadership within the tribe have all contributed to the revitalization and rebirth of a Pequot tribal nation within the state of Connecticut. From this triumph of democratic process and America's enlightenment values, a new tribal tradition is emerging around a successful casino enterprise and tribal museum and research facility.[36] In an era often guided by identity politics, a politics the tribes did not create but have been forced to engage, a continual articulation of Mashantucket Pequot identity has attended each phase of the tribe's reemergence. The recent developments that have transpired in and around the reservation's boundaries, signaling the termination of one epoch of history and the beginning of another, have forever altered the landscape of southeastern Connecticut, a geographical locale that has already been, and will continue to be, the site of dramatic confrontation and change.

Part Three.

Gamblers

On the "Indianness" of Bingo 5.

Gambling and the Native American Community

Since the late 1970s, the expansion of the Indian gambling industry has raised concerns among tribal and nontribal peoples alike. As the controversy surrounding Foxwoods indicates, the redistribution of wealth and the transformation of local and state politics generate debate over a variety of legal, economic, and social questions. Reservation gambling can be equally controversial within the tribes. These controversies might involve disagreements over the organization and management of a tribal gaming facility or debates over whether or not a tribal nation should pursue high-stakes, for-profit gaming as a path toward self-determination. There are those among the indigenous community who are deeply concerned that the lure of easy money and the obsession with gambling will erode the traditional, community-based ethics at the core of Native society. Questions have also been raised over the political consequences of a thriving gambling trade. While high-stakes reservation gambling is an expression of tribal sovereignty, some Indians fear that the industry will ultimately diminish, rather than enhance, the long-term ability of the tribes to retain their status as separate nations within the territorial boundaries of the United States.

As it is understood today, Indian nation sovereignty refers to the formal relationship of modern Indian communities to local, state, and federal governments. As such, sovereignty was created in the crucible of indigenous-colonial relations. Yet sovereignty is based on an independence of Indian communities that predates European contact. "What does sovereignty mean," Seneca scholar John Mohawk asks, "when it finds its roots in Indian traditions and not in the courts and congresses of the United States and Canada?"[1] According to

Mohawk, traditional sovereignty is something held by all citizens in common.[2] It is rooted in shared experiences in the land and expressed in origin stories, ceremonial cycles, lifestyles, and languages. It encompasses the peoples' sense of themselves as a distinct human population with a unique and divinely sanctioned purpose in the world.

There can be no doubt that Europeans viewed Indian nations as sovereign entities. Colonial governments recognized their indigenous counterparts and engaged in government-to-government relations with them for the purposes of trade and war. Europeans presupposed that Native peoples formed culturally distinct communities. They respected the Indians' right to make governmental arrangements that furthered their own political and social goals. This understanding was codified in treaties between Indian nations and European-derived colonial, state, and federal governments. For example, in 1794, the Six Nations of the Haudenosaunee Iroquois confederacy and the United States established a treaty of peace and friendship. Ratified by Congress and signed by George Washington, the Treaty of Canandaigua guarantees the Haudenosaunee "the free use and enjoyment" of the territories, which shall remain theirs "until they choose to sell the same to the People of the United States, who have the right to purchase."[3] This agreement continues to be recognized by both parties. In accordance with Article 6 of the treaty, the United States yearly delivers $4,500 worth of treaty cloth to the Haudenosaunee, who distribute it among their members. Confirming their nation-state status, the Haudenosaunee are the only American Indian nation to hold a seat on the United Nations and issue an internationally recognized passport.

Conversely, in Europe, the concept of sovereignty refers to the divine right of kings to rule their nation states and to their independence from other such states. In an empire, sovereignty is invested in the ruling nation, which limits the independence and self-government expressed by states within its dominion. Thus, while sovereignty was a presupposed condition of indigenous life, the colonists, through military conquests, agreements, and the pressures associated with their social and economic institutions, gradually diminished the scope of Indian nation sovereignty. In some places, as in southeastern Connecticut, that sovereignty was supposed to be extinguished.

In the United States, the limits of tribal sovereignty were established in the 1830s in a series of landmark Supreme Court decisions involving removal. The

Court presupposed the sovereign rights of Indian peoples in pre- and postcontact times. In *Worcester v. Georgia,* Chief Justice John Marshall described Native Americans as distinct peoples divided into separate nations who were independent of each other and of the rest of world.[4] According to Marshall, the Indians retained "their original natural rights, as the undisputed possessors of the soil from time immemorial," long after contact. The one exception that altered this right was the condition "imposed by irresistible power."[5] In other words, the Indians lost their sovereign right to the land when they lost the power to defend their borders. However, even in their weakened state, Indian nations retained a degree of their original independence. In *Cherokee Nation v. Georgia,* Marshall conceptualized this abridged tribal sovereignty in the term "domestic dependent nations."[6] As Charles F. Wilkinson explains, the Supreme Court's ruling assumed the United States' dominion of the tribes and thus abolished the tribes' right to ally with other nations.[7] But as nations, they retained the right to engage in government-to-government relations with local, state, and federal assemblies. In subsequent decisions, U.S. courts extended federal jurisdiction over Indian country in cases involving specified crimes.[8] The courts also assumed stewardship over Indian peoples and treated them as wards of the state. As minors, Native peoples were effectively denied most of their group and individual rights.

Despite the diminishment of tribal sovereignty in the United States, the principle of independence has been kept alive by indigenous peoples refusing to relinquish total control of their social, cultural, and economic resources to authoritarian, colonialist regimes. As the history of the Pequots demonstrates, the principles of traditional sovereignty, including the right to self-government and the right to claim possession of a territory, have survived in even the most hostile environments. In the United States, these limited powers were given standing in federal courts through the passing of the Indian Reorganization Act in 1934. A reversal of the government's allotment policy, the act was designed for the express purpose of "restor[ing]" the "incalculable damage" caused by allotment.[9] It instructed the tribes to organize on behalf of their own welfare and to adopt their own constitutions and bylaws.[10] In addition, it instructed the federal government to provide legal and financial services to help the tribes reclaim lost acreage and to develop their economic resources. In this way, the federal government committed itself to improving the conditions of the tribes by providing them with funding, services, and recognition as legitimate governing bodies within the constitutional framework of the United States. While reorganization gave tribal governments real legal and political clout, it did so by encouraging the tribes to adopt governmental procedures that facilitated interactions with federal agencies like the Bureau of Indian Affairs. By investing authority in federally mediated councils, tribalism has contributed to the ongoing evolution of Indian self-government. This evolution has led to a decline in traditional governing structures and the social organizations that supported them.

Because reservation gambling is an expression of both the limited sovereignty the federal government allows Indian tribes and an expression of the political and social independence enjoyed by Native communities in the times before conquest, it begs a number of important yet unanswered questions. Insofar as it is a creation of federal tribalism, will reservation gambling support the proliferation of a federally mediated tribal culture to the detriment of Indian nation sovereignty and self-government? As an expression of the traditional independence of Native communities, will tribal gambling support indigenous identities and traditions, or contribute to the erosion of traditional cultures by encouraging greater assimilation into the mainstream values of the United States? Along with making the reservations the epicenter of a lucrative gambling trade, tribal gambling creates new leaders who are often politically and economically independent of both elected and traditional governing councils. Are these "bingo chiefs" appropriating a corporate tribal sovereignty for personal gain or expressing their own fundamental rights as tribal people? To put the question in broader terms, will high-stakes gambling stimulate the growth of viable economies for whole reservation communities or will it contribute to a greater disparity in the distribution and use of tribal resources? The debate over reservation gambling has also informed an intratribal debate on "Indianness" itself. In the new tribal world of consumer economics, federal subsidies, and wage labor, what can be recognized as authentically Indian? If gambling operators lack Indianness, where does Indianness reside?

A tribal appropriation of a European-American gambling industry, reservation gambling introduces to reservation communities one of the most defining and problematic of American cultural institutions. The kinds of games played in Indian casinos are not native to North America, but are based on the traditional games of Europe. The first European visitors quickly introduced these games to indigenous American peoples. Columbus's sailors are reported to have gambled aboard ship on their way to the New World.[11] When forced to throw their cards into the water, they fashioned new ones from the leaves of Caribbean island plants. Faced with the risks of sailing into uncharted seas, Columbus's sailors practiced ancient gambling rituals originating in pre-Christian and precapitalistic societies. Games of chance had long served as both diversions and rites of divination in the European countries from which they sailed. This tradition is evident in ancient Greek and Hebrew literatures[12] and indicates the serious role gambling has played in Western cultural traditions. Perceiving this role, Johan Huizinga, a historian of play in human culture, described gambling as an innate human urge that influenced the development of religion, law, the performing arts, and foreign policy. For Huizinga, play created order, and was itself, the principle of order.[13] In his 1935 work *Homo Ludens* (Man the Player) he assigned dice and other gambling games to the domain of "sacred play," an important function of which was to help groups maintain the cosmic order.[14]

The connection that Huizinga discerned between order and play provides insight into the social role of gambling in the United States. In some ways embodying the core values of American culture, gamblers have helped to define the independence, acquisitiveness, competitiveness, and optimism of the national character.[15] Perceiving this link, Alexis de Tocqueville described Americans as a people of chance. "Those who live in the midst of democratic fluctuations," he wrote in the 1840s, "have always before their eyes the image of chance, and they end by liking all undertakings in which change plays a part."[16] Driven by a desire to achieve financial gain, as well as the pure enjoyment of gaming, Americans engage in commerce "not only for the sake of the profit it holds out to them, but for the love of the constant excitement occasioned by that pursuit."[17] In such a social system, commerce was comparable to a "vast lottery."[18] The proliferation of gambling in contemporary American culture, both as a pastime and as a legitimate way to make money, lends currency to Tocqueville's thesis.

Along with providing rituals and metaphors that order the social and economic universe, games of chance have served as an effective means of raising money. By harnessing the self-interest of colonists, lotteries provided funding for some of the most celebrated institutions in Anglo-American history. The Jamestown Colony, Yale University, and a host of other prominent East Coast colleges were all partially funded by lottery ticket sales. A lottery helped to fund the Continental Army during the Revolutionary War.[19] Until the early nineteenth century, when banking became an established institution, a lottery was the normal way to raise funds for all sorts of local, state, and federal projects.[20] Thomas Jefferson once described lotteries to be among the most democratic of practices because they "layed taxation only on the willing."[21]

Until the expansion process was complete, gambling establishments prospered on successive frontiers and stimulated the taste for risk and speculation that continues to fuel the American economy. Eventually, the small-time frontier gambling hall found a permanent home in Las Vegas, the modern mecca of American gamblers. In the early nineteenth century, frontier gambling towns along the Mississippi River were a celebrated feature of American life, and remained so until farmers, businessmen, and bankers transformed frontier outposts into respectable towns and cities.[22] In the late nineteenth and early twentieth centuries, gambling houses and operations in New York City thrived under Anglo, Irish, and Italian gangs. Although gambling was eventually outlawed in most American cities, the public did not lose interest in gambling. As the success of Las Vegas demonstrated, whole cities could be built on gambling wealth. By the late twentieth century, gambling had gained unprecedented acceptance in American culture, so much so that when Billy Graham brought his "Crusade for Christ" to Las Vegas in 1978, he carefully avoided criticizing the city for its gambling-based economy. Pointing out that the Bible says nothing definitive against the practice, he expressed his concern for those who gambled their souls, not tourists playing in the casinos or employees working in the resort industry.[23]

At the beginning of the twenty-first century, games of chance have achieved unprecedented legitimacy. As John M. Findlay points out, "revenue shortfalls, tax revolts, interest in economic revitalization, and greater tolerance for betting" have led to a lifting of state restrictions against gambling.[24] Consider the case in Connecticut. Before the Mashantucket Pequot Tribe established its high-stakes bingo hall, offtrack betting, greyhound racing, jai alai, and the lottery were established sources of state revenue, employment, and private profit. As defense contractors like Groton's Electric Boat were being forced to curtail their work force, the Pequot casino helped to fill the employment and revenue gap.

Despite its popularity, gambling inspires deeply ambivalent feelings among Americans. At the heart of this ambivalence is a tension between the dictates of the Protestant work ethic, which rewards hard work with the slow accumulation of riches, and the spirit of risk and speculation at the heart of American capitalism. Although risk taking is viewed as a necessary element of success, it is considered detrimental when reduced to mere gambling. These attitudes are evident in the practices of the New England Puritans, a people who, as William Wood demonstrates, opposed Massachusetts gaming practices with their own virtuous speculations. While the Puritans succeeded by speculating on the value of lands, timber, agricultural products, and furs, among other commodities that had value on European and world markets, they viewed gambling as both a moral and commercial threat to society. This attitude persisted throughout the antebellum period in American history, when Christian virtues were called upon to limit the potentially corrupting influences of the marketplace. The distinction between gambling and commercial risk taking, however, is not always clear. As Ann Fabian argues, the lines separating virtuous capitalistic speculation and vicious gambling cannot be maintained with any absolute degree of certainty.[25] Not only do the two categories merge into each other, but, depending on the circumstances, it is possible to conceive of virtuous gamblers and vicious speculators. In the United States, gamblers can be heroes and villains, while speculators can serve as both captains of industry and confidence men.

The distinction between virtuous speculation and vicious gambling reflects not only racial and ethnic biases, but class biases as well. While wealthy elites have been generally unrestricted in their enjoyment of games of chance, laborers have been censured for their interest in gaming. This attitude is preserved in a British government order to ban lotteries in its American colonies in the 1760s. According to a mandate sent to colonial governors, "[Lotteries] doth tend to disengage those who become adventurers therein from that spirit of industry and attention to their proper callings and occupations on which the public welfare so greatly depends."[26] In 1826, Britain attempted to ban its own lotteries because they were believed to "corrupt the morals, and encourage a spirit of Speculation and Gambling among the lower class of people."[27] In both cases the concern was that the labor class would become unmanageable and unproductive if allowed to cultivate its interest in gambling. The censure of gamblers thus helped to control workers and to contain threats to those at the top of the social hierarchy. Ironically, if the advancement of a new commercial economy was incompatible with the laborer's natural propensity for games and gambling, the new emphasis on money only stimulated the desire to gamble.[28]

One of the most dramatic confrontations between gambling and anti-gambling factions in the United States occurred in Vicksburg, Mississippi, in 1835. Founded in 1819, early Vicksburg was little more than a steamboat landing and farmer's market. Fueled by a boom in land speculation, its economy grew rapidly. Newly conquered Indian territories attracted settlers and businessmen to the cotton-rich lands nearby, and Vicksburg became a community of speculators vying for stakes in the town's future. The speculative environment also attracted a class of professional gamblers. In the first wild decades of growth, their operations thrived alongside those of other entrepreneurs. However, to the self-defined respectable class of citizens—Vicksburg's plantation owners, bankers, and merchants—gamblers presented obstacles to growth and the acquirement of eastern social refinements. Despite the increasing hostility to their presence, the gamblers refused to curtail their operations or to subject themselves to the rulings of the town court. The tensions between the two groups were aggravated by the fear of slave revolt; many regarded the egalitarianism of the "blacklegs" as proof of their association with abolitionists. On July 4 1835, the citizenry decided to run the gamblers out of town. The threat of violence was enough for most gamblers, who immediately abandoned the area and reestablished themselves farther west. Those who refused to leave, however, killed a member of the group sent to arrest them. By the end of the day, five gamblers were hanged and their equipment was destroyed.[29]

Not surprisingly, public comment on the Indian gaming industry has tended to emphasize vicious gambling over virtuous speculation. This attitude is the product of envy, legitimate concerns about the social and economic effects of for-profit gaming, and the habit of applying the stigmas European-Americans attach to their own practices and behaviors to Native cultural institutions. This is most clearly illustrated in the historical commentary on traditional Indian gaming. When viewed through the vicious gambling/virtuous speculation paradigm, such practices are associated with wastefulness and the lack of thrift and industry, and never with productive risk and speculation. By the early seventeenth century, Indian gaming was already the focus of censure for incoming settlement communities. The gambling, lazy, and wasteful Indian male that William Wood described eventually became a stock character in European-

American representations of Indians. Among the most notable scholars to proliferate this stereotype were Thomas Jefferson, Francis Parkman, and Lewis Henry Morgan. Commenting on the subject of Indian gambling, Jefferson declared the Natives' "vivacity and activity of mind" to be equal to that of whites; "hence, his eagerness for hunting, and for games of chance."[30] While Jefferson intends to prove that Indians are endowed with the same talents as whites, an important consideration for him as he sought to defend aboriginal man from the degeneracy theory of European naturalists, he can find few better examples of the Indians' intellectual and physical capacities than their penchant for gambling.

Writing about his travels through Lakota/Sioux territories in the 1840s, New England historian Francis Parkman recalls one night when "a monotonous thumping of Indian drum, mixed with occasional sharp yells, and a chorus chanted by twenty voices,"[31] kept him anxiously awake. These ceremonies, which Parkman uses to illustrate a savage frenzy, were actually part of a ritual Lakota game, most likely *hanpa-pe-cunpi*," the "moccasin" or "hand game" described by Luther Standing Bear in *My People the Sioux.*[32] For Standing Bear, hanpa-pe-cunpi was a communal celebration and wholesome entertainment. He relates how the entire camp would attend the matches, with everyone watching intently as the adults played on into the night. "No drinks were served," he stresses, "which took away the senses of our men and women, so no one grew boisterous. We had no bad words in our language, so none were used."[33] Writing in the twentieth century, Standing Bear clearly is aware of the negative associations his white readers may have about Indian ceremonies. Typical of this biased viewpoint, Parkman compares the proceeding at the Lakota camp to the "desperate gambling" that occurs in the "hells of Paris."[34] Although based on an eyewitness account of the Lakota gambling contest, Parkman's analysis reflects a preexisting discourse on Indianness that designated Native gaming practices a sign of cultural pathology.

Lewis Henry Morgan, a contemporary of Parkman, sounded a similar note in his 1851 work, *League of the Ho-De-No-Sau-Nee or Iroquois.* A founding father of American ethnography, Morgan wrote his book with the intention of encouraging a "kinder feeling towards the Indian, founded upon a truer knowledge of his civil and domestic institutions."[35] Nonetheless, Morgan saw nothing praiseworthy in Indian gaming practices. Betting, as he writes, was never "reprobated" by Native religious teachers; instead, they encouraged it. According to Morgan, this led a dangerous overindulgence: "It often happened that the Indian gambled away every valuable article which he possessed; his tomahawk, his medal, his ornaments, and even his blanket. The excitement and eagerness with which he watched the shifting tide of the game, was more uncontrollable than the delirious agitation of the pale-face at the race-course, or even the gambling table."[36] Like most commentators of their day, Parkman and Morgan see Native gambling only in European-American terms and never attempt to understand the practice from a Native perspective. As we will see in both this and the subsequent chapter, Native Americans countered such representations by favorably comparing their own gambling practices to those of white Americans. In the mid-nineteenth century, however, the pejorative representations of Native American gambling practices proliferated by white writers dominated the discourse.

A radical shift in the way whites perceived Indian gaming practices occurred near the turn of the nineteenth century. As Kathryn Gabriel reports, a chance meeting at the 1893 Columbian Exposition in Chicago between two American ethnologists, Stewart Culin and Frank Hamilton Cushing, led to a dramatic reappraisal. It was there that Culin had on display some games of chance he had collected from Asia and Europe. Cushing, who recently had served as a field collector under the explorer John Wesley Powell, noticed a similarity between these games and the ones he had been exposed to during his field work at Zuni. Mutually intrigued by this discovery, the two men decided to collaborate on an exhaustive study of games. What resulted was Culin's tomelike work, *Games of the North American Indians*. Published in 1903 by the Smithsonian's Bureau of American Ethnology, this book included material on 229 different Native groups in North American and Mexico. It identified thirty-six different types of games, which Culin divided into two categories: games of skill and dexterity, and games of chance.[37]

Although Culin devoted most of his text to describing individual games, he did offer an interpretation of the cultural aspects of indigenous gaming practices. Culin correctly perceived them to be "rites pleasing to the gods to secure their favor, or as processes of sympathetic magic, to drive away sickness, avert other evil, or produce rain and the fertilization and reproduction of plants and animals, or other beneficial results."[38] Unlike the earlier commentaries, Culin's ethnographical discourse offers no hint of condemnation. Writing at a time when Indians were no longer a threat to expansion, his views reflect a developing interest in Native American culture as an object of study. With the passing of the Indian Gaming Regulatory Act (IGRA) some eighty years later, this more open-minded perspective has been supported by federal statutes. The act formally defines traditional forms of gaming as "Class One Gaming": "social games solely for prizes of minimal value or traditional forms of Indian gambling engaged in by individuals as a part of, or in connection with, tribal ceremonies and celebrations."[39] The act distinguishes these games from "Class Two Gaming," which includes bingo, pull-tabs, and lotteries, and "Class Three Gaming," which includes high-stakes casino gambling.

As Culin pointed out to his non-Indian readers, gaming has ancient roots in native North America. Associated with rituals of play and storytelling, games of chance connect the people to their communal origins and destiny. This tradition is most profoundly evident among Haudenosaunee who consider Gus-ka-eh, the Sacred Bowl Game, a divine amusement made by the Creator for the happiness of the people.[40] Taught to humans when the world was young, it is an important rite of the *Midiwis,* or Mid-winter Ceremony. According to Trudie Lamb, a Schaghticoke Indian writer, "the Midiwis concludes the end of one cycle and marks the beginning of another. The Sacred Bowl Game is one of the Four Sacred Rituals of Mid-winter and symbolizes the struggle of the Twin Boys to win control over the earth. The Mid-winter is a time of praying and awaiting the rebirth, a renewal of life. It is a time of giving thanks to the spirit forces and to the Creator."[41] Also known as the Peach Stone Game, Gus-ka-eh is played with a wooden or cane bowl and flat stones, fruit pits, nut shells, or some other flat, two-sided object. Players take turns shaking the bowl and betting on the probability of different showings of the pieces. Each bowl shaker has a set number of bean or corn seeds, a portion of which is staked on each round of the game. The winning player is the one who collects all the beans or kernels.[42] When played during the four-day Mid-winter, the game is said to amuse the life-giving forces, please the plant and animal kingdoms, and make the Creator laugh.

The twin boys referred to by Lamb are known in Iroquoian as Teharonhi-awako (Skyholder) and Sawiskera (Troublemaker). The grandchildren of Sky-Woman, the earth mother who remakes the world in the image of the Sky-World, the twins are born with opposite personalities; continual conflict is the result. Their ongoing rivalry, symbolizing the dualism of nature, is creative and destruc-

tive by turns. The bowl game is played to end their feuding.[43] In a version of the
story summarized for me by Mike McDonald of Akwesasne's North American
Indian Travelling College, Skyholder gains a winning edge when he substitutes
the regular playing pieces for the severed heads of some small birds he had created. Killing the birds is a great sacrifice for Skyholder, but a necessary one if he
is to defeat his powerful twin. Troublemaker, having been defeated in this sacred
game, is relegated to the darkness, where he continues to exercise considerable
power.[44] When played in its ceremonial contexts, Gus-ka-eh commemorates
this divine struggle. The game's cosmological significance is further emphasized
in the rules governing play. According to some traditionals, the game cannot
accurately be described as a gambling contest or a game of chance, but as a ritual
game that explains the balance of nature.[45] Because the game is played to honor
the Creator, and not for the personal gain of its contestants, money must never
be staked. Only culturally significant objects that hold intrinsic value are acceptable wagers.

As the ceremonial nature of Gus-ka-eh demonstrates, traditional Indian
gaming practices are associated with communal rituals and celebrations. According to Barbara Kanatiiosh Gray, a researcher with the Haudenosaunee Environmental Task Force, the game creates solidarity between the clans and unites
the entire Longhouse.[46] Generally speaking, gambling ceremonials are team
competitions to be participated in by whole communities. This social aspect
of traditional Indian gaming is evident in Mourning Dove's description of the
Salishan stick game:

> In the evening, people made large bonfires in the open air and challenged
> other tribes to play stick games. Lively songs were sung by both sides, and
> each team tried to distract the other while it was trying to hide the two
> bones. The object of the game was for the other side to guess which hand
> had a particular bone. Each side had a long pole stretched across in front
> and pounded on it with a short stick, keeping time with the songs. Bets of
> robes, blankets, coins and so forth were piled in the middle. Anyone could
> bet on a team, even women. Women also had their betting games, which
> could last for a few hours or several days. All bets had to be absolutely
> matched. Anyone who wanted to make a bet had to match it against
> one for the other side. After the game, a winner got back double on the

*bet. . . . All gambling required good sportsmanship. It was shameful for a
poor loser to grieve. They would get no sympathy.*[47]

The Haudenosaunee bowl game is likewise practiced as a team competition.
In the mid-nineteenth century, Morgan reported that it was routinely played
between neighboring communities and different clans within a particular town.
The victory belonged to both the gambler and his clan, town, or nation. Thus,
based on their skill at betting or throwing dice, gamblers were chosen by the
whole group.[48]

The kind of social and sacred gambling described by Standing Bear, Lamb,
and Mourning Dove has little in common with Las Vegas–style gambling, high-
stakes bingo, and video slots. As Gerald Vizenor explains, "pull tabs are not
moccasin games and bingo is far from a traditional tribal giveaway to counter
materialism."[49] Rather, reservation gambling is an exercise of tribal sovereignty
for the purposes of moneymaking. Because of its overtly capitalistic value, traditionalists fear that reservation gambling will foster materialism, acquisitiveness,
and self-interest divested of the group. Along with eroding the core values on
which Native society is founded, tribal gaming is a controversial political issue
that has had the unfortunate effect of increasing tensions between Indian and
non-Indian groups. Because of their vulnerability to legislative action and unfavorable court decisions, tribal governments must be wary of the legal and
political consequences of running high-stakes gambling facilities.

Unknown in Indian country just a generation ago, the tribal gaming industry is an appropriation of both European-American gambling practices and the
American high-stakes gambling industry. The first reservation gambling facilities appeared in the late 1970s, when the Penobscot Indians of Maine and the
Seminole Indians of Florida established high-stakes Indian bingo operations.
Soon, tribal councils throughout the United States were developing plans of their
own. Their progress was hindered by growing opposition in the states. Before the
emergence of Indian bingo, state governments had complete regulatory control
over public gambling within their borders. By claiming sovereign rights of their
own, the tribes challenged that authority. The issue was resolved in federal court
when the Seminole Indians sued the State of Florida for closing down its bingo
hall. In 1983, the Fifth Circuit Court of Appeals ruled that Seminole bingo could
continue because the federal government had never transferred to Florida civil

jurisdiction over Indian lands. This decision hinged on the finding that Indian bingo in Florida fell under civil, not criminal, law. Since bingo wasn't a crime, the state could take no action.[50] Four years later, in 1987, the Cabazon Band of Mission Indians in California filed suit against the State of California over the right to run a casino. The case hinged on the nonprofit status of the tribal government and the state's policy of allowing casino-night fund-raisers for nonprofit organizations. Again, the federal judge ruled in favor of the tribe, a decision that paved the way for Indian casinos nationwide.[51]

Although state lawmakers and law enforcement officials continually fought to limit the development of the Indian gambling industry, federal courts consistently ruled in favor of the tribes. Bruce Johansen argues that the judges' rulings reflect initiatives within the government to reduce federal expenditures on Indian tribes and the deregulation of the gambling industry that occurred during Ronald Reagan's presidency.[52] In 1988, these policies led to the passing of the Indian Gaming Regulatory Act. According to the IGRA, states must negotiate gambling compacts with tribal governments if the proposed form of gambling is legal in the state. Because tribal governments are nonprofit organizations, this fact requires states that allow high-stakes bingo and Las Vegas–night gambling for nonprofit fund-raising to negotiate gaming compacts with any recognized Indian tribe within their borders. The teeth of the act were provided by earlier legislation that allowed tribes to sue the states in federal court. The IGRA thus provided the states a measure of regulatory control without denying the Indians the right to own and operate the games.

In the wake of the rulings and legislation, the number of reservation gambling establishments grew dramatically. By 1985, approximately 80 of the more than 300 federally recognized American Indian tribes in the United States were running a high-stakes bingo operation. After 1988, table games, slot machines, poker, and pari-mutuel betting were routinely incorporated into existing tribal operations and full-scale, Las Vegas–style gambling casinos cropped up across North America. By the end of the 1990s, hundreds of high-stakes Indian gambling operations could be found in the United States. More would emerge as state-recognized tribes won federal recognition. Before the decade was over, roughly 190 of the more than 550 federally recognized tribes were running some type of high-stakes gambling operation.[53]

By testing the limits of the law as well as the limits of their own political power, tribal governments (with the support of non-Indian lawyers, legislators, and entrepreneurs) have altered the nature and size of tribal economies throughout the United States. Many reservation communities, the Pequots among them, have enjoyed tremendous financial benefits. After the establishment of a tribal gaming hall, members of the Shakopee Mdewakanton Dakota tribe, in Minnesota, who had been earning a meager $1.95 an hour stripping copper, were netting approximately $1 million each.[54] Dramatic increases like this promise a positive change for communities plagued by chronic poverty, drug and alcohol abuse, and discrimination. On more remote reservations, Indian gambling is much less profitable. As Katherine A. Spilde, former Director of Research for the National Indian Gaming Association, points out, the top twenty Indian casinos earn 50 percent of all Indian gaming revenues.[55] The rest earn small profits or just enough to pay off service on their debt. In all cases, however, tribal gambling has dramatically cut unemployment rates and provided more jobs for Indian peoples than any other economic development program in history.

Notwithstanding its potential to reverse cycles of poverty and provide unprecedented economic opportunities for Indian peoples, reservation gambling has contributed to increased tensions between tribal and nontribal groups. For many non-Indian Americans, the success of tribal entrepreneurs has raised questions about the fairness of laws that give Indians advantages in the gambling trade. Nevada's Senator Henry Reid, one of the authors of the IGRA, has publicly stated that "the law has been twisted and turned in so many ways that now Indians have far more rights than non-Indians. That was never the intent of the law."[56] In Connecticut, some of the same lawmakers who supported the Mashantucket Pequots' bid for federal recognition opposed the establishment of bingo and casino operations in Ledyard. Citizens in the towns surrounding Foxwoods are often resentful of the changes of lifestyle that result from the tribe's development and growth. These "casino envies," as Vizenor terms them, have motivated efforts to curtail tribal gaming rights nationwide.[57] A suit filed by Donald Trump in federal court contended that the IGRA violates the sovereign right of states to "tax, regulate and police gambling activities conducted within their borders."[58] Designed to protect Trump's own substantial casino market, this suit helped to swing the balance of power back in favor of the states. In March of 1996, the Supreme Court curtailed congressional authority to resolve disputes about gaming on Indian reservations by a 5–4 vote. Consequently, tribes can no longer sue a state in federal court if the state refuses to negotiate a gaming compact. The law still allows the tribes the dubious right to petition the secretary of the interior. In the long run, however, the new ruling threatens to place the tribes at the mercy of the state courts, their traditional nemeses.[59]

The court's ruling demonstrates the fickle nature of federal Indian reforms. While the IGRA was considered an equitable solution to the conflicts generated by tribal gambling initiatives, the tribes' successes have engendered resentment and backlash. Given the history of Indian–white relations, this situation is ironic yet unsurprising. As Leonard Prescott, former chairman of the National Indian Gambling Association has commented, in their dealings with whites, fairness and the so-called "level playing field" have mostly eluded Native peoples: "Were they concerned about a level playing field when there were more suicides on reservations than anywhere else? When there was more sickness and disease on reservations than anywhere else? When there was poverty? Where were they then to say 'we got to have them on a level playing field?'"[60] As Prescott points out, the tribes' recent gains have not begun to offset their tremendous losses. Although tribal gaming has the potential to alleviate some chronic problems, a reluctance among whites to allow indigenous peoples a genuine stake in the gambling trade threatens the tribes' long-term prospects for development and growth.

Along with aggravating external conflicts, reservation gambling has contributed to social tensions within the tribes. While the so-called "new buffalo" has enabled reservation tribal leaders to provide badly needed jobs, services, and capital, not all Native Americans agree that gambling is a long-term benefit to Indian peoples. Along with fears that high-stakes gambling will contribute to the erosion of core values, traditional Indian people are concerned about the potentially negative side effects high-stakes gambling may have on treaty-based sovereignty. As James V. Fenelon has pointed out, the objection is not necessarily to gambling itself, but with the economic institutions, social practices, and political cultures that develop in the wake of capitalistic enterprises.[61] Wary of the consequences of total assimilation, tribal critics of reservation gambling are also critics of Bureau of Indian Affairs policies, as expressed through Indian Reorganization Act councils, that have dominated the social and political life of Indian America in the twentieth century. As a manifestation of government mandates, tribal gambling is viewed with the same suspicion that attends other forces that erode traditional culture and threaten Indian national sovereignty. Among the Navajo, this traditionalist view helped to defeat a tribal referendum to establish a reservation gambling facility. While the Navajo were able to settle their differences peacefully, the clash of ideas and interests has disrupted reservation life and caused bitter division within communities. In the most dramatic example, the establishment of high-stakes gambling at Akwesasne divided the Mohawk community into gambling and antigambling factions. At the height of the controversy, two men were killed in an all-night firefight.

At Akwesasne, the violence over gambling can be traced to domestic conflicts rooted in the disastrous consequences of European contact. Among the Haudenosaunee, there is no greater expression of the evils of contact than that which is found in the *Gaiwiio,* or *Code of Handsome Lake.* Handsome Lake emerged as a leader of the Seneca Nation in the years following the Revolutionary War. Although the Six Nations Confederacy was never conquered by the United States, the aftermath of the war left it impoverished and virtually powerless. Its once extensive territory was reduced to a handful of small reserves that existed on the fringes of the new economic system. In this postconfederacy environment, many traditional attitudes and practices were threatened. Although fundamental changes to Haudenosaunee culture had already occurred, and others were imminent, it was unpractical and more unwise for the Longhouse people to simply model the lifestyles of the Americans. Yet something needed to be done. As Mary Jemison's biography illustrates, morale among Haudenosaunee men was at an all-time low and alcoholism at an all-time high. Bruce Johansen writes that it was not uncommon for an entire winter harvest of furs to be sold for hard liquor.[62] Handsome Lake himself had a near-fatal bout with alcoholism. His teachings were meant to counter this evil, as well as to provide the people with the means to resist economic and cultural subordination, retain their lands, and remain at peace with their white neighbors.

In his efforts to accomplish what he regarded as the necessary reform of Haudenosaunee society, Handsome Lake attempted to constrain a new mode of living within a code of ethics that combined his original Seneca traditions with elements of Quakerism and Christianity. While he sanctioned such time-honored ceremonials as the Great Feather Dance, the Harvest Dance, and the Peach Stone Game, he counseled his people to adopt some of the technological and social practices of the Quakers he admired. Thus, he advocated the building of frame houses, the keeping of livestock, and the implementation of white farm- ing methods.[63] However, while Seneca farmers were to adopt new agricultural practices, they were to reject the profit motive of rural capitalism. As Anthony F. C. Wallace explains, Handsome Lake envisioned an indigenous village com- munity that "depended upon reciprocal gift–giving rather than commercial sale as the mechanism of internal distribution."[64] Thus, the people were counseled not to "sell anything they raised off the ground, but give it away to one another, and to the old people in particular," as they must possess everything in common, including the land itself, whose title was to be reserved to the Nation as a whole.[65]

The suspicion of money and profit motives are indicated in the opening pages of Handsome Lake's teachings, as it was translated by Seneca ethnologist Arthur C. Parker in 1905, from Chief Edward Cornplanter's version.[66] In the section entitled, "How the White Race Came to America and Why the *Gaiwiio* Became a Necessity," Cornplanter retold the European discovery myth from a Native point of view. In Cornplanter's version, a modern version of Sawiskera, here referred to as the Evil One, dupes a young European preacher into import- ing to North America five deadly objects: playing cards, money, fiddles, rum, and witchery. The preacher, having confused this devil with the savior, believes these objects will be used to good purpose: "Bring these to the people," he is told, "and make them as white men are."[67] The preacher, who could not accomplish this mission alone, enlists the help of Christopher Columbus, who carries the evil objects across the water. Having set this process in motion, the Evil One stops to admire his work: "Then did he laugh and then did he say, 'These cards will make them gamble away their wealth and idle their time; this money will make them dishonest and covetous and they will forget their old laws; this fiddle will make them dance with their arms about their wives and bring about a time of tattling and idle gossip; this rum will turn their minds to foolishness and they will barter their country for baubles; then will this secret poison [the witchery] eat the life from their blood and crumble their bones.'"[68] With this catalogue of evil objects, the code attempts to identify the European goods and practices that are most damaging to the people. Describing a casinolike environment in which gambling, drinking, and dancing are prevalent, it describes how the breakdown of traditional culture leads directly to the loss of the land. *Handsome Lake* may in fact describe the type of atmosphere that speculators created when they came to negotiate with Indians. In identifying this link between European gambling practices and the machinations of land speculators, the code offers a traditional perspective on the role of gambling in Native society. When practiced within a traditional framework, games like Gus-ka-eh affirm Haudenosaunee culture and support the long-term survival of the people; when practiced irresponsibly and in a nontraditional manner, gaming can lead to disaster.

Although each object in Handsome Lake's catalogue deserves a thorough analysis, the cards explicitly involve the issue of European-American gambling practices. By 1500, playing cards were common in every European country and were among the first things that traders and trappers introduced to North America. Native peoples, expert at their own games of chance, easily learned the new games. Despite the apparent ease with which Native peoples took up cards, the European game threatened to change the attitudes that people brought to their gaming practices. Handsome Lake believed that card playing was a profane and destructive activity that encouraged the people to "gamble away their wealth and idle their time." But ritual gaming, as we have seen, is not prohibited by Haudenosaunee tradition or Handsome Lake. When practiced within the framework of tradition, Gus-ka-eh constitutes an affirmation of Haudenosaunee culture and identity. In this context, "wealth" refers to both social and economic stock, and should be distinguished from the mere acquisition of money.

While the teachings of Handsome Lake revitalized the Haudenosaunee's traditional way of life, the code is by no means universally accepted. Handsome Lake was and continues to be controversial among Six Nations people. This is particularly true at Akwesasne. According to Parker, there is no record of Handsome Lake having visited St. Regis, the New York town on the American side of the reserve. He described the Akwesasne Mohawks of his day as a "progressive" people whose "Indianness" was largely gone. While they possessed Indian blood and spoke an Iroquois dialect, their material culture was nearly identical to that of their white neighbors and they retained "no Indian customs."[69] Parker must surely have overstated the case for Akwesasne Mohawk assimilation, as traditionalism continues to play an important role in the social and political life of the community. This became apparent in the mid-1980s, when Haudenosaunee traditionalists protested the development of gas stations, smoke shops, and bingo halls on the reserve. For the operators, these enterprises allowed Mohawks to remain competitive and economically self-sufficient in a modern capitalistic society. For traditionalist adherents of Handsome Lake, they constituted a threat to the community-centered values that form the backbone of Haudenosaunee culture. The bingo halls were the most controversial of these ventures. The inability of Mohawks to reach a consensus on their operations and role in the community eventually resulted in civil unrest and violence.

As many observers have pointed out, tensions over gambling at Akwesasne have been aggravated by colonial edicts made in the nineteenth century. In the aftermath of the War of 1812, England and the United States agreed to divide the reserve between them. As a result, the over 8,000 Mohawks who inhabit this twenty-seven-square-mile territory live under the jurisdiction of at least five different non-Indian governmental agencies. On the New York side of the line, the New York State government and the federal government in Washington, D.C., claim certain rights and responsibilities. Non-Indian jurisdiction on the Canadian side is divided between Ontario Province, Quebec Province, and the Canadian federal government in Ottawa. In addition, Mohawks routinely deal with local municipal governments on both sides of the boundary, raising the total number of non-Indian governmental agencies with which the Mohawks treat to well over a dozen.

Divided in this way, from the outside, internal authority at Akwesasne is contested among five distinct groups. The oldest of these bodies is the Mohawk Nation Council of Chiefs. Led by traditionalists who accept the teachings of Handsome Lake, the Nation Council operates under the "Great Law of Peace," the original political constitution of the Six Nations' confederacy. While the Mohawk Nation Council is the only governing body at Akwesasne that claims to represent Mohawks on both sides of the international border, it is not recognized by state, federal, or provincial authorities. That recognition is vested in two other councils. The oldest of these is the St. Regis Tribal Council in New York. Created in 1802 by the State of New York to serve as a trustee of documents and as a liaison for timber sales and negotiations of land, the council is recognized by U.S. state and federal agencies.[70] The Mohawk Council of Akwesasne, recognized by Ottawa, Ontario Province, and Quebec Province, constitutes the reserve's third government. In addition to these governmental entities, two other nongovernmental groups also enjoy wide influence. These include the quasi official Mohawk Sovereignty Security Force, or "Warriors," and entrepreneurial Mohawks, including gas station operators, smoke shop owners, smugglers, and casino owners and operators.

The emergence of high-stakes gambling at Akwesasne created conditions under which the lack of a central authority, combined with the competing goals of the reserve's different factions, led to violent disagreements and a deadlocked political process. The start of the gambling war can be traced to 1983, when the St. Regis Tribal Council, then led by a progambling faction, licensed the Mohawk Bingo Palace, the reserve's first high-stakes gambling facility. By 1989, six other casino, bingo, and electronic slot machine facilities had been established by independent businessmen. Built on tribal lands, these new facilities operated without formal agreements with either the tribal council or the State of New York. Nonetheless, the emerging bingo chiefs, as some people referred to them, had a great deal of support within the Mohawk community. They provided important new sources of income and channeled a great deal of cash into the reserve's struggling economy.[71]

The success of high-stakes bingo quickly divided the reserve into anti- and progambling factions. The antigambling factions included three main groups, the Mohawk Nation Council, the Mohawk Council of Akwesasne (Canada), and antigambling factions within the St. Regis Tribal Council (New York). Many of these "antis" viewed independent gambling operators as opportunists who were exploiting a corporate tribal sovereignty for individual gain. By rejecting traditional proscriptions against alien forms of gambling, they not only showed little regard for Haudenosaunee tradition, but encouraged the acquisitiveness, materialism, and entrepreneurial self-interest that is characteristic of American social philosophy. The lack of accountability caused further alarm. For Barbara Barnes, director of the North American Indian Travelling College, Akwesasne was becoming a frontier gambling town: "We were in the midst of a glitter-gulch strip, [with] no community controls, no government approval, no tribal regulations, and no profits to the people."[72] In addition to disrupting patterns of life, gambling operators were undermining the traditionalists' attempts to establish a single government on the territory. By disregarding Canadian laws that then banned casinos, progambling Mohawks were aggravating the jurisdictional problems caused by the international boundary. Not all of those who protested the unbridled proliferation of casino gaming desired a total ban on gambling in the territory. Antigambling activists within New York's St. Regis Tribal Council were primarily interested in restoring equity, fairness, and tribal control to the gambling trade, not in ending the games altogether.

The progambling factions at Akwesasne were led by progambling groups within the St. Regis Tribal Council, independent gambling operators, cigarette and alcohol smugglers, and the Mohawk Sovereignty Security Force, or "Warriors." The progambling chiefs in the tribal council supported the negotiation of state compacts and a regulated gambling economy. However, they did little to limit the operation of unlicensed facilities. The operators themselves ignored pressure from an increasingly active antigambling faction to shut down and refused to limit operations until state compacts could be reached. Positioning themselves as entrepreneurs with the true interests of the people at heart, they claimed to have created hundreds of well-paying jobs and a Mohawk economy no longer dependent on state and federal welfare programs or the unpredictable fluctuations of the building industry, the single most important source of wages among Mohawk men.

As progambling Mohawks are quick to point out, traditional ways of making a living at Akwesasne have been undermined by encroachments on Mohawk land and the industrialization of the surrounding area. In 1903, the Aluminum Company of America (ALCOA) built its first smelter less than a mile from the reserve. Completion of the St. Lawrence Seaway in the 1950s and the subsequent availability of inexpensive hydropower attracted more plants to the area. Three aluminum smelting plants and a GM casting factory continue to operate on the borders of Akwesasne.[73] Through the discharge of polychlorinated biphenyl (PCB), a cancer-causing substance that accumulates in the environment, into the St. Lawrence River, and the release of fluorides into the atmosphere, the fisheries were gradually ruined, the cattle poisoned, and the crops contaminated. Before the seaway was completed, the reserve supported approximately 100 commercial fishermen and 120 farmers; by the 1990s, only about ten fishermen and twenty farmers remained.[74] The people themselves suffered from higher rates of cancer and other ailments. Mohawk children were born with cleft palates, deafness, and intestinal abnormalities.[75] Industrialization also changed the work habits of the Mohawk men who were hired as helpers on projects to construct iron bridges and steel-frame buildings in Canada, as well as to build the factories. These laborers quickly became expert ironworkers in their own right, and the legendary Mohawk high steelworker was born.[76] Construction-related jobs eventually filled the employment and resource void created by the environmental problems.

Many progambling Mohawks are former steelworkers who became active in the reserve's flourishing underground economy. Before gambling came to Akwesasne, cigarette smugglers had been exploiting Akwesasne's special legal and political resources for years. Profiting both from their tax-exempt status as Mohawks and high Canadian taxes on tobacco sales, these "butt-leggers" thrived on a commodity no one else could supply—cheap cigarettes for Canadian smokers. Mohawk smugglers also developed a thriving trade in liquor, another commodity highly taxed by the Canadian government. For these Mohawks, the international boundary line was actually a financial resource, as it allowed Mohawks to fill a profitable economic niche, albeit an illegal one. The most prominent of these entrepreneurs was Tony Laughing. Beginning when he was just thirteen years old, Laughing walked the high steel. In the 1970s and 1980s, he made a small fortune running liquor and cigarettes across the border. In the late 1980s, he would open the reserve's first high-stakes, Las Vegas–style casino, Tony's Vegas International (TVI). Having upped the ante, Laughing found himself targeted by antigambling activists and state and federal authorities. Eventually, TVI was raided by the antis and shut down by the police. Laughing was arrested, tried, and sentenced to twenty-seven months in prison on federal gaming charges.[77]

The Warriors represent themselves as descendants of ancestral braves and protectors of Mohawk sovereignty.[78] In the early 1970s, they won two major confrontations with provincial and state police. The first was at Kahnawake, the Mohawk reserve near Montreal. At that time, the Canadian-backed tribal council at Kahnawake was supporting the efforts of non-Mohawks to settle on the territory. The Warriors, protesting this development, eventually forced a standoff with Canadian police. In the end, it was the tribal council that altered its position. With this success, the Warriors emerged as a political force. Their next major initiative involved a tract of land near Moss Lake, in New York, where the state had purchased some 600 acres for a wilderness preserve. In 1974, the Warriors occupied this land and declared it a sovereign Mohawk territory. Although the resulting standoff with state police threatened to erupt into violence, a peaceful settlement was negotiated. After three years of talks, the Warriors reached an agreement with the state that allowed Mohawks to hunt, fish, and grow crops at Ganienkeh, 5,000 acres of state-owned land west of Moss Lake.[79]

Having established themselves as an effective political force at Ganienkeh and Kahnawake, the Warriors began to extend their influence at Akwesasne. In 1989, when antigambling Mohawks invited state police and FBI agents to crack down on the unlicensed operators, the Warriors established roadblocks to prevent the arrest of casino operators and the confiscation of their property. Although they never officially supported unlicensed gambling at Akwesasne, the Warriors opposed intervention of any kind from federal agents and border police. Funded by the underground economy and flourishing butt-legging trade, they had economic interests of their own at stake.

The Warrior's progambling stance reveals a schism between themselves and other traditionalists at Akwesasne, and points to another important division within the Mohawk community. In the late 1970s, state police, with allies in the St. Regis tribal office, blockaded a group of Akwesasne traditionalists on Racquette Point. The traditionalists had provoked elected tribal officials by confiscating chain saws and stopping work on a project to remove timber from the area. Backed by widespread public support, the Longhouse people won this test of wills.[80] Ten years later, however, many of these same traditionalists backed intervention by state and federal officials against gambling operators. Their resolution cemented a developing distinction between themselves and the Warriors. In the early 1980s, Peter Matthiessen's article on the Racquette Point controversy drew no distinction between the Haudenosaunee traditionalists of Akwesasne and the Warriors who had occupied Moss Lake. In Rick Hornung's 1991 account of the Akwesasne gambling controversy, *One Nation Under the Gun,* as well as in Bruce E. Johansen's more detailed study, *Life and Death in Mohawk Country,* Warriors and Handsome Lake–affiliated traditionalists are represented as two distinct and unallied groups.

The controversy came to a head when antigambling activists and their supporters became increasingly forceful in opposing the powerful gambling interests. When demonstrations, roadblocks, and the destruction of gaming equipment failed to get results, the antis invited the state police onto the reserve to arrest the operators and confiscate their equipment. Not only did this action fail to stop gambling, but it also increased tensions between the two groups. The Warriors, now openly sympathetic to the gambling operators, attacked the roadblocks and allegedly set fire to the offices of the antigambling *Akwesasne Notes* and the archives of the North American Indian Travelling College. With the violence escalating, people began to evacuate the reserve. Some 2,000 residents would eventually take refuge in the surrounding towns and cities. Refusing to abandon the roadblocks, the antis sought outside intervention a second time. In January of 1990, the last antigambling chief on the tribal council wrote the president of the United States, requesting his "personal attention and assistance" in resolving the crisis. In his letter to President George H. W. Bush, Chief Harold Tarbell stated that the unresolved conflict would "undermine the sovereign rights of all Indian tribes, jeopardize the integrity of IGRA, and destroy economic benefits to legitimate Indian gambling activities on a national basis."[81]

The crisis reached its low point on the evening of 1 May 1990, when, in an all-night gun battle, two men were killed: Matthew John Wenhisseriio Pyke, a twenty-two-year-old supporter of the antis; and Harold Edwards Jr., a Mohawk who is not believed to have been affiliated with either side of the controversy.[82] As a result of the killings, about 500 state and provincial troops were sent into the area. The New York side was occupied by New York state police under a declaration of martial law; the Canadian side by the Royal Canadian Mounted Police, Ontario Provincial Police, and the Surete du Quebec.[83] Akwesasne was now under foreign occupation. Its governments had failed to unite its people, its rivers and lands were polluted, and its economy was not benefiting from the boom in tribal gaming.

While it was an infringement of Mohawk Nation sovereignty, the occupation by state and federal troops provided the community with an opportunity to regroup and heal. In the aftermath of the civil violence, new agreements were reached between the St. Regis Tribal Council and operators of the Mohawk Bingo Palace.[84] The council also began negotiations for a state gaming compact. An agreement was eventually reached with Governor George Pataki, and, in 1999, the Akwesasne Mohawk Casino opened its doors to the public. A Class Three facility, the medium-sized casino employs approximately 950 people, 60 percent of whom are tribal members.[85] Hoping to take advantage of the governor's desire to license more Indian casinos, the tribe has also been negotiating for a Mohawk casino in the lucrative Catskills market. At the writing of this book, the Mohawk economy, bolstered by its gaming enterprises, is one of the strongest in the depressed Northway. Rather than remaining at the mercy of market forces, Akwesasne has become an economic engine in its own right.

Progress has also been made on the environmental front. Since 1995,

industrial polluters have spent over $500 million on the remediation of polluted sites in the area. Two hundred million has been spent on upgrades to air
pollution filter equipment alone. As part of the cleanup effort, GM and Reynolds Aluminum have removed contaminated sediments from the river. ALCOA
is currently working on a feasibility study for remediation of its own industrial
pollutants. Fishing has made a comeback as surface feeders like perch are now
considered safe for human consumption.[86] Through the combined efforts of the
St. Regis Tribal Council's environmental office and the Haudenosaunee Environmental Task Force, the reserve's natural resources are healthier and more
abundant than they have been in years.

Despite these encouraging developments, a virtual cold war exists between
the Mohawk Nation Council supporters and the St. Regis Tribal Council.
Conflicts within the tribal council itself have led to the emergence of People's
Government and Constitutional Government factions.[87] The Mohawk's gambling operations have also been threatened. A powerful anti-Indian gaming
coalition that includes the Saratoga County Chamber of Commerce, the
Coalition Against Casino Gambling, the evangelical Christian group New
Yorkers for Constitutional Freedoms, and a number of state legislators have
brought a suit challenging the tribal-state gaming compact. In May of 2002,
the Appellate Division of the Supreme Court in Albany ruled in favor of the
coalition and declared the compact to be illegal. Attorneys for the plaintiffs have
since called for a federal injunction to remove the casino's video lottery terminals.[88] Negotiations for a Mohawk casino in the Catskills have also stalled. In
addition to unfavorable court rulings, the chances of reaching a state compact
have been undermined by out-of-state tribes claiming territory and casino
rights in New York. Aggravating its own internal conflicts, sovereignty and self-
determination at Akwesasne are being threatened and compromised by powerful
outside forces.

If Akwesasne's future is anything like its past, the reserve will continue
to be a place where competing attitudes toward traditionalism and modernization will clash. While the traditions upheld by Mohawk Nation Council leaders
provide the basis of its political sovereignty, entrepreneurialism provides better
jobs and wages, increased educational opportunities, and economic self-
determination. However, while traditionalism and modernization are often
in conflict, it does not follow that they can not coexist in ways that serve the

common good. As other tribes have shown, it is possible for casinos and vibrant cultural traditions to support each other. Among the Mashantucket Pequots, for example, casino profits have provided the means to revive long-dormant cultural traditions. Yet the relationship between gaming and traditional culture will not be an easy one. As Fenelon argues, while traditional people who live and act in the modern world may utilize the potent forces of casino profits to maintain and resurrect their cultural values, the modernization processes represented by those same casinos will be a continual source of threat to their values.[89] These tensions are not likely to be resolved soon. Given the competing demands that vex Indian peoples everywhere, important questions remain: Will the appropriation of the American gambling industry by tribal peoples be accomplished in a manner that advances self-determination without destroying the aboriginal character of indigenous communities? Or, will the high-stakes gambling trade contribute to the erasure of tribal identities and the complete assimilation of the people they distinguish?

Contesting the Evil Gambler   6.

Gambling,   Choice,   and

Survival   in   Native   American   Indian   Literature

The dramatic proliferation of the tribal gambling industry has coincided with the flowering of Native American literary art. As the fortunes of many tribal communities have been bound up with the economic, legal, and social implications of gambling, Native American writers have exploited the dramatic and symbolic potential of traditional gambling stories. While this is largely a contemporary phenomenon, it can be traced to Indian novelists writing almost a century and a half ago. John Rollin Ridge offered the first example of an Indian novel informed by traditional attitudes toward gambling in his 1854 work *The Life and Adventures of Joaquin Murieta*. In the early twentieth century, Chrystal Quintasket, a Salishan writer working under the pen name Mourning Dove, made a yet more complex use of tribal gambling practices in her allotment era novel, *Cogewea, the Half-Blood,* first published in 1927. In the contemporary period, some of the best examples of the influence of traditional gambling stories are found in works published since the late 1970s, when high-stakes gambling operations first began to appear on tribal lands. Among the most popular of these writers are Gerald Vizenor, Leslie Marmon Silko, and Louise Erdrich. Vizenor, the most prolific Indian writer on gambling, weaves his own Chippewa/Anishinabe traditions into such works as *Bearheart: The Heirship Chronicles* (1978), *Heirs of Columbus* (1991), and *Dead Voices* (1992). In works by Silko, gambling stories from Keres-speaking cultures figure prominently. The most famous of these is *Ceremony,* her 1977 novel about an American Indian veteran of World War II. Also of Chippewa descent, Louise Erdrich, in *Love Medicine* (1984, expanded and republished in

1993), *Tracks* (1988), and *The Bingo Palace* (1994), has dramatized how tribal gambling traditions can be reenacted through European-American games like poker and bingo.

For each of these writers, traditional gambling practices and stories serve as key symbols, ideological touchstones, and plot-shaping devices. By suggesting strategies of resistance and survival to colonial domination and genocide, the stories and the metaphors they generate provide what Vizenor has termed an "agonistic" space where Indian writers contest assimilation. Gambling stories are among the most useful narratives for this purpose because they describe conflicts that are settled through dialogue, negotiation, and skill. As in the Haudenosaunee Peach Stone myth, gaming stories pit good gamblers against destructive opponents. Good gamblers gamble for the sake of the people and the land they inhabit. Destructive gamblers are associated with traditional tribal enemies, European-American culture, and traditional social vices. Having multiple significations, a destructive gambler might appear as a figure from tribal lore, a white man, or another Indian. In addition to providing moral distinctions and guidance, gambling stories establish the importance of ritual play in ensuring the long-term survival of individuals and groups. For Indian writers, the survival of stories is necessary for the survival of the people.

The social, dramatic, and symbolic dimensions of Native American gambling metaphors were first sketched out by John Rollin Ridge, a Cherokee who published under the pen name Yellow Bird. The story of an honest man turned outlaw by the system, his *Life and Adventures of Joaquin Murieta, the Celebrated California Bandit* captures the frustrations of non-Anglo Californians newly subjected to colonial domination. Ridge based his novel on the journalistic accounts of an historical Joaquin Murieta. A scourge to white miners and settlers, he was a Robin Hood to Mexicans and Indians who found themselves increasingly oppressed by inrushing Anglos.[1] Ridge understood the sources of Murieta's actions and sympathized with his crusade. Born in Oklahoma Indian Territory in 1827, he experienced firsthand the violence that resulted from hostile colonial takeovers. The son of John Ridge and grandson of Major Ridge, the two principal leaders of the proremoval party, he witnessed the murder of his father by other Cherokees who harbored resentment against the removal party.[2] As a young man, Ridge was himself accused of murder. Moving to California to avoid trial, he found a job writing for the newspapers.[3]

In the novel, Murieta is characterized as having a mild, peaceable, and generous disposition. Inclined to admire the Anglos, he joins the California gold rush and pursues the American dream. The young man soon discovers that the newcomers view him as an inferior. Rather than noble pioneers, the settlers behave like "lawless and desperate men" who look upon "any and all Mexicans . . . as no better than conquered subjects of the United States."[4] "Having no rights which could stand before a haughtier and superior race," Murieta is literally thrown out of his own house by Americans, who "peremptorily bade him leave his claim, as they would allow no Mexicans to work in that region" (10). Regrouping from this setback, Murieta establishes a farm, from which he is again driven by Americans who offer "no other excuse than that he was 'an infernal Mexican intruder!'" (10).

Denied access to the opportunities coveted by his Anglo peers, and forced to survive on the margins of the economic system, Murieta becomes a professional gambler and earns his livelihood dealing monte. While professional gamblers in the mid-nineteenth century were often viewed as social pariahs, the narrator insists that monte dealing "is considered by the Mexican in no manner a disreputable employment, and many well-raised young men from the Atlantic States have resorted to it as a profession in this land of luck and chances" (11). Reflecting the characteristics of the gentleman gambler of Western lore, Murieta is known for playing the game on "very fair and honest principles" (11). According to the narrator, he won others' money with such "skill and grace, or lost his own with such perfect good humor that he was considered by all the very beau ideal of a gambler and the prince of clever fellows" (12). Stripped of its pejorative associations, gambling in Ridge is a reflection of the Western landscape in which it is practiced; in a hostile world of "luck and chance," life itself is a gamble.

Murieta gives up monte dealing after he is falsely accused of horse stealing and whipped by an Anglo mob. Drawing back into the California landscape, he becomes an agent of vengeance and retribution. Equally adept at maneuvering in the vast landscapes of the West and the "restricted space" of the saloon, he boldly turns the tables on his colonial adversaries.[5] At the height of his powers, Murieta masters the poker table, an agonistic space that John Lowe describes as a "double altar with the gods of money above and guns below."[6] Murieta's good fortune is attributed to his "magical luck" (51). As his reputation grows, his "extraordinary successes" lend credence to "the old Cherokee superstition that there were some men who bear charmed lives and whom nothing can kill but a silver bullet" (139). As Lowe notes, these qualities identify Murieta as a manifestation of the tribal trickster who is also a gambling hero.

Despite his supernatural qualities, Murieta is subject to mortal wounds. After a reward is posted for his capture, he becomes the subject of an intense manhunt. Eventually, he is tracked down and killed by the agents of the law. Despite its tragic overtones, the novel rejects the inevitability of Murieta's demise. Rather than the irresistible work of fate, his death is attributed to an "extreme carelessness" born of confidence in his own ability (153). While overconfidence provides Ridge's hero with a tragic flaw, *The Life and Adventures of Joaquin Murieta* expresses a profound if cautionary optimism characteristic of tribal gambling stories. While Murieta does not survive, the story holds out the possibility of success for those who actively resist colonial domination.

If Ridge introduced the tribal gambling metaphor to American Indian literature, Mourning Dove showed how it could provide more than an ideological touchstone. Written in collaboration with Lucullus Virgil McWhorter, *Cogewea* is organized around a series of gambling rituals. Among them are poker, monte, and traditional tribal games. At a box social, the men bid on picnic baskets anonymously prepared by the women. For the single members of the community in search of husbands and wives, this ritual of courtship is a type of high-stakes guessing game. The novel also offers a cross-cultural analysis of gambling decorum. In a horse racing scene, Mourning Dove considers the differences between Native and white gamblers. While whites crowd to the judges' table "disputing, in language more emphatic than elegant," tribal gamblers have learned to accept "winnings and losses alike with stoic indifference."[7] The perceived lack of good sportsmanship among the white track bettors foreshadows the tactics of Alfred Densmore, a white man who plays the role of the evil gambler.

The novel is set during the allotment period of American Indian history, a time when speculations on Indian lands and federal Indian policies combined to divest Native peoples of some 90 million acres, 60 percent of the lands they held prior to the passing of the General Allotment Act in 1887.[8] The title character is described as a twenty-one-year-old mixed-blood woman and recent graduate from Pennsylvania's Carlisle Indian Industrial Arts School. At the outset of the novel, she is working on her sister's ranch, her brother-in-law being a white rancher who married into the community during allotment. Her Indian mother has long since passed away; her white father has abandoned her and her two sisters for the Alaskan gold rush. Throughout the story, Cogewea faces choices involving lifestyle, work, and marriage. She describes these in terms of gambling and fishing metaphors. "Life is a gamble," she reflects, "a chance, a mere guess. Cast a line and reel in a splendid rainbow trout or a slippery eel" (21). The phrase "Life is a gamble" is repeated later in the novel when Cogewea is on the verge of making her own near-fatal guess. As in the stick games that Mourning Dove described in her autobiography, Cogewea must choose a hand, which in this case is a metaphorical hand in marriage. One hand is represented by Alfred Densmore, a charming and sophisticated Easterner who represents an opportunity for the young woman to travel to Paris and make the most of her boarding school education; the other is represented by James LaGrinder, a fellow mixed-blood. As well as being the most skilled cowboy on the ranch, Jim is a man of courage, modesty, and honor. His affection for Cogewea and proven ability to care for her make him an ideal match. Despite these good qualities, Cogewea does not view him in a romantic light. Rebuffed, he takes solace in the idea that he might "yet have a chance" (30).

While he plays the part of loving suitor, Densmore has only a sporting interest in the young woman. Having come west in search of the opportunities and adventures no longer available to him in the increasingly ossified business and social climates of the East, he views Cogewea as potential sources of income. To achieve his economic goals, he plans to marry her in what he considers to be an illegitimate Indian marriage rite. By doing so, he hopes to stake a claim to her allotment. Like the archetypal confidence man of Western lore, Densmore will use any stratagem to trap his game. As well as being a sign of the degenerate white speculator, he signifies the evil gambler of tribal stories. "Consumed by insatiable desires," writes Martha L. Viehmann, he is a coyote-like figure.[9] Densmore's greedy, self-interested, and mendacious nature earns for him the nickname Shoyahpee, an Indian word that is translated to mean "one who eats up everything he sights" (289).

Having come west to see the "painted and blanketed aborigines of history and romance," Densmore first meets Cogewea on a chance visit to the H-B Ranch, where he plans to "rough it awhile among the Indians and cowboys" (44). The mixed-blood cowhands, doubtful that Densmore possesses the skills of which he boasts, trick him into riding Croppy, a wild horse that only Jim, the most talented cowboy on the ranch, has been able to ride. Croppy throws Densmore, who breaks his arm on the fall. Accepting no responsibility for his misfortune, Densmore secretly plots revenge. The young woman unwittingly aids his scheme when she nurses the Easterner through his rehabilitation.

Densmore's seduction, disguised as courting, proceeds like a high-stakes game of chance. As foreshadowed by the fishing metaphor in Cogewea's opening speech, the couple is found fishing on the banks of a river and betting on who will land the first trout. Densmore hooks one first, but it breaks the line before it can be reeled in. Cogewea lands her own fish and thus wins the first round. In jest, Densmore ups the ante by betting $5,000 against her hand in marriage on the next fish. Cogewea wins again. Densmore asks, "Would you have been as prompt in delivering, had I won?" (158). Her response reminds Densmore of the moral implications of play: "An *honest* gambler is supposed to meet all obligations unequivocally" (158). What Cogewea fails to realize is that Densmore is operating under no similar set of beliefs. Like the evil gamblers of the tribal stories, or the white speculator-confidence man, he is only concerned with winning. At his suggestion, the ante is once again upped. Ten thousand dollars or Cogewea's hand is bet on the next trout. Again she wins, but only by a fraction. Densmore is willing to bet higher, as he has no intentions of ever paying his debt. The game ends when she declares that betting is off.

While Densmore loses the fishing bets, he inches closer to his prey. As Cogewea's friends and family well know, the young woman is increasingly drawn to the white man. The Stemteema, Cogewea's tribal grandmother and guardian, warns her against pursuing the relationship. While Cogewea respects her grandmother's wishes, she eventually agrees to elope with Densmore. On the couple's ill-fated ride into the night, he discovers that her allotment is much smaller than rumored. Angry and frustrated in his desires for economic gain, he beats Cogewea and leaves her to perish in the woods. At the prompting of the Stemteema, the young woman is rescued by Jim and nursed back to health. While Cogewea is severely demoralized by the realization that Densmore was playing her for a fool, her story ends on a comic note. At the end of the novel, she receives a notice that her long-lost white father struck it rich before he died. With this twist of fate, a sizable fortune is left to his Indian daughters. The last laugh is on Densmore, who can only read about Cogewea's good fortune in the papers (284). With this hopeful and ironic finish, the novel demonstrates how the community can provide a hedge against the schemes of the white trickster.

From a social and political standpoint, *Cogewea* can be read as a critique of federal allotment policies. By dramatizing the threat posed to Indian women by predacious white speculators masquerading as loving suitors, the novel highlights the effects of white laws that allowed for the cession of Indian land to white husbands of Indian brides. Because allotment defined Indians as the patentees of private lands, lands owned by an Indian woman became, upon marriage, the property of her white husband. This transfer of ownership was not always possible before allotment, when lands were held by treaty with the federal government. The new laws thus provided a motivation for white men to secure Indian brides. This placed Indian women at increased risk. Rather than introducing them to the benefits of civilization, allotment made Indian women targets of white male speculators.

Mourning Dove's use of tribal gambling practices suggests the methods of later Native American writers like Silko, Vizenor, and Erdrich. Writing from a Pueblo Indian perspective, Silko culls her gambling metaphors from ancient Pueblo and Navajo cultures. As Kathryn Gabriel reports in *Gambler Way,* Indian gaming politics in the Southwest existed hundreds of years before the arrival of Europeans. As evidence, she cites excavation reports from the late nineteenth century that turned up hundreds of wooden and bone gambling sticks and dice chips at Pueblo Bonito.[10] At about the same time, folklorists recorded a Navajo origin story that describes a gambling temple being built in Chaco Canyon for a gambler god known as Noqo'ilpi, a figure preserved in numerous folklore journals and excavation reports.[11] According to stories recorded from Navajo and Pueblo speakers, the region was once lorded over by a gambler of great power and wealth. Some archaeologists believe that Pueblo Alto, known to local Navajos as *niyiilbiihi bighan,* or "home of the one that wins (you) by gambling," was a center of gambling in the ancient Southwest.[12]

The gambling referents in Silko's writing can be traced to traditional Keres stories. According to Keres tradition, games of chance were invented by Iyatiku, the Corn Woman or Earth Mother, during a time of drought. As reported by Paula Gunn Allen, Iyatiku hoped to distract the people from their troubles, but the new pastime became an obsession among the men of the community, who devoted all of their time to gambling. Angered by the neglect of their communal obligations, Corn Woman returned to the underworld; the town was soon destroyed by a flood and the people were forced to evacuate their homes. Out of compassion and pity for her people, Corn Woman left behind her power, the Irriaku, or corn fetish, which, she explained, was her heart. She told them to share the fruits of her body and to remain at peace in their hearts, as the rains come only to peaceful people.[13] In this story, gambling is presented as a legitimate social entertainment that threatens the survival of the community when it is abused.

Another Keres story collected by Elsie Clews Parson in the 1910s describes the career of an evil gambler known as C'ky'o Kaup'a'ta who rises to great power through a combination of gambling skill and witchery.[14] An expert gambler, C'ky'o Kaup'a'ta increases his advantage by tricking his mortal opponents into eating cornmeal seasoned with the blood of their own slain relatives. Under his spell, they gamble away both their possessions and their lives. Not content to destroy the people through gambling, C'ky'o Kaup'a'ta steals the rain clouds. The ensuing drought causes all the earth to suffer. It is at this point in the story that Sun Man, the hero of the people, comes forth to contest the gambler and win back the clouds.

Sun Man does not work alone to save the world. Before journeying to the gambler's lair, he is instructed by Grandmother Spider. Also known as Thought Woman, Grandmother Spider symbolizes the life-creating force, which is also the generative source of tribal stories.[15] The Gambler, she tells Sun Man, will first challenge him at dice. Sun Man will lose this contest. Thinking he has the advantage, the Gambler will then challenge him to guess the contents of two bags hanging from the walls of his lodge. If Sun Man guesses correctly, he wins the clouds; a wrong guess will forfeit his life. Grandmother Spider knows that the bags contain the constellations Orion and the Pleiades. Armed with this knowledge, the good gambler has an advantage over his evil opponent, but he is still at risk. His chance, or gamble, is not knowing the future as it has been fore-told to him: "Indeed?" he remarks to the grandmother's plan; she responds with a challenge, "Go ahead, be a man."[16] In the journey that follows, Sun Man reen-acts the story exactly as it had been told to him. Spider Woman's instructions, combined with his own compassion, courage, and skill, allow him to defeat the Gambler and releases the rain clouds. The Gambler loses his eyes, but survives to play again.

As Gabriel argues, the evil gambler of tribal lore is continually transformed to embody the current dominating party.[17] Among Navajo and Pueblo peoples, gambler archetypes are often related to white incursions into the region by Spanish and Anglo colonists. The stories thus "grapple with the ebb and flow of power and fortune and to warn against hostile religious takeover."[18] We see this process at work in *Ceremony*. In the novel, C'ky'o Kaup'a'ta is associated with a variety of forces, including mainstream American culture, that threaten the survival of the people. Sun Man's counterpart is Tayo, a Native man living in the relocation era of American Indian history. In the course of the novel, the story gradually becomes a part of Tayo's mental framework as he negotiates a dangerous world of choices. These choices involve the possible engagement with two basic forces, described by Gunn Allen as "the feminine life force of the universe and the mechanistic death force of the witchery."[19] For Tayo to succeed, he must recall the stories that advance the creative life force and reenact them in terms of his own life. As the storyteller explains in the beginning of the novel, "stories,/ ... aren't just entertainment./Don't be fooled./They are all we have, you see,/all we have to fight off/illness and death."[20]

At the beginning of the novel, Tayo is suffering from post-traumatic stress disorder. A World War II veteran and survivor of a Japanese prisoner-of-war camp, he is unable to cope with the death of his cousin Rocky, who died in the Philippines, and the death of his uncle Josiah, who died while the young men were away fighting the war. Tayo feels responsible for both deaths, as well as for the long drought that has persisted at home. Placing the situation of these modern characters in a traditional setting, Silko weaves into the novel a Keres story about another C'ky'o medicine man, known as Pa'caya'nyi, and two brothers, Ma'see'wi and Ou'yu'ye'wi, figures whom Allen identifies as the war twins of the Keres tradition. In this story, Pa'caya'nyi convinces the brothers to practice a new and dazzling kind of magic. Obsessed with performing these tricks, they neglect their traditional responsibilities to the Corn Mother. As a reprimand to them, she collects the life-giving things, the plants and rain clouds, and retires to the world below. Drought and suffering are again visited upon the land (46–49). Unwittingly, Tayo and Rocky reenact this story, playing the part of the foolish brothers, while the role of the C'ky'o medicine man is played by the army recruiter, a would-be agent of assimilation. Tayo and Rocky enjoy their new way of life in the army and take full advantage of the status the uniform confers upon them. While Rocky loses his life for the uniform, Tayo has the chance to complete a redemptive journey that reenacts Sun Man's sacred gamble for the return of the rain clouds.

Tayo's first identification with the Sun Man–Gambler story occurs in the summer before the war, when he visits a spring to make a prayer offering. While there, he watches the spiders, frogs, dragonflies, and hummingbirds drink from a pool. The spider reminds him of Sun Man's sacred gamble, and how Spider Woman had told Sun Man how to win the storm clouds back from the Ka't'sina's mountain prison. As Tayo watches the animals, he sees a world made of stories, "a world alive, always changing and moving" (95). Soon after, he hears the rumble of thunder from Tse-pi'na (renamed Mount Taylor by the Anglos), the place where the Gambler imprisoned the clouds: "The wind came up from the west, smelling cool like wet clay. Then he could see the rain. It was spinning out of the thunderclouds like gray spider webs and tangling against the foothills of the mountain" (96). In this passage, Tayo's prayer offering coincides with the end of the dry spell. Later that same day, as the rain continues to fall, he makes love to Night Swan, a woman associated with the healing powers of the mountain rain.[21] From these experiences, Tayo becomes aware of his own vital role in aiding the earth's regenerative cycles.

Tayo's development into a traditional person is interrupted by the war and the sickness it causes. When the white doctors fail to help him, his grandmother guides him to Ku'osh and Betonie, two traditional healers. Under their guidance, Tayo embarks on a redemptive mission to retrieve his uncle's stolen cattle. Before the war, Tayo and Josiah tended the herd together. With Tayo absent, and the older man unable to care for them himself, the cattle are stolen by Floyd Lee, a white rancher who keeps them fenced in on the high pastures of Tse-pi'na, the traditional mountain home of C'ky'o Kaup'a'ta. In a ritual reenactment of the Sun Man-Gambler story, Tayo performs the role of Sun Man. The following passage, often quoted, epitomizes that transformation of time, space, and vision that occurs as Tayo completes the ceremony:

> *The ride into the mountains had branched into all directions of time. He knew then why the old timers could only speak of yesterday and tomorrow in terms of the present moment: the only certainty; and this present sense of being was qualified with bare hints of yesterday or tomorrow, by saying, "I go up to the mountain yesterday or I go up to the mountain tomorrow." The C'ky'o Kaup'a'ta somewhere is stacking his gambling sticks and waiting for a visitor; Rocky and I are walking across the ridge in the moonlight; Josiah and Robert are waiting for us. This night is a single night; and there has never been any other (192).*

As sacred time merges with ritual action, the journey becomes increasingly dangerous for Tayo. With the white police force closing in, he knows he will have only "one chance" to win the release of the cattle (190). In this context, the white rancher and his security patrol are identified with the forces of the evil gambler. With snow beginning to fall, Tayo drives the cattle through the fence. As the metaphorical counterpart to the rain clouds, the herd, once returned to the pueblo, signals an end to the drought.

Collectively, the stories of the pueblo embody a cultural and spiritual identity that provides meaning and context to Tayo's ongoing struggle against the witchery, a force that Silko has described as a "metaphor for the destroyers or the counter force, that force which counters vitality and birth."[22] Tayo's continued survival will depend on his ability to avoid being subsumed into white stories that traditionally assign Indian peoples to isolation, despair, and death (231–32). As Ts'eh, another Native healer, informs him, whites "have their stories about us—Indian people who are only marking time and waiting for the end. And they would end this story right here, with you fighting to your death alone in these hills" (231–32). Reminding Tayo that violence will only further evil's plans, she provides a moral for the story. For Tayo to contribute to the continuance of the earth and its people, he must learn to control his rage and direct his energies in a positive manner. By modeling nonviolent means of resistance and survival, gambling ceremonies and storytelling traditions reinforce this lesson.

In *Bearheart*, Gerald Vizenor reworks a Chippewa/Anishinabe story describing a gambling contest between the trickster-creator Manabozho and an evil gambler known as the Nita Ataged. As in the Keres story, the hero is called upon to save the people from the cannibal. Before journeying into the Nita Ataged's lair, Manabozho consults with his grandmother, who warns him against undertaking such a dangerous task. In this case, the trickster does not take his elder's advice: "the folk hero of the *anishinabe* felt that he was brave and should know no fear. The warning words of *nokomiss*, his grandmother, were unheeded."[23] Upon reaching the Gambler's lodge, Manabozho is challenged to play a version of the woodland bowl game. In the bowl are four figures representing the four ages of man. The players will take turns tossing the pieces in the bowl. The winning player will be the one who makes the pieces stand on four successive tosses. The Nita Ataged wastes no time in demanding that Manabozho stake his life on the outcome of the contest: "there is but one forfeit I demand of those who gamble with me and lose, and that forfeit is life. I keep the scalps and ears and hands, the rest of the body I give to my friend the *wiindigo* and their spirits I consign to *Niba Gisiss.*"[24] This speech, intended to frighten Manabozho, elicits laughter instead. As Nora Barry explains, the evil gambler would destroy the comic, yet sacred, survival strategies that Vizenor's texts celebrate. A potentially tragic trope, the Nita Ataged is defeated by the comic trickster, who balances the world with humor.[25] Defeat for the Nita Ataged, however, will not signal the end of the game. In one form or another, the Gambler's spirit will survive to play again.

Vizenor creates a futuristic version of the evil gambler in the figure of Sir Cecil Staples, the Monarch of Unleaded Gasoline. Sir Cecil is a type of the white confidence man-speculator who sets traps for people by disguising them as opportunities. A manifestation of the Nita Ataged, he is a trickster who tricks to enslave and destroy. In postapocalyptic America, the Gambler's talent for murder and destruction thrive. As Sir Cecil explains, "the plastic film known as social control hanging over the savage urge to kill was dissolved when the government failed and the economic world collapsed. . . . When the value of material possessions were useless . . . there were no common values to bind people together and hold down their needs for violence and the experience of death."[26] In this passage, Vizenor critiques what Barry describes as the "social and spiritual cannibalism of the dominant culture."[27] By emphasizing pathologies evident in European-American society, he turns the tables on those who describe tribal gambling as a sign of Native degeneracy.

Sir Cecil is contested by a group of crossblood pilgrims led by Proude Cedarfair, the counterpart to Manabozho, the compassionate trickster of the stories. The pilgrims first encounter the Gambler at What Cheer Trailer Ruins, where he is said to have a hidden stockpile of gasoline. The pilgrims hope to acquire enough fuel to continue their journey. Having no way to take the gasoline by force (and, as we later learn, unaware that no gasoline actually exists) they agree to gamble their lives against a chance to win five gallons of gas. First, they must decide on who will gamble for the group. Little Big Mouse argues that goodness must contest evil: "The most good person should be the gambler" (110). In retrospect, her suggestion is a good one, but it is not seconded. Another member of the group, Belladonna Darwin-Winter Catcher, argues that the good gambler should be chosen by chance. This initiates a debate on the meaning of chance. "Nothing is chance," Proude argues, "there is no chance in chance. . . . Chances are terminal creeds" (110–11). . . . Fools praise chance to avoid the fear of death. . . . We must fear the living to leave so much death to chance. . . . We are fools with terminal creeds when we gamble with chance" (112). Elaborating on Proude's statement, Louis Owens writes that "a mere capitulation to chance would deny the emphasis upon our ultimate responsibility for ordering and sustaining the world we inhabit that is central to Native American ecosystemic cultures."[28] By contrast, Belladonna's understanding of chance seems to rely on a blind faith that goodness will overcome evil. Thus, in lieu of a volunteer, and in an attempt to choose the good gambler fairly, the pilgrims devise a system for drawing lots. In this way, Lilith Mae Farrier is selected to be the group's good gambler.

Proude's objection to Belladonna's proposal introduces to the novel two interrelated concepts: terminal creeds and cultural narcissism. As they are defined in the novel, terminal creeds are "terminal diseases" that silence questions and force agreement. Changeless and unadaptive, they are tragic tropes, embedded in formulaic phrases, that lead their bearers to isolation and death. Similarly, cultural narcissism is a form of mental isolation that "rules the possessor" (191). Belladonna reveals her own terminal creeds and cultural narcissism when she recites a litany of positive "Indian" traits. While these characteristics may indeed identify some tribal peoples, they are stereotypes nonetheless. As her auditors point out, her rules have too many exceptions: "You speak from terminal creeds," they conclude, "[and are] not a person of real experience and critical substance" (196). They reward her speech by feeding her poisoned cookies. In her gamble against Sir Cecil, Lilith Mae likewise falls victim to terminal creeds. Terrified of facing the evil gambler, she sets her mind to "luck and chance" (116). When she does win a round of the game she takes "personal pleasure in winning;" the egocentric response causes her to lose her place in the "energies of sacred time" (118). Sir Cecil immediately recognizes the weakness of his first opponent. "Chance and luck are the game of fools," he declares after winning her life.

A more potent dialogue on terminal creeds occurs during Proude's gamble against Sir Cecil. In this contest, Proude takes the initiative when he announces to Sir Cecil that he has come to speak with him about "evil and death" (129). As Sir Cecil points out, Proude's is not a simple game of death: "You would change minds and histories and reverse the unusual control of evil power" (130). Sir Cecil is confident, however, that he will not be beaten by Proude and that the game will at least end in a draw. In this case, "evil will still be the winner because nothing changes when good and evil are tied in a strange balance" (131). "We are equals at this game of good and evil mister proude. Nothing is lost between equals" (132). Proude rejects the evil gambler's reasoning: "But we are not equals. We are not bound in common experiences. We do not share a common vision. Your values and language come from evil. Your power is averse to living. Your culture is death" (132). In this dialogue, Proude deconstructs the binary thinking that informs the evil gambler's philosophy. The game follows the pattern of their speech. When Sir Cecil tosses the figures in the bowl, they fall into its cracked center. When Proude throws, the figures stand back-to-back, facing out toward the edge of the bowl, which itself is a symbol of the earth. The placement of the figures demonstrates his own outward-looking philosophy. Like Tayo in *Ceremony,* he does not gamble for sheer amusement, power, or gain, but for the sake of creation and the people.

In later works, *Heirs of Columbus,* a 1991 novel, and "The Moccasin Game," a companion story published in 1993, Vizenor applied tribal gambling metaphors to the tribal gambling controversy. By foregrounding the effects on the tribes of reservation gambling, these texts join an exploration of tribal art and politics to a meditation on the roles of ritual games and for-profit gambling in contemporary tribal culture. As discussed in chapter 4, the heirs referenced in the novel's title represent a modern crossblood community that combines indigenous traditions and modern technologies. The tribal descendants of Christopher Columbus, they own and operate Santa Maria Casino, a floating casino caravel and replica of the explorer's flagship. Through the success of the gambling operation, the entrepreneurial heirs fund genetic research to heal the world's children and isolate the gene for tribal survivance. Large public works projects include a giant statue of the Trickster of Liberty and a laser hologram show.

Along with running a modern casino, the heirs play a traditional tribal moccasin game. Described as the game that "saved the heirs from the water demons,"[29] it is accompanied by the story of the tribe's contest against Wiindigoo, a cannibal spirit associated with winter starving.[30] With his blond hair and perfect smile, Wiindigoo is deceptively attractive. His sly methods, combined with his European appearance, associate him with the white confidence man and speculator. At the same time, Wiindigoo is an ancient and familiar enemy of the people. In *Ojibway Heritage,* Basil Johnston describes Wiindigoo as an ordinary man driven mad by hunger. With the help of a magic hunting potion, he eventually finds plentiful game, but having lost his reason, he eats it all and leaves nothing for his starving family and village.[31] Wiindigoo is eventually killed, but his spirit lives on as an incorporeal being, the "spirit of excess" that captivates and enslaves anyone too preoccupied with sleep, work, play, drink, or other pursuit.[32] According to Johnston, children and the young were often warned, "Don't play too much, Wiindigoo will get you." Though Wiindigoo was fearsome and visited punishment upon those committing excesses, he nevertheless conferred rewards upon the moderate. He was excess that encouraged moderation.[33]

In *Heirs of Columbus,* the people's sacred gamble against Wiindigoo is recalled through a ceremonial moccasion game. Much like the tribal stick game, the players take turns guessing which moccasin hides the ceremonial object, in this case, a coin that bears the image of Columbus. As the game progresses, the players narrate a story that describes how the children were staked on the outcome of a contest with the evil gambler. According to the traditional story, the people were a poor match for the powerful spirit. Despite their efforts to confuse the cannibal, Wiindigoo soon reached for the winning moccasin. However, before he could turn it, he was frozen solid by Mikwan, a winter spirit that came to the tribe's aid. The frozen Wiindigoo and the accoutrements of the game are hidden in her cave. By this "breath of winter in the summer" (21) the tribe is saved. The game, however, is not over; nor has Wiindigoo been defeated. Later in the novel, he will return to finish the game.

In the short story "The Moccasin Game," Vizenor elaborates on the story as it is presented in *Heirs of Columbus.* Evoking the pre-Columbian context and origins of tribal moccasin games, this story has no white characters or references to Europe or European-Americans. It begins near a fire circle on the shores of a moonlit lake, where "Native American Silent People" sign the moccasin game story; their hand movements are translated by Nawina, a tribal woman, whose narration is the printed text.[34] Intending to draw attention to the play of signification that constitutes a text in the oral tradition, Vizenor reminds the reader that the story, as read, is several places removed from the lived experience of hearing a moccasin game story told in real time.

The first round of the game is initiated by Wiindigoo, who steals a copper ring engraved with "seventeen tribal figures carved on the wide rim" (45). This circle, described as the "sacred tribal history" (45), is staked against a newly fashioned canoe. The tribal player guesses wrong and the canoe is lost. Wiindigoo offers the tribe another chance to win the ring, but only if they stake the children; if they wish to reclaim the past, as represented by the ring, they must risk their future, as represented by the children. Unwilling to relinquish history to the cannibal, the tribe agrees to his terms, knowing full well that it can ill afford to lose the children. It is only by Mikwan's intervention that the children are temporarily safe.

In the midst of the game, the tribal players participate in a Mediwewin, or Medicine Lodge Ceremony. With this episode, Vizenor joins gambling, medicine, and storytelling as parts of one curative ritual. Johnston describes the Mediwewin as a ceremonial that commemorates the knowledge of medicine and the healing of disease.[35] Moccasin games and tribal tricksters are associated with the ceremony. As Nora Barry reports, Manabozho, the good gambler of the stories, was sent with the gift of medicine to the Anishinabe by the Creator, Kitche Manitou.[36] In Vizenor's story, the candidates are teased by Wiindigoo as they make their way into the Midewigaan, or Grand Medicine Lodge. Taunting them with "human temptations, mongrel names, and the treacherous powers of nature" (49), he attempts to turn them from the path of goodness. The word *Mediwewin* is probably a contraction of *mino,* meaning "good," and *daewaewin,* meaning "hearted."[37] As the etymology of the word suggests, knowledge of medicine is not enough to ensure good health and well-being; one must also lead a moral life. Through the moccasin game, the people demonstrate their goodheartedness by balancing the destructive capability of Wiindigoo.

At the conclusion of *Heirs of Columbus,* the suspended moccasin game is resumed when federal agents release the frozen cannibal. As Wiindigoo again reaches for the winning moccasin, Stone Columbus, the tribal player, warns him that the marked coin has been placed with a dangerous war herb (181), which is described as the "soldier weed" of "brute force and termination" revealed to Black Elk in his vision (178). At first Wiindigoo suspects that Stone is bluffing, but hesitates long enough to be convinced that victory would result in his own demise. According to Stone,

> *"The war herb would terminate the world, a bioactivated evanescence, only you and the robots would survive, and you would be mocked by the robots forever."*
>
> *"Who would you be without the heirs and the children to menace?*
> . . . *"*
>
> *"Your choice would be your last moccasin game, nothing would remain if you reveal the war herb, nothing more human than the robots, and our memories in the stone, but even a demon needs humans."*
>
> *"The soldier weed would end your game forever"* (181–82).

Swayed by Stone's words, Wiindigoo raises his hand and "moves back into the shadows," but cautions the tribe that "the game will never end" (182). In this context, the suspension of the game suggests that the long-term survival of the community depends upon the survival of its games and stories. By emphasizing the moccasin game as a sign of "survivance," Vizenor dramatizes the importance of ritual play to well-being. Like the word *performance*, the coined term uses the noun modifier "-ance" to emphasize the actions, processes, and functions by which the tribes continue.

In a more recent work, *Dead Voices: Natural Agonies in the New World* (1992), Vizenor offers more dialogues on the relationship between survival and gambling. In this text, gambling rituals and storytelling traditions find themselves at home on the urban streets of Oakland, California. The central character is Bagese, a tribal woman and storyteller. Her stories are introduced by Laundry, a university lecturer on tribal philosophies. While Laundry is positioned as an expert on tribal affairs and culture, Bagese describes him as a "wordy" bound to printed books and the "dead voices" of classroom recitations.[38] She nicknames him Laundry because he has the generic smell of television soap: "The sweet smell of laundry," she informs him, "is a dead voice" (16). With this comparison, Bagese distinguishes the language of a literate culture bound by printed words from the language of a culture that records and transmits its collective experience aurally.

For Bagese, storytelling is related to a game of wanaki chance. Invented by a manidoo spirit in a time when the world was young, wanaki connects Bagese and Laundry to the sources of tribal experience, language, and power. Laundry describes it as Bagese's game of "natural meditation" that "liberate shadows and the mind":

> Chance is an invitation to animal voices in a tribal world, and the word wanaki means to live somewhere in peace, a chance at peace.
>
> She turned seven cards in the game, one each for the bear, beaver, squirrel, crow, flea, praying mantis, and the last was the trickster figure, a wild card that transformed the player into an otter, a rabbit, a crane, a spider, or even a human. The animals, birds, and insects were pictured in unusual poses on the cards. The bear, for instance, was a flamenco dancer, the crow was a medical doctor, and the praying mantis was the president. The cards and creatures were stories, and she insisted that nothing was ever personal in a game of wanaki chance.
>
> Bagese told me that the poses of the creatures were the common poses of civilization, the stories and shadows of the animals and birds in the mirrors. She compared the wanaki peace cards to tarot cards that depict the vices and virtues of human adventures, but tarot was in the eye and wanaki was in the ear. The fortunes were never the same as the animal stories (16–17).

Every morning, Bagese turns one of the seven cards and concentrates on the picture. As she becomes the creatures in the cards, she narrates her adventures in the first-person plural. Gathering bits of nature—leaves, stones, flower petals, and the like—and arranging them on the floor of her apartment, she creates a natural map of the surrounding urban terrain. Through this practice, Bagese reconstructs the features of an indigenous, pre-Columbian world in the midst of a "cold and chemical" civilization (7). Describing a new "wilderness" in the city, her stories reclaim the urban space as tribal (10).

Making different uses of Chippewa gambling traditions, Louise Erdrich's writings reenact gambling stories and practices among the trappings of contemporary reservation life. With no mention of evil gamblers or traditional games of chance, poker, a New Orleans card game with roots in European culture, provides the form of the sacred gamble in *Love Medicine*. In this text, the contestants are King and Lipsha, half brothers and the sons of June Kashpaw, a tribal woman who dies in the novel's opening pages. Their gamble is for her inheritance, as represented by a Pontiac Firebird that King, the son recognized by the courts as June's legitimate heir, has purchased with the money he collected from her life insurance policy. Self-centered, violent, and untrustworthy, King represents the evil gambler of the stories. Compassionate, gentle, and honest, Lipsha represents the good gambler, whose powers are associated with healing and growth. Presiding over the game is Gerry Nanapush, Lipsha's father and King's tribal nemesis.

The sacred gamble begins without apparent ceremony. In search of information about Gerry, Lipsha pays a visit to King's Minneapolis apartment, a setting that functions as the symbolic lair of the evil gambler. Quite by chance, it seems, he discovers a deck of cards on the sill of the air shaft window. Later in the scene, Gerry, as the embodiment of the trickster-creator Nanapush, enters the apartment through this hole. To pass the time, the brothers begin an idle game of poker, betting on pieces of Lucky Charms cereal. King calls for a game of five-card stud; Lipsha designates deuces wild, because he liked that "puny little card becoming strategy."[39]

Unbeknownst to King, Lipsha is an expert gambler with inherited talents. In Erdrich's second novel, *Tracks,* we meet his great-grandmother, Fleur Pillager, a tribal shaman who reveals the traces of the good gambler when she beats four white men at poker. Fleur's skill is inherited by her daughter, Lulu, Lipsha's grandmother, who teaches Lipsha the art of card playing. The training includes lessons on keeping the odds in his favor. As Proude Cedarfair suggests, the good gambler must take the chance out of chance. Lipsha does this by marking the deck. By the time something of worth is staked on his game with King, the cards are virtually transparent in his hands.

The game reaches higher levels of significance when Gerry enters the scene. As his last name suggests, Gerry is an embodiment of the Great Hare, the compassionate trickster of the Chippewa. His power is demonstrated in a miraculous leap from a three-story hospital window, through which he squeezes himself like a "fat rabbit disappearing down a hole" (169). He reappears in King's apartment in a similarly magical and mysterious fashion. In his presence, the game is continued, but the stakes have been increased dramatically:

> "We must decide," said Gerry seriously, "What we are playing for."
> "I got money," King said.

"We're not playing for your rubber check," Gerry said. "You prob-
ably used your payoff up by now. We won't play for money, but we got to
play for something. Otherwise there's no game." (261)

Lipsha suggests the car. Compelled by his fear of Gerry, King agrees to these terms. The game will thus decide the following question: Should June's legacy be awarded to King, by right of the white man's law, or to Lipsha, by virtue of his compassion and caring? The answer, of course, is Lipsha. Now holding all the cards, he deals King a pair, Gerry a straight, and himself a royal flush, a hand he describes as a "perfect family." As the king, queen, and jack suggest, Lipsha has imaginatively reconstructed his family through the game. This is literally true insofar as the Firebird, the symbol of June, serves as the vehicle by which Lipsha helps Gerry escape into Canada. Amid all the disunities and disruptions imposed upon the community by contact with white America, a simple card game becomes a symbol of agency and hope.

Erdrich's commentary on the role of traditional gambling stories and practices in the modern world continues in *Tracks* and *The Bingo Palace*. Set in the allotment era, *Tracks* follows the career of Fleur Pillager, a tribal gambler of great power. Demonstrating that the good gambler can be any gender, Fleur gambles to save the land from the grasp of the speculators. As we have seen in *Cogewea,* speculations on tribal land are related to speculations on tribal women. Suggesting this connection, Fleur's gambling opponents are four white men who manage a butcher's shop. The men allow Fleur to join their game, thinking she will be an easy mark. To their great surprise, she proves herself to be an excellent card player. For several consecutive nights she wins a dollar on low hands such as pairs and straights. Increasingly frustrated with their inability to dominate the tribal woman, the men decide to raise the stakes of the game. This is the oppor-tunity for which Fleur has been waiting. With more money on the table than ever before, she plays the winning cards. Her success brings out the worst in the men. Frustrated, angry, and lacking any semblance of good sportsmanship, they beat and rape her for winning. Despite this ill treatment, Fleur keeps the money and uses it to pay the annual fees on Pillager allotments.[40] In this way, she turns the tables on the vicious speculations that were produced by allotment. Justice is served to the men, who pay a heavy price for their misdeeds. During a tornado seemingly conjured by Fleur, they are trapped in a meat locker, where all but one are frozen to death.

Although the men have been killed, their spirits do not perish, but wait in

the next world for an opportunity to continue the game. Their chance comes later
in the novel. In labor in the midst of a winter famine, Fleur is brought to the brink
of death by pregnancy complications. As narrated by Pauline, a mixed-blood
Catholic convert, the shaman's spirit travels to Chippewa heaven, where the
men are found waiting with their cards. In the game that follows, Fleur gambles
for her own life, her newborn child's, and her three-year-old daughter's. Of
these, only the infant's is lost. Although she again survives, Fleur's troubles are
not over. In the end, she is beaten out by the speculators, who charge late fees
on overdue allotment payments. Unable to pay the penalty, Fleur is forced to
relinquish the land. In a last gesture of defiance, she wrecks the logging crews
by causing the trees to fall on them. While Fleur must turn away, her gambler's
talent will be passed on to future generations, who will use it to make their own
acts of resistance and survival.

In *The Bingo Palace,* Erdrich joins a meditation on the role of traditional
gambling practices in the modern world with an exploration of the effects that
high-stakes tribal gambling may have on reservation communities. Centered
around a tribal bingo facility, the action in the novel dramatizes a variety of
personal and ethical dilemmas related to reservation gambling. The first of
these involves Lipsha's successful gamble for a grand prize bingo van. As in the
contest in *Love Medicine,* Lipsha's gambling raises questions about the proper
uses of the gambler's skill. Unlike his sacred gamble for June's Firebird, which
reunites a broken family, his play for the van lacks a moral purpose. Initially,
Lipsha saw the winning of the van as a chance to impress Shawnee Ray, a young
woman with whom he has fallen in love. He had intended to bring it to Shawnee
Ray as a token of his love, but instead finds that the personal satisfaction of driv-
ing a luxury automobile encourages a more selfish response. Intoxicated with his
newfound power, he goes out to party. His celebration is cut short by an encounter with some white youth. Lipsha's triumph is turned to mockery when they total
the van. True to the ethos of a tribal gambler, he stoically accepts the loss and is
optimistic about his future: "It makes no sense, but at this moment I feel rich . . .
it seems like everything worth having is within my grasp. All I have to do is reach
my hand into the emptiness."[41] For Lipsha, it would seem, mastery of the game,
if only for brief intervals, is worth more than the prizes that can be won. Rather
than a means for material gain, his gambling adventures offer a path toward self-
discovery and wisdom.

A more degenerate form of gambling is illustrated by Lyman Lamartine, a tribal gambling operator who loses everything at an Indian Gaming Conference in Reno, Nevada. While Lipsha gambles at his own peril, Lyman risks the future of the tribe itself. In an orgy of compulsive gambling, Lyman gambles away a loan from the Bureau of Indian Affairs intended to finance a tribal gambling operation. As Karen L. Wallace argues, he "succumbs to the lure of easy money and the control it seems to allow him."[42] Describing the episode as a commentary on emerging gambling addictions among tribal peoples, she suggests that Erdrich uses Lyman to illustrate how the dangers of reservation gambling are compounded by a lack of options.[43] In order to continue gambling, Lyman next pawns his grandfather's sacred pipe for $100. Not only has he jeopardized his tribe's means of self-determination, but he has given up a tribal heirloom, a communal symbol of survival, continuity, and identity.

Erdrich balances the misguided and irresponsible gambling of Lipsha and Lyman with the socially productive gambling of Lulu and Fleur. According to Lipsha, Lulu is one of those rare Chippewas who profits from bingo. Stoic and businesslike at the gaming table, she banks her winnings, which then serve as a family fund (61–62). Before Lipsha begins his play for the van, she warns him against foolishly trusting in his luck: "Everybody wins once," she admonishes him, "It's the next time and the next time you got to worry about" (62). Fleur, as an incarnation of the mythic gambler, returns to the reservation to gamble for the return of the land. Her opponent is Jewett Parker Tatro, the former Indian agent who bought the reservation land, "land for which he had cheated so carefully and persistently" (142). As Wallace asserts, through this characterization, Erdrich "reveals the history of mismanagement . . . [and] legacy of government intervention" that has undermined the principles of tribal sovereignty and self-determination.[44] Fleur's contest with Tatro is an attempt to reassert those principles.

Fleur has grown more powerful with age. Now an old woman, she appears as a composite figure. In addition to being a type of *Nanapush*, the tribal trickster and good gambler of the stories, she is associated with Mikwan, the Ice Woman Vizenor associates with the cleansing powers of winter, the Nita Ataged, and Wiindigoo himself, a figure here referred to as Fleur's cousin and with whom she shares a cave on the frozen shores of Matchimanito Lake. In her gamble with Tatro, Fleur appropriates the powers of these spirit beings. She is attended by a small white boy whose odd manners and appearance mark him as no ordinary child. As he expertly shuffles the deck with hands that are "long and pale, strong, spidery, and rough," his true identity is revealed. As Wallace suggests, his appearance is reminiscent of the Nita Ataged, that "curious being . . . almost round in shape, smooth and white," that serves as the basis for Sir Cecil Staples."[45]

In some respects, Lipsha's mistake in pressing his luck and Lyman's collapse at Reno's gaming tables preview Tatro's losses to Fleur. The defeat of all three men is predicated on an impurity of action and motive. Driven by a self-interest divested of the groups they ostensibly serve, each succumbs to the worst effects of his own bad intentions, as the mythic paradigm demands that such gamblers ultimately wind up losers. The ease with which Tatro has acquired the tribe's inheritance, "beaded moccasins, tobacco bags, clothing, drums, rare baskets, [and] property," has led to overconfidence. He now hopes to gain possession of Fleur's Pierce-Arrow (143). Seduced into playing for the antique luxury automobile, he is defeated by his more powerful opponent, whose motive, the return of stolen reservation lands, and superior skill at gambling, trump the avariciousness of the white man.

Fleur's sacred gamble for the return of the reservation functions as a metaphor for the land reacquisition potential of high-stakes reservation gambling. This connection is made explicit through Lyman's dreams of Fleur exhorting him to focus on the land: "Land is the only thing that lasts life to life. Money burns like tinder, flows off like water, and as for the government's promises, the wind is steadier. . . . This time, don't sell out for a barrel of weevil-shot flour and a mossy pork. . . . Put your winnings and earnings in a land-acquiring account. Take the quick new money. Use it to purchase the fast old ground" (148–49). As Wallace points out, this episode reemphasizes "the importance of self-determination and the danger of losing sight of future improvement in the face of immediate personal gain."[46] Lyman quickly grasps Fleur's message. Despite his recent losses, he is optimistic about his chances to capitalize on the new opportunities before the tribe. Focusing on a self-determination that is based on an aggressive land reacquisition policy, he maps out a new plan of action: "Use a patch of federal trust land somewhere, anywhere near his employee base. Add to it, diversify, recycle what money came in immediately into land-based operations" (149).

As a group, these texts demonstrate the fundamental relationship between gambling rituals, tribal storytelling traditions, and tribal literature. For tribal writers, gambling stories and the powerful metaphors they generate provide a means to comment upon a whole range of issues involving politics, philosophy, religion, and art. As we have seen in the course of this study, questions about gambling are inextricably linked to land claims conflicts generated by the aggressive settlement policies of European colonists, policies that place tribal peoples at the mercy of market forces that sometimes allowed for individual, but rarely group, success. Through a process of stereotyping proliferated by white-controlled media, the perceived-to-be vicious gambling of the Indians was contrasted unfavorably with the assumed-to-be virtuous speculations of colonists.[47] This process not only contributed to the erosion of Native cultures, the principle means of group solidarity, but ensured that Native peoples were limited in their opportunities to compete in America's capitalistic social system. In the contemporary period, it has been by an assertion of land-based tribal sovereignty that Native peoples have claimed rights of self-determination. High-stakes gambling is just one of these rights. Given the history of indigenous-colonial relations in North America, it is both ironic and telling that the fortunes of so many tribal corporations have been joined to an appropriation of the American gambling industry. For Native peoples, dealing with hostile colonial forces has always been a high-stakes game of chance. Narrative traditions, in both their spoken and written forms, combined with traditional gambling practices, instruct the players on how to play that game.

Epilogue.

What is the future of Indian gaming? One may as well ask, what is the future of indigenous-colonial relations? As this study has shown, those relations are not static, but have responded dynamically to a variety of social, economic, and political forces. For the most part, the colonials engineered Indian policies that served their own ends. Aside from early collaborations in trade and war, Indians were subject to policies of removal and assimilation. That began to change in the 1930s, when the Bureau of Indian Affairs, under John Collier, recognized the failure of allotment and instituted policies designed to mitigate some of its worst effects. While the termination of federal reservations in the 1940s and 1950s undermined some of the gains that occurred as a result of the Indian Reorganization Act, self-determination had become the focus of tribal peoples throughout North America. In the contemporary period, Indian leaders have been remarkably inventive in finding ways to take advantage of the tribes' unique political and economic resources. This has led to some genuine improvements in the lives of Indian peoples.

To apply this study's central metaphor to the current state of affairs, it can be said that Indians have learned to play the game well. Working within a system that was largely devised to confine, limit, and destroy them, they have found ways to reclaim lost territories, position themselves in politically advantageous ways, and resist outside dominance. Rejecting the dominant culture's assumption of the inevitability of Indian extinction, they have remained in the game and shown that, rather than being in a continual state of decline, Indian nations have the power to reverse their fortunes. In this context, gambling metaphors can provide meaningful frameworks for understanding Indian/non-Indian relations over time and the role of chance in the realm of policy and colonialism. As the national discussion of "what gambling means" intensifies, it is important to recognize that gambling is not simply a pathological response to perceived powerlessness, but a natural human response to the inherent chaos of living. Indian gambling metaphors are particularly apt tropes for recognizing the elements of chance and gambling that affect all human endeavors. Originating in noncapitalistic societies, they provide a framework for decision-making processes that work toward outcomes that advance a community's common goals, and not just the needs of its individual members.

By listening to the complex messages of history, literature, and their own oral traditions, Native peoples can better resist hegemonic images and position themselves politically in new and powerful ways. On the one hand, Indians must remain true to their own cultural traditions, which provide the basis for their status as nation-states and their identity as distinct and sovereign peoples. On the other, they must understand how those traditions both contradict and reflect the cultural traditions of the non-Indian society that surrounds them. Indian writers can play an important role in this process. By supplementing oral traditions with written records, they can help to keep essential cultural traditions alive in the memory of the people. Rather than undermining the oral tradition, Indian writers can provide a richer body of knowledge from which Indian leaders might draw inspiration as they develop new strategies of survival, resistance, and growth.

Non-Indians must learn to turn their attention away from reservation casinos, those fetishized symbols of Indian power, and toward the wider history of indigenous-colonial relations from which reservation gambling has emerged. Focusing on the immediate effects of Indian nation gaming, non-Indians have tended to ignore the complex and unpredictable historical forces that have led to this recent development. In part, this study is intended to counter that trend by revealing the processes that have shaped the current state of tribal affairs. Non-Indians must also learn to share power with tribal entities, for it is only by recognizing each other as coequal partners in America's future that both groups of people will be able to move forward.

Finally, it is hoped that the attention to Native history and literature will provide non-Indians with insight into some of their own cultural institutions and little-understood aspects of their history. Considering that so much of that history is shrouded in myth, and that debates over the recent proliferation of gambling on tribal and nontribal territories have emerged throughout the United States, the time is ripe for a more nuanced approach to understanding Indian gaming, Indian identity, and Indian nation politics.

Notes.

Introduction

1. Mourning Dove, *Cogewea,* 21.
2. Prucha, *Documents,* 171–74.
3. Prucha, 173.
4. McNickle, *Native American Tribalism,* 82–83.
5. Ibid.
6. Melville, *Moby-Dick,* 67.
7. Vizenor, "Trickster Discourse," 188.
8. Vizenor, "A Postmodern Introduction," 13.
9. Vizenor, *Crossbloods,* 7–8.

1. "Could Yee Blame Us for Revenging So Cruell a Murder?"

1. Wood, *New England's Prospect,* 103.
2. Wood, 105.
3. Wood, 103.
4. Wood, 104.
5. Starna, "The Pequots in the Early Seventeenth Century," 46.
6. DeForest, *History of the Indians of Connecticut,* 160.
7. Ibid.
8. Melville, 67.
9. Krupat, *New Voices in Native American Literary Criticism,* 9.
10. Krupat, *Ethnocriticism,* 18.

11. David Murray, *Forked Tongues,* 2–4.

12. David Murray, 16.

13. Salisbury, *Manitou and Providence,* 9–10.

14. Salisbury, 10–11.

15. Salisbury, 35.

16. Ibid.

17. Salisbury, 45–46.

18. David Murray, 2.

19. Starna, 34.

20. Wood, 80.

21. Jennings, *The Invasion of America,* 190–91.

22. Ceci, "Wampum as a Peripheral Resource," 58–59.

23. Cave, *The Pequot War,* 28.

24. Jennings, 188–89.

25. Ibid.

26. Cave, 72.

27. Winthrop, *Winthrop's Journal,* 102; Cave, 72–73.

28. Winthrop, 102.

29. Winthrop, 108.

30. Winthrop, 139.

31. John Mason, *A Brief History,* 9.

32. Cave, 71.

33. Winthrop, 139.

34. Cave, 115.

35. Deloria, *Custer Died for Your Sins,* 178.

36. Churchill, *Indians Are Us?* 29.

37. Pearce, *Savagism and Civilization,* 21.

38. Pearce, 242.

39. Cronon, *Changes in the Land,* 54–126.

40. Cronon, 86.

41. Cronon, 76–77.

42. Jennings, 82.

43. Jennings, 186–201.

44. Ceci, 59–60.

45. Winthrop, 118.

46. Starna, 46.

47. Hauptman, "The Pequot War and Its Legacies," 72.

48. Drinnon, *Facing West,* 37.

49. Cave, 105–06.
50. Underhill, *Newes from America,* 8. Subsequent references to Underhill are cited from this edition.
51. Winthrop, 186.
52. Cave, 117.
53. Gardener, *Lion Gardener His Relation of the Pequot Warres,* 141–42.
54. Cave, 135.
55. Salisbury, 219.
56. Cave, 135.
57. Cave, 137.
58. Cave, 176.
59. Ibid.
60. Simmons, "The Mystic Voice," 151–52.
61. Ibid.
62. Drake, *Indian Biography,* 319.
63. Apess, *A Son of the Forest,* 4.
64. Hauptman, "The Pequot War and Its Legacies," 76.
65. Slotkin, *Regeneration Through Violence,* 72.
66. Vincent, *A True Relation,* 107.
67. White, *Tropics of Discourse,* 81–99.
68. Vincent, 109–10.
69. Rountree, *Pocahontas's People,* 75. According to Rountree, the Powhatan attack on colonial settlements followed in the wake of a smallpox epidemic, intense efforts to missionize the Powhatans, and increasing English claims to Native lands desired for tobacco cultivation. Forced to withdraw to their forts, the English would later mount counterattacks, targeting Indian corn fields in an effort to starve the Natives into submission. The fighting would continue for some twenty years (67–68).
70. Hauptman, "John Underhill," 102.
71. Effingham and DeForest, *Captain John Underhill,* 18.
72. Slotkin, 70.
73. Hauptman, "John Underhill," 107.
74. Hauptman, 104–05.
75. Hauptman, 101.
76. Hauptman, 102.
77. Hauptman, 103.
78. Selma R. Williams, *Divine Rebel,* 80.
79. Selma R. Williams, 45.
80. Heimert and Delbanco, *The Puritans in America,* 149.

81. Selma R. Williams, 45.

82. Heimert and Delbanco, 154–56.

83. Slotkin, 70.

84. Owens, *Other Destinies,* 7.

85. Cave, 6.

86. Ibid.

87. Slotkin, 75.

88. Churchill, 246.

89. Hauptman, "John Underhill," 104.

90. Lepore, "Dead Men Tell No Tales," 479–512.

91. Cave, 101.

92. Cave, 114–15.

93. Drinnon, 40.

94. Slotkin, 183–87.

95. Jennings, 198.

96. Jennings, 186–201.

97. Orr, *History of the Pequot War,* ix.

98. Louis B. Mason, *The Life and Times,* 246.

99. Louis B. Mason, 269; Trumbull, *The Public Records,* 570–72.

100. *Black's Law Dictionary,* 7th ed., s.v. "brief."

101. *The American Heritage Dictionary of the English Language,* New College ed., s.v. "brief."

102. John Mason, *A Brief History,* 7. Subsequent references to Mason are cited from this edition.

103. Louis B. Mason, 259.

104. Slotkin, 184.

105. Drinnon, 38.

106. Gardener, 140. Subsequent references to Gardener are cited from this edition.

107. Cave, 167.

108. William T. Williams, "Introduction," 135.

109. Ibid.

110. Cave, 174–75.

111. William T. Williams, 135.

112. William T. Williams, 134–35.

113. William T. Williams, 134.

2. "Lost in the Deep, Voiceless Obscurity"

1. Bellamy, *The Duke of Stockbridge,* 47–49.
2. Maddox, *Removals,* 39–43.
3. Dwight, *Greenfield Hill,* 96.
4. Dwight, 97.
5. Dwight, 104.
6. Pearce, 62.
7. Boudinot, *A Star in the West,* 15–16.
8. Vanderwerth, *Indian Oratory,* 62–63.
9. Dannenberg, "'Where, then, shall we place the hero of the wilderness?'" 72–73.
10. Frazier, *The Mohicans of Stockbridge,* 2.
11. Frazier, 4.
12. Frazier, 4–5.
13. Frazier, 5.
14. Frazier, 7.
15. Frazier, 16–17.
16. Frazier, 18–23.
17. Axtell, *The Invasion Within,* 198.
18. Frazier, 13.
19. Sedgwick and Marquand, *Stockbridge,* 9.
20. Ibid.
21. Frazier, 42.
22. Axtell, 197.
23. Axtell, 197–98.
24. Axtell, 197.
25. Frazier, 117
26. Mynter, "Leaving New England," 32.
27. Segwick and Marquand, 137.
28. Frazier, 234–36.
29. Frazier, 236.
30. Catharine Maria Sedgwick, *Hope Leslie,* 86. Subsequent references to the novel will be identified in the text by page number in parentheses.
31. Axtell, 200–01.
32. Sedgwick and Marquand, 213.
33. Axtell, 197.
34. Sedgwick and Marquand, 2.
35. Nelson, "Sympathy as Strategy," 202.

36. Green, "The Pocahontas Perplex," 699.

37. Green, 703.

38. Ibid.

39. Nelson, "Sympathy as Strategy," 200.

40. Kolodny, *The Land before Her,* 81.

41. Kolodny, 80−81.

42. Demos, *The Unredeemed Captive,* 51.

43. Seaver, *A Narrative of the Life of Mrs. Mary Jemison,* 77.

44. Axtell, 309.

45. Axtell, 302; Demos, 166.

46. Demos, 165−6; Allen, *The Sacred Hoop,* 30−42.

47. Wood, 115.

48. Jefferson, *Notes on the State of Virginia,* 96−97.

49. Jefferson, 97−98.

50. Bellamy, 300−01.

51. Bellamy, 74.

52. Bellamy, 217.

3. Land, Literacy, and the Lord

1. Owens, 9−10.

2. Ibid.

3. Hochbruck and Dudensing-Reichel, "'Honoratissimi Benefactores,'" 1.

4. Bragdon, "Vernacular Literacy," 26−34.

5. Ibid.

6. McBride, "The Legacy of Robin Cassacinamon," 81.

7. McBride, 76−77.

8. McBride, 81.

9. McBride, 84.

10. Ibid.

11. McBride, 82.

12. Ibid.

13. DeForest, 423−25.

14. Connecticut Archives, *Indian Papers,* 1st ser., 1:95A.

15. *Indian Papers,* 1:231A.

16. *Indian Papers,* 1:234A

17. *Indian Papers,* 1:167.

18. *Indian Papers,* 1:227.

19. *Indian Papers,* 1:239A.
20. *Indian Papers,* 1:238.
21. Connecticut, *Acts and Laws,* 97.
22. Nelson, "'(I speak like a fool . . .),'" 45.
23. Ibid.
24. Nelson, "'(I speak like a fool . . .),'" 44.
25. *Indian Papers,* 1st ser., 2:53A.
26. *Indian Papers,* 2:118G.
27. *Indian Papers,* 2:119A.
28. *Indian Papers,* 2:243A.
29. *Indian Papers,* 2:248
30. Love, *Samson Occom,* 316–34.
31. *Indian Papers,* 2d ser., 2:36A.
32. *Indian Papers,* 2:33A.
33. O'Connell, *On Our Own Ground,* 15.
34. O'Connell, "'Once More Let Us Consider,'" 167–68.
35. Dannenberg, 67.
36. Vizenor, *Manifest Manners,* 92.
37. Vizenor, "A Postmodern Introduction," 13.
38. O'Connell, *On Our Own Ground,* 14.
39. Campisi, *The Mashpee Indians,* 104.
40. Campisi, *The Mashpee Indians,* 105
41. Ibid.
42. Mather, *Magnolia Christi Americana,* 576.
43. Vaughan and Clark, *Puritans among the Indians,* 26.
44. Irving, *The Sketchbook,* 239.
45. Irving, 240.
46. Irving, 198.
47. Stone, *Metamora,* 16.
48. David Murray, 38; Laura J. Murray, "The Aesthetic of Dispossession," 219.
49. Lepore, *The Name of War,* 211.
50. Apess, *Eulogy on King Philip,* 277.
51. Dannenberg, 72.
52. Dannenberg, 80.
53. Jaskoski, *Early Native American Writing,* xii.
54. DeForest, 138–39.
55. DeForest, 421.
56. DeForest, 490.

57. Campisi, "The Emergence of the Mashantucket Pequot Tribe," 131.

58. Campisi, "The Emergence of the Mashantucket Pequot Tribe," 132.

59. Ibid.

4. Fashioning a Tribal Utopia

1. Carlson, "Good-bye, John Mason," 5.

2. Ibid.

3. Deloria, 251.

4. Bee, "Connecticut's Indian Policy," 196.

5. Ibid.

6. Bee, 197.

7. Ibid.

8. Bee, 198–99.

9. Prucha, 14–15.

10. Eisler, *Revenge of the Pequots,* 74–75.

11. Campisi, "New England Tribes," 183–84.

12. Clifford, *The Predicament of Culture,* 279.

13. Clifford, *The Predicament of Culture,* 300.

14. Clifford, *The Predicament of Culture,* 278.

15. Clifford, *The Predicament of Culture,* 333–35.

16. Clifford, *The Predicament of Culture,* 321.

17. U.S. House Committee on Interior and Insular Affairs, *Settlement of Indian Land Claims,* 62.

18. Campisi, "New England Tribes," 184.

19. U.S. House Committee on Interior and Insular Affairs, 23–24.

20. Campisi, "New England Tribes," 184–85.

21. Ibid.

22. Vizenor, *Crossbloods,* vii.

23. Ibid.

24. Vizenor, *Crossbloods,* viii.

25. Vizenor, *Heirs of Columbus,* 3.

26. *New Pequots, The,* CPTV, 1988.

27. Vizenor, *Crossbloods,* 91.

28. John Mason, *A Brief History,* 20–21.

29. Campisi, "The Emergence of the Mashantucket Pequot Tribe," 138.

30. Clifford, *The Predicament of Culture,* 9.

31. Clifford, "Four Northwest Coast Museums," 245.

32. Clifford, "Four Northwest Coast Museums," 216.
33. Clifford, "Four Northwest Coast Museums,"240.
34. Ibid.
35. De Uriarte, "Taking Chances at Mashantucket," 6.
36. Ibid.

5. On the "Indianness" of Bingo

1. Mohawk, "On Sovereignty," 9.
2. Ibid.
3. Jemison and Schein, *Treaty of Canandaigua,* 299.
4. Wilkinson, *American Indians, Time, and the Law,* 55.
5. Wilkinson, 56.
6. Wilkinson, 55.
7. Ibid.
8. Wilkinson, 57.
9. Prucha, 225.
10. Prucha, 224.
11. Sifakis, *Encyclopedia of Gambling,* 56
12. Gabriel, *Gambler Way,* 159.
13. J. B. Jackson, "The Places We Play," 76.
14. Ibid.
15. Findlay, *People of Chance,* 50–51.
16. Tocqueville, *Democracy in America,* 165.
17. Ibid.
18. Tocqueville, 248–49.
19. Brenner and Brenner, *Gambling and Speculation,* 10–14.
20. Ibid.
21. Brenner and Brenner, 1.
22. Findlay, 50.
23. Findlay, 203.
24. Findlay, 205.
25. Fabian, *Card Sharps,* 5.
26. Brenner and Brenner, 12.
27. Brenner and Brenner, 13.
28. J. B. Jackson, 85.
29. Findlay, 64–69.
30. Jefferson, 96.

31. Parkman, *The Oregon Trail*, 177.

32. Standing Bear, *My People the Sioux*, 34–35.

33. Standing Bear, 37.

34. Parkman, 177.

35. Morgan, *League of the Ho-De-No-Sau-Nee*, ix.

36. Morgan, 293.

37. Gabriel, 155.

38. Culin, *Games of the North American Indians*, 809.

39. Prucha, 316–17.

40. Parker, *The Code of Handsome Lake*, 41.

41. Lamb, "Games of Chance", 10–11.

42. Barbara Kanatiiosh Gray, letter to author, 1 November 2002.

43. *Legends of Our Nations*, 78–79.

44. It should be noted that Troublemaker is not the indigenous counterpart to evil as found in the Western tradition, nor is the brothers' feud a struggle between good and evil, in the Christian sense. According to Barbara A. Mann, Troublemaker is associated with good things, like medicine, herbs, and tobacco. Both Skyholder and Troublemaker are necessary in the chain of life and for nature to remain in balance. (Barbara A. Mann, "The Fire at Onondaga: Wampum as Proto-Writing," *Akwesasne Notes Magazine*, n.s., 1, no. 1: 43.)

45. Mohawk Nation Council, interview with the author, 22 May 2002.

46. Gray, letter to author.

47. Mourning Dove, *A Salishan Autobiography*, 102.

48. Morgan, 292.

49. Vizenor, *Crossbloods*, xii.

50. Johansen, *Life and Death*, xxviii–xxix; 185–91.

51. Gabriel, 186.

52. Johansen, *Life and Death*, xxiii.

53. Spilde, "Educating Local Non-Indian Communities," 88.

54. Gabriel, 3.

55. Spilde, 88.

56. *Reservation Roulette*, 1992.

57. Vizenor, *Manifest Manners*, 138–48.

58. Carlson, "Donald Trump," 7.

59. Eisler, *Revenge of the Pequots*, 241.

60. *Reservation Roulette*, 1992.

61. Fenelon, "Traditional and Modern Perspectives," 109.

62. Johansen, 115.

63. Parker, 38.

64. Anthony F. C. Wallace, *The Death and Rebirth*, 282.

65. Anthony F. C. Wallace, 264.

66. Parker, 14.

67. Parker, 17.

68. Parker, 18.

69. Parker, 14.

70. Mohawk Nation Council, interview with the author.

71. Hornung, *One Nation*, 22.

72. Johansen, 26.

73. "Transnational Investments and Operations," 18.

74. Johansen, 14.

75. Ibid.

76. Hill, "Skywalkers," 124–42.

77. Johansen, 53.

78. Hornung, 21–22.

79. Hornung, 23.

80. Matthiessen, "Akwesasne," in *Indian Country*, 127–164.

81. Johansen, 51.

82. Johansen, 92.

83. Johansen, 96.

84. Johansen, 128.

85. St. Regis tribal office, interview with the author, 22 May 2002.

86. Mohawk Nation Council, interview with the author.

87. Drew, "Three Chiefs," 1, 3.

88. Drew, "Court Action," 1, 3.

89. Fenelon, 116.

6. Contesting the Evil Gambler

1. Joseph Henry Jackson, "Introduction," xix–xxi.

2. Joseph Henry Jackson, xiii.

3. Joseph Henry Jackson, xiv.

4. Ridge, *The Life and Adventures of Joaquin Murieta*, 9. Subsequent references to the novel will be identified in the text by page number in parentheses.

5. Lowe, "'I Am Joaquin!'" 116.

6. Ibid.

7. Mourning Dove, *Cogewea*, 17. Subsequent references to the novel will be identified in the text by page number in parentheses.

8. McNickle, 82–83.
9. Viehmann, "'My People . . . My Kind,'" 211.
10. Gabriel, 93.
11. Gabriel, 91.
12. Gabriel, 97.
13. Allen, 17–18.
14. The following summary of the Sun Man-Gambler story is taken from two sources, Franz Boas's translation in *Keresan Texts,* 76–82; and Leslie Marmon Silko's translation, appearing in *Ceremony,* 170–76. In *Storyteller,* Silko credits Elsie Clews Parsons with having collected the story that Boas later published: "In 1918 Franz Boas, ethnologist and linguist, passed through Laguna. His talented protege Elsie Clews Parsons stayed behind to collect Laguna texts. . . . Boas, as it turns out, was tone-deaf and the Laguna language is tonal so it is fortunate he allowed Ms. Parsons to do the actual collecting of the stories," (254).
15. Scarberry, "Grandmother Spider's Lifeline," 100.
16. Boas, *Keresan Texts,* 82.
17. Gabriel, 120.
18. Gabriel, 136.
19. Allen, 119.
20. Silko, *Ceremony,* 2. Subsequent references to the novel will be identified in the text by page number in parentheses.
21. Allen, 121.
22. Bruchac, "Indian Storyteller," 104.
23. Vizenor, *Anishinabe Adisokan,* 140.
24. Vizenor, *Anishinabe Adisokan,* 148.
25. Barry, "Chance and Ritual," 13.
26. Vizenor, *Bearheart,* 189–91. Subsequent references to the novel will be identified in the text by page number in parentheses.
27. Barry, 20.
28. Owens, 234.
29. Vizenor, *Heirs of Columbus,* 20. Subsequent references to the novel will be identified in the text by page number in parentheses.
30. Barry, 13.
31. Johnston, *Ojibway Heritage,* 165–67.
32. Johnston, 167
33. Ibid.
34. Vizenor, "The Moccasin Game," 40. Subsequent references to the story will be identified in the text by page number in parentheses.

35. Johnston, 83.
36. Barry, 18.
37. Johnston, 84.
38. Vizenor, *Dead Voices,* 5–21. Subsequent references to the novel will be identified in the text by page number in parentheses.
39. Erdrich, *Love Medicine,* 254. Subsequent references to the novel will be identified in the text by page number in parentheses.
40. Erdrich, *Tracks,* 36.
41. Erdrich, *The Bingo Palace,* 62. Subsequent references to the novel will be identified in the text by page number in parentheses.
42. Karen L. Wallace, "The Bingo Palace," 153.
43. Ibid.
44. Karen L. Wallace, 155–56.
45. Vizenor, *A People Named the Chippewa,* 5.
46. Karen L. Wallace, 46.
47. Fabian, 5.

Bibliography.

Allen, Paula Gunn. *The Sacred Hoop: Recovering the Feminine in American Indian Traditions.* Boston: Beacon Press, 1986.

Apess, William. *Eulogy on King Philip.* 1836. Reprinted in *On Our Own Ground: The Complete Writings of William Apess, a Pequot.* Ed. Barry O'Connell. Amherst: University of Massachusetts Press, 1992.

———. *The Experiences of Five Christian Indians of the Pequot Tribe.* 1833. Reprinted in *On Our Own Ground: The Complete Writings of William Apess, a Pequot.* Ed. Barry O'Connell. Amherst: University of Massachusetts Press, 1992.

———. "An Indian Looking-Glass for the Whiteman." In *On Our Own Ground: The Complete Writings of William Apess, a Pequot.* Ed. Barry O'Connell. Amherst: University of Massachusetts Press, 1992.

———. *Indian Nullification of the Unconstitutional Laws of Massachusetts Relative to the Marshpee Tribe; or, the Pretended Riot Explained.* 1835. Reprinted in *On Our Own Ground: The Complete Writings of William Apess, a Pequot.* Ed. Barry O'Connell. Amherst: University of Massachusetts Press, 1992.

———. *A Son of the Forest.* 1831. Reprinted in *On Our Own Ground: The Complete Writings of William Apess, a Pequot.* Ed. Barry O'Connell. Amherst: University of Massachusetts Press, 1992.

Axtell, James. *The Invasion Within: The Contest of Cultures in Colonial North America.* New York: Oxford University Press, 1985.

Barry, Nora. "Chance and Ritual: The Gambler in the Texts of Gerald Vizenor." *Studies in American Indian Literature.* 5, no. 3 (1993): 13–22.

Bee, Robert L. "Connecticut's Indian Policy." In *The Pequots in Southern New England: The Fall and Rise of an American Indian Nation.* Ed. Lawrence M. Hauptman and James D. Wherry. Norman: University of Oklahoma Press, 1990.

Bellamy, Edward. *The Duke of Stockbridge: A Romance of Shays' Rebellion.* New York: Silver, Burdett and Co., 1900.

Boas, Franz. *Keresan Texts.* New York: The American Ethnological Society, 1928.

Boudinot, Elias. *A Star in the West; or, A Humble Attempt to Discover the Ten Lost Tribes of Israel, Preparatory to Their Return to Their Beloved City of Jerusalem.* Trenton, N.J.: D. Fenton, S. Hutchinson, and J. Dunham, 1816.

Bragdon, Kathleen. "Vernacular Literacy and Massachusetts World View, 1650–1750." *Dublin Seminar in New England Folklife.* Annual Proceedings 16 (1991): 26–34.

Brenner, Reuven, and Gabrielle A. Brenner. *Gambling and Speculation: A Theory, a History, and a Future of Some Human Decisions.* Cambridge: Cambridge University Press, 1990.

Bruchac, Joseph, ed. "Indian Storyteller Wins Pot of Gold." *Greenfield Review.* 9 (Winter 1981–82): 104.

Campisi, Jack. "The Emergence of the Mashantucket Pequot Tribe." In *The Pequots in Southern New England: The Fall and Rise of an American Indian Nation.* Ed. Lawrence M. Hauptman and James D. Wherry. Norman: University of Oklahoma Press, 1990.

———. *The Mashpee Indians: Tribe on Trial.* Syracuse, N.Y.: Syracuse University Press, 1991.

———. "New England Tribes." In *The Pequots in Southern New England: The Fall and Rise of an American Indian Nation.* Ed. Lawrence M. Hauptman and James D. Wherry. Norman: University of Oklahoma Press, 1990.

Carlson, Richard G., ed. "Donald Trump Targets Indian Gaming Rights." *The Eagle: New England's Indian Journal* 11, no. 3 (1993): 7.

———. "Good-bye, John Mason." *The Eagle: New England's Indian Journal* 11, nos. 5, 6 (1993): 5.

Cave, Alfred. *The Pequot War.* Amherst: University of Massachusetts Press, 1996.

Ceci, Lynn. "Wampum as a Peripheral Resource." In *The Pequots in Southern New England: The Fall and Rise of an American Indian Nation.* Ed. Lawrence M. Hauptman and James D. Wherry. Norman: University of Oklahoma Press, 1990.

Churchill, Ward. *Indians Are Us? Culture and Genocide in Native North America.* Monroe, Maine: Common Courage Press, 1994.

Clifford, James. "Four Northwest Coast Museums: Travel Reflections." In *Exhibiting Cultures: The Poetics and Politics of Museum Display.* Ed. Steven D. Levine and Ivan Karp. Washington, D.C.: Smithsonian Institution Press, 1991: 216–45.

———. *The Predicament of Culture: Twentieth-Century Ethnography, Literature and Art.* Cambridge, Mass.: Harvard University Press, 1988.

Connecticut. *Acts and Laws Passed by the General Court or Assembly of Her Majesties Colony of Connecticut, in New England.* New London: Printed and sold by T. Green, 1770.

Connecticut Archives. *Indian Papers.* 1st and 2d series. Trans. Paul Costas. Mashantucket Pequot Ethnohistorical Project.

Cronon, William. *Changes in the Land: Indians, Colonists, and the Ecology of New England.*
New York: Hill and Wang, 1983.

Culin, Robert Stewart. *Games of the North American Indians.* 1907. Reprint. New York:
AMS Press, 1973.

Dannenberg, Anne Marie. "'Where, then, shall we place the hero of the wilderness?'" In
Early Native American Writing: New Critical Essays. Ed. Helen Jaskoski. New York:
Cambridge University Press, 1996.

De Uriarte, John Bodinger. "Taking Chances at Mashantucket: Tradition and Nation as
Representational Strategies." National Indian Gaming Association Library and
Resource Center. *www.indiangaming.org/library/events/speaker.* 2001.

DeForest, John W. *History of the Indians of Connecticut from the Earliest Known Period to
1850.* 1851. Reprint. Hamden, Conn.: The Shoestring Press, 1964.

Deloria, Vine, Jr. *Custer Died for Your Sins.* Norman: University of Oklahoma, 1968.

Demos, John. *The Unredeemed Captive: A Family Story from Early America.* New York: Vintage Books, 1994.

Drake, Samuel G. *Indian Biography.* Boston: Josiah Drake, 1832.

Drew, Neil. "Court Action Threatens Catskill Casino." *Indian Time* 20, no. 18 (2002):
1, 3.

———. "Three Chiefs vs. Constitutional 'Decision' Denied." *Indian Time* 20, no. 20
(2002): 1, 3.

Drinnon, Richard. *Facing West: The Metaphysics of Indian Hating and Empire Building.* New
York: Schocken Books, 1990.

Dwight, Timothy. *Greenfield Hill: A Poem in Seven Parts.* New York: Childs and Swain,
1794.

Effingham, L., and Anne Lawrence DeForest. *Captain John Underhill, Gentleman—Soldier
of Fortune.* New York: Underhill Society of America, 1985.

Eisler, Kim Isaac. *Revenge of the Pequots: How a Small Native American Tribe Created the
World's Most Profitable Casino.* New York: Simon and Schuster, 2001.

Erdrich, Louise. *The Bingo Palace.* New York: Harper Collins, 1994.

———. *Love Medicine.* New York: Bantam, 1984.

———. *Tracks.* New York: Harper and Row, 1988.

Fabian, Ann. *Card Sharps, Dream Books, and Bucket Shops: Gambling in Nineteenth-Century
America.* Ithaca, N.Y.: Cornell University Press, 1990.

Fenelon, James V. "Traditional and Modern Perspectives on Indian Gaming." In *Indian
Gaming: Who Wins?* Ed. Angela Mullis and David Kamper. Los Angeles, Calif.:
UCLA American Indian Studies Center, 2000.

Findlay, John M. *People of Chance: Gambling in American Society from Jamestown to Las Vegas.* New York: Oxford University Press, 1986.

Frazier, Patrick. *The Mohicans of Stockbridge.* Lincoln: University of Nebraska Press, 1992.

Gabriel, Kathryn. *Gambler Way: Indian Gaming in Mythology, History and Archaeology in North America.* Boulder, Colo.: Johnson Books, 1996.

Gardener, Lion. "Lion Gardener His Relation of the Pequot Warres." In *Massachusetts Historical Society Collections.* Ed. William T. Williams. 3d. ser., 3. Cambridge, 1833.

Green, Rayna. "The Pocahontas Perplex: The Image of Indian Women in American Culture." *Massachusetts Review* 16 (Autumn 1975): 698–714.

Hauptman, Lawrence M. "John Underhill: A Psychological Portrait of an Indian Fighter, 1597–1672." *Hudson Valley Regional Review* 9 (1992): 2.

———. "The Pequot War and Its Legacies." In *The Pequots in Southern New England: The Fall and Rise of an American Indian Nation.* Ed. Lawrence M. Hauptman and James D. Wherry. Norman: University of Oklahoma Press, 1990.

Heimert, Alan, and Andrew Delbanco, eds. *The Puritans in America: A Narrative Anthology.* Cambridge, Mass: Harvard University Press, 1985.

Hill, Richard. "Skywalkers." In *New Voices from the Longhouse.* Ed. Joseph Bruchac. Greenfield Center, N.Y.: Greenfield Review Press, 1989.

Hochbruck, Wolfgang, and Beatrix Dudensing-Reichel. "'Honoratissimi Benefactores,'" In *Early Native American Writing: New Critical Essays.* Ed. Helen Jaskoski. New York: Cambridge University Press, 1996.

Hornung, Rick. *One Nation under the Gun.* New York: Pantheon, 1991.

Irving, Washington. *The Sketchbook.* Vol. 2. Paris: A. And W. Galignani, 1825.

Jackson, J. B. "The Places We Play." *Wilson Quarterly* 21, no. 3 (1997): 72–89.

Jackson, Joseph Henry. Introduction to *The Life and Adventures of Joaquin Murieta, the Celebrated California Bandit,* by John Rollin Ridge. Norman: University of Oklahoma Press, 1955.

Jaskoski, Helen. Preface to *Early Native American Writing: New Critical Essays.* New York: Cambridge University Press, 1996.

Jefferson, Thomas. "Notes on the State of Virginia." In *The Portable Thomas Jefferson.* Ed. Merrill D. Peterson. New York: Penguin, 1975.

Jemison, Peter G., and Anna M. Schein, eds. *Treaty of Canandaigua, 1794: Two-Hundred Years of Treaty Relations between the Iroquois Confederacy and the United States.* Santa Fe, N.Mex.: Clear Light Publishers, 2000.

Jennings, Francis. *The Invasion of America: Indians, Colonialism, and the Cant of Conquest.* New York: Norton, 1975.

Johansen, Bruce E. *Life and Death in Mohawk Country.* Golden, Colo.: North American
Press, 1993.

Johnston, Basil. *Ojibway Heritage.* Lincoln: University of Nebraska Press, 1990.

Kolodny, Annette. *The Land before Her: Fantasy and Experience of the American Frontiers,
1630–1860.* Chapel Hill: University of North Carolina Press, 1984.

Krupat, Arnold. *Ethnocriticism: Ethnography, History, Literature.* Berkeley: University of
California Press, 1992.

———. Introduction to *New Voices in Native American Literary Criticism.* Washington,
D.C.: Smithsonian Institution Press, 1993.

Lamb, Trudie. "Games of Chance and Their Religious Significance among Native
Americans." *Artifacts* 8, no. 3 (1980): 1, 10–11.

Legends of Our Nations. Cornwall Island, Ontario: North American
Indian Travelling College, 1984.

Lepore, Jill. "Dead Men Tell No Tales: John Sassamon and the Fatal Consequences of
Literacy." *American Quarterly* 46, no. 4 (1994): 479–512.

———. *The Name of War: King Philip's War and the Origin of American Identity.* New York:
Alfred A. Knopf, 1998.

Love, W. DeLoss. *Samson Occom and the Christian Indians of New England.* New York:
Syracuse University Press, 2000.

Lowe, John. "'I Am Joaquin!': Space and Freedom in Yellow Bird's *The Life and Adventures of Joaquin Murieta.*" In *Early Native American Writing: New Critical Essays.* Ed.
Helen Jaskoski. New York: Cambridge University Press, 1996.

Maddox, Lucy. *Removals: Nineteenth-Century American Literature and the Politics of Indian
Affairs.* New York: Oxford University Press, 1991.

Mason, John. *A Brief History of the Pequot War.* Boston: S. Kneeland & T. Green, 1736.

Mason, Louis B. *The Life and Times of Major John Mason of Connecticut, 1600–1672.* New
York: G. P. Putnam's Sons, 1935.

Mather, Cotton. *Magnolia Christi Americana.* Hartford, Conn.: Silas Andrus & Son,
1853.

Matthiessen, Peter. *Indian Country.* New York: Penguin, 1984.

McBride, Kevin A. "The Legacy of Robin Cassacinamon: Mashantucket Pequot Leadership in the Historic Period." In *Northeastern Indian Lives, 1636–1816.* Ed. Robert
S. Grumet. Amherst: University of Massachusetts Press, 1995: 74–92.

McNickle, D'Arcy. *Native American Tribalism: Indian Survivals and Renewals.* New York:
Oxford University Press, 1973.

Melville, Herman. *Moby-Dick; or, the Whale.* 1851. Reprint. New York: W. W. Norton,
1967.

Mohawk, John. "On Sovereignty." *Akwesasne Notes Magazine* n.s. 1, no. 3–4 (1995): 8–9.

Morgan, Lewis Henry. *League of the Ho–De–No–Sau–Nee or Iroquois.* Secaucus, N.J.: The Citadel Press, 1975.

Mourning Dove. *Cogewea, the Half–Blood: A Depiction of the Great Montana Cattle Range.* 1927. Reprint. Lincoln: University of Nebraska Press, 1981.

———. *A Salishan Autobiography.* Ed. Jay Miller. Lincoln: University of Nebraska Press, 1990.

Murray, David. *Forked Tongues: Speech, Writing and Representation in North American Indian Texts.* Bloomington: Indiana University Press, 1991.

Murray, Laura J. "The Aesthetic of Dispossession: Washington Irving and Ideologies of (De)Colonization in the Early Republic." *American Literary History* 8, no. 2 (1996): 205–30.

Mynter, Ken. "Leaving New England: The Stockbridge Indians." In *Rooted like the Ash Tree: New England Indians and the Land.* Ed. Richard G. Carlson. Naugatuck, Conn.: Eagle Wing Press, 1987: 30–32.

Nelson, Dana. "'(I speak like a fool but I am constrained).'" In *Early Native American Writing: New Critical Essays.* Ed. Helen Jaskoski. New York: Cambridge University Press, 1996.

———. "Sympathy as Strategy in Sedgwick's Hope Leslie." In *Culture of Sentiment: Race, Gender, and Sentimentality in Nineteenth–Century America.* Ed. Shirley Samuels. New York: Oxford University Press, 1992.

The New Pequots. Produced by CPTV. Directed by Ken Simon. 1988. Videocassette.

O'Connell, Barry. Introduction to *On Our Own Ground: The Complete Writings of William Apess, a Pequot.* Amherst: University of Massachusetts Press, 1992.

O'Connell, Barry. "'Once More Let Us Consider': William Apess in the Writing of New England Native American History." In *After King Philip's War: Presence and Persistence in Indian New England.* Ed. Colin G. Calloway. Hanover, N.H.: University Press of New England, 1997. 162–77.

Orr, Charles, ed. Introduction to *History of the Pequot War: The Contemporary Accounts of Mason, Underhill, Vincent and Gardener.* Cleveland, Ohio: Helman–Taylor Co., 1897.

Owens, Louis. *Other Destinies: Understanding the American Indian Novel.* Norman: University of Oklahoma Press, 1992.

Parker, Arthur C. *The Code of Handsome Lake.* 1913. Reprinted in *Parker on the Iroquois.* Ed. William N. Fenton. Syracuse, N.Y.: Syracuse University Press, 1975.

Parkman, Francis. *The Oregon Trail.* New York: New American Library, 1964.

Pearce, Roy Harvey. *Savagism and Civilization: A Study of the Indian and the American Mind.* Baltimore: Johns Hopkins Press, 1967.

Prucha, Francis Paul, ed. *Documents of United States Indian Policy.* 2d ed. Lincoln: University of Nebraska Press, 1990.

Reservation Roulette: Indian Gaming. Prod. News and Community Affairs Office of KLVX Television. Las Vegas, Nev.: December 1992. Videocassette.

Ridge, John Rollin. *The Life and Adventures of Joaquin Murieta, the Celebrated California Bandit.* Ed. Joseph Henry Jackson. Norman: University of Oklahoma Press, 1955.

Rountree, Helen C. *Pocahontas's People: The Powhatan Indians of Virginia through Four Centuries.* Norman: University of Oklahoma Press, 1990.

Salisbury, Neal. *Manitou and Providence: Indians, Europeans, and the Making of New England, 1500–1643.* New York: Oxford University Press, 1982.

Scarberry, Susan J. "Grandmother Spider's Lifeline." In *Studies in American Indian Literature.* Ed. Paula Gunn Allen. New York: Modern Language Association, 1983.

Seaver, Thomas E. *A Narrative of the Life of Mrs. Mary Jemison.* Ed. June Namias. Norman: University of Oklahoma Press, 1995.

Sedgwick, Catharine Maria. *Hope Leslie; or, Early Times in the Massachusetts. 1827.* Reprint. Ed. Mary Kelly. New Brunswick, Canada: Rutgers, 1987.

Sedgwick, Sarah Cabot, and Christina Sedgwick Marquand. *Stockbridge, 1739–1939: A Chronicle.* Great Barrington, Mass.: Berkshire Courier, 1939.

Sifakis, Carl. *Encyclopedia of Gambling.* New York: Facts on File, 1990.

Silko, Leslie Marmon. *Ceremony.* New York: Penguin, 1977.

———. *Storyteller.* New York: Arcade, 1981.

Simmons, William S. "The Mystic Voice." In *The Pequots in Southern New England: The Fall and Rise of an American Indian Nation.* Ed. Lawrence M. Hauptman and James D. Wherry. Norman: University of Oklahoma Press, 1990.

Slotkin, Richard. *Regeneration through Violence: The Mythology of the American Frontier, 1600–1860.* Middletown, Conn.: Wesleyan University Press, 1973.

Spilde, Katherine A. "Educating Local Non-Indian Communities." In *Indian Gaming: Who Wins?* Ed. Angela Mullis and David Kamper. Los Angeles: UCLA American Indian Studies Center, 2000.

Standing Bear, Luther. *My People the Sioux.* Lincoln: University of Nebraska Press, 1975.

Starna, William A. "The Pequots in the Early Seventeenth Century." In *The Pequots in Southern New England: The Fall and Rise of an American Indian Nation.* Ed. Lawrence M. Hauptman and James D. Wherry. Norman: University of Oklahoma Press, 1990.

Stone, John Augustus. "Metamora; or, the Last of the Wampanoags: An Indian Tragedy in Five Acts as Played by Edwin Forrest." In *America's Lost Plays*. Ed. Barrett H. Clark. Princeton, N.J.: Princeton University Press, 1940.

Tocqueville, Alexis de. *Democracy in America*. Vol. 2. Ed. Phillips Bradley. New York: Vintage Books, 1945.

"Transnational Investments and Operations on the Lands of the Indigenous Peoples." Report of the United Nations Transnational Corporations and Management Division to the Working Group on Indigenous Populations. *The Eagle: New England's Indian Journal* 10, no. 6 (1992): 3, 18.

Trumbull, J. Hammond. *The Public Records of the Colony of Connecticut*. Vol. 1. Hartford, Conn.: Brown and Parsons, 1850.

Underhill, John. *Newes from America*. 1638. Reprint. New York: De Capo Press, 1971.

U.S. House Committee on Interior and Insular Affairs. *Settlement of Indian Land Claims in the States of Connecticut and Louisiana: Hearings on H.R. 6612*, 97th Cong., 2d sess., 15 July 1982.

Vanderwerth, W. C., ed. *Indian Oratory: Famous Speeches by Noted Indian Chieftains*. Norman: University of Oklahoma Press, 1971.

Vaughan, Alden T., and Edward W. Clark, eds. *Puritans among the Indians: Accounts of Captivity and Redemption, 1676–1724*. Cambridge, Mass.: Belknap Press of Harvard University Press, 1981.

Viehmann, Martha L. "'My People . . . My Kind': Mourning Dove's Cogewea, the Half-Blood as a Narrative of Mixed Descent." In *Early Native American Writing: New Critical Essays*. Ed. Helen Jaskoski. New York: Cambridge University Press, 1996.

Vincent, Philip. "A True Relation of the Late Battle Fought in New England." In *History of the Pequot War: The Contemporary Accounts of Mason, Underhill, Vincent and Gardener*. Ed. Charles Orr. Cleveland, Ohio: The Helman-Taylor Co., 1897.

Vizenor, Gerald. *Anishinabe Adisokan: Tales of the People*. Minneapolis: Nodin Press, 1970.

———. *Bearheart: The Heirship Chronicles*. Minneapolis: University of Minnesota Press, 1978.

———. *Crossbloods: Bone Courts, Bingo and Other Tribal Reports*. Minneapolis: University of Minnesota Press, 1990.

———. *Dead Voices: Natural Agonies in the New World*. Norman: University of Oklahoma Press, 1992.

———. *Heirs of Columbus*. Hanover, N.H.: University Press of New England, 1991.

———. *Manifest Manners: Postindian Warriors of Survivance*. Hanover, N.H.: Wesleyan University Press, 1994.

———. "The Moccasin Game." In *Earth Song, Sky Spirit: Short Stories of the Contemporary Native American Experience*. Ed. Clifford E. Trafzer. New York: Doubleday, 1993: 40–53.

———. *A People Named the Chippewa*. Minneapolis: University of Minnesota Press, 1984.

———. "A Postmodern Introduction." In *Narrative Chance: Postmodern Discourse on Native American Indian Literatures*. Ed. Gerald Vizenor. Albuquerque: University of New Mexico Press, 1989: 3–16.

———. "Trickster Discourse: Comic Holotropes and Language Games." In *Narrative Chance: Postmodern Discourse on Native American Indian Literatures*. Ed. Gerald Vizenor. Albuquerque: University of New Mexico Press, 1989: 187–212.

Wallace, Anthony F. C. *The Death and Rebirth of the Seneca*. New York: Vintage Books, 1972.

Wallace, Karen L. "The Bingo Palace: Indian Gaming as Literary Device." In *Indian Gaming: Who Wins?* Ed. Angela Mullis and David Kamper. Los Angeles, Calif.: UCLA American Indian Studies Center, 2000.

White, Hayden. *Tropics of Discourse: Essays in Cultural Criticism*. Baltimore: Johns Hopkins Press, 1978.

Wilkinson, Charles F. *American Indians, Time, and the Law: Native Societies in a Modern Constitutional Democracy*. New Haven, Conn.: Yale University Press, 1987.

Williams, Selma R. *Divine Rebel: The Life of Anne Marbury Hutchinson*. New York: Holt, Rinehart and Winston, 1981.

Williams, William T. Introduction to "Lion Gardener His Relation of the Pequot Warres," by Lion Gardener. In *Massachusetts Historical Society Collections*. Ed. William T. Williams. 3d. ser., 3. Cambridge, Mass.: 1833.

Winthrop, John. *Winthrop's Journal: History of New England, 1630–1649*. Vol. 1. Ed. James Kendall Hosmer. New York: Barnes and Noble, Inc., 1953.

Wood, William. *New England's Prospect*. 1634. Reprint. Ed. Alden T. Vaughan. Amherst: University of Massachusetts Press, 1977.

Index.

acculturation, 63; Handsome Lake and, 127–28; to Indian society, 53–54, 55–56

"Act for the Preservation of Indians, and the Preservation of their Property, An," 87–88

activism: Indian, 89, 91–92, 108

advocacy, 73; William Apess's, 80–82; Pequot tribal, 65–66, 71, 78, 86–87; tribal, 85–86

African-Algonquians, 75, 77, 104

African-Americans, 75, 77, 100

Akwesasne, xiv, xv, xvii, 127; environmental problems in, 135–36; gambling controversy at, 131–35; traditionalism vs. modernism in, 129–30, 136–37

Akwesasne Mohawk Casino, 135

Akwesasne Notes, 134

Albany, 42

ALCOA. *See* Aluminum Company of America

alcohol consumption, 43, 127

Algonquians: economic culture of, 7–8. *See also various groups/tribes by name*

Allen, Paula Gunn, 145

alliances: Pequot-Massachusetts Bay Colony, 9, 14

allotment period, xi–xii, 163; as literary theme, 142, 145, 158–59

Aluminum Company of America (ALCOA), 132, 136

American Indian movement, 91–92

American Indian Museum, 6

Anglo-Pequot War, xv–xvi, 4, 6–7, 14–16, 28; causes of, 11, 13; commemoration of, 89, 107; Gardener's narrative of, 31–32; histories of, 8–9; Mason's narrative of, 30–31; symbolism of, 39–40; Underhill's narrative of, 21–28; Vincent's narrative of, 17–19

antigambling factions, 117–18; Mohawk, xiv, xv, xvii, 127, 131–35, 136

Antinomian Controversy, 19, 20–21

Apess, William, xvi, 39, 64, 75, 108; advocacy of, 80–82; on King Philip, 83–85; self-identity of, 76–77, 79–80; and social status issues, 78–79

Arnold, Benedict, 86

assimilation, 126, 129

Avery, James, 69, 70, 77

Axtell, James, 96

Bakhtin, Mikhail, 6, 21

banishment, 10, 19, 20, 21

Index

BAR. *See* Branch of Acknowledgement and Research

Barnes, Barbara, 131

Bearheart: the Heirship Chronicles (Vizenor), xvii, 139, 149–52

Bee, Robert L., 98

Bellamy, Edward: *The Duke of Stockbridge,* 37, 58–59

Benedict, Ruth, 9

bingo, 123–24; Akwesasne Mohawk, 129, 130, 131

Bingo Palace, The (Erdrich), xvii, 140, 159–61

Block, Adriaen, 9

Block Island: raid on, 14–15, 23, 26, 29

Boudinot, Elias, 39; *A Star in the West,* 40

bound servitude: of William Apess, 79–80

Bragdon, Kathleen, 65

Branch of Acknowledgement and Research (BAR), 94, 95, 98

Brief History of the Pequot War, A (Mason), 8, 28, 30–31

Brooke, Lord, 29

Brotherton (N.Y.), 46, 75

Bunker Hill, Battle of, 45

Bureau of Indian Affairs, 94, 98, 114, 126–27

Bush, George H. W., 135

businesses: Mohawk, 129–30

Cabazon Band, 124

Caleb, Hannah, 77–78, 85, 108

California, 124

Campisi, Jack, 96, 98

Canada: Mohawks and, 130, 131, 133

Cape Cod, 96

captives: acculturation of, 54–55; Anglo-American, 53–54; Pequot, 16–17, 66

card playing, 129

casinos, 5, 124

Cassacinamon, Robin (father), 90, 107–8; as mediator, 66–67; Winthrops and, 65–66

Cassinnamint, Robin (son), 85, 97; and land claims, 67–69

Cave, Alfred, 11, 16; *The Pequot War,* 8–9

Ceci, Lynn, 98

ceremony: gaming as, 121–23

Ceremony (Silko), xvii, 139, 147–49

Chaco Canyon, 145

Charles II, 29

Cherokee Nation v. Georgia, 113

Cherokees, 140

Child, Lydia Maria, 85; *Hobomok,* 38

children: interracial, 56, 57

Chippewa/Anishinabe: moccasin game in, 152–55; trickster-creator in, 149–50

Christianity, 43, 63, 96, 136; Indian view of, 77–78

Christianization: William Apess and, 76, 77–78; literacy and, 64–65, 70–71; of Mashantucket Pequots, 72–73

Church, Benjamin: *Entertaining Passages on the King Philip's War,* 31, 82

cigarette smuggling, 133

civilization, 56; American, 39–40; Mohicans and, 44–45

civil rights, 39; Pequot, 64, 78, 80–81

C'ky'o Kaup'a'ta, 146

Coalition Against Casino Gambling, 136

Code of Handsome Lake, xvii, 127–28

Cogewea, the Half-Blood (Mourning Dove), xi, xvii, 139; gambling rituals as theme in, 142–45

Coldiron, William M., 98

Collier, John, 163

colonialism, 3, 6, 13; criticism of, 48–49; fur trade and, 42–43; Pequots and, 4–5, 14; violence of, 86–87

colonies: boundaries of, 28–30

Columbus, Christopher, 11–12, 99

Index

Index